Communism and Political Change in Spain

Communism and Political Change in Spain

Eusebio
Mujal-León

INDIANA UNIVERSITY PRESS

Bloomington

Manufactured in the United States of America

Library of Congress Cataloging in Publication Data

Mujal-León, Eusebio, 1950-
    Communism and political change in Spain.

    Bibliography: p.
    Includes index.
1. Partido Comunista de España—History. 2. Communism—Spain—
History. I. Title.
JN8395.C6M84 1983   324.246075   81-48616
ISBN 0-253-31389-9   AACR2
1 2 3 4 5 87 86 85 84 83

Contents

Acknowledgments

My interest in radical movements and politics is longstanding. Undoubtedly it began in my earnest childhood discussions with a father whose life
breathed politics, and developed further after my family and I had to
leave Cuba in 1959. My interest in politics matured when, as an under-
graduate at the Catholic University of America, I had the good fortune to
work with Joan Barth Urban. The opportunities she provided helped me
through an otherwise frustrating three years in law school. She
encouraged me to pursue graduate studies at M.I.T., a choice I have never
regretted. In Cambridge, various people gave me intellectual stimulation
and guidance. William E. Griffith was unstinting in his support and
encouragement. Suzanne Berger and Donald L. M. Blackmer influenced
my development and are also responsible for much of what is good about
this book.

Heartfelt thanks are also in order to various foundations and groups that
have given me financial support over the last five years. Without that assistance, I could not have researched or written this work. Thanks, then,
to the Council for European Studies for a Pre-Dissertation Fellowship
Award (Summer 1975), to the Social Science Research Council for an International Doctoral Fellowship Award for Western Europe (1977–78), to
the Helen Dwight Reid Foundation for a Grant (1978–79), and to the H.
B. Earhart Foundation for a Fellowship Award (1978–79).

This book could also not have been completed without the help of other
friends and colleagues. Jeane Kirkpatrick, Evron Kirkpatrick, and Howard
Penniman of Georgetown University have been helpful in ways large and
small. Juan Linz has been kind in sharing his insights and encyclopedic
knowledge of things Spanish. Edward Malefakis read the manuscript over
carefully and made numerous suggestions on how to improve it. Ray
Caldwell and I have talked about the PCE and Spanish politics so often by

now that we could probably recite each other's views and arguments almost by heart. José María Mohedano Fuertes probably does not agree with some of the opinions I express in these pages, but our differences have never stopped him from extending openness, friendship, and patience to me. Many others, too numerous to list here, or desirous of anonymity, should but cannot be mentioned. To them, a silent but sincere thanks. The Georgetown University Publications Fund helped me prepare the manuscript for publication, and Alneater Gilliam typed it. Andrea Mathews and Devon Gaffney helped me with editing.

Parts of this book have been published previously, and I should like to thank the publishers for permission to use the materials here: an earlier version of chapter 1 appeared in George Schwab (ed.), *The Ideological and Political Theoretical Foundations of Eurocommunism* (Greenwood Press); parts of chapter 5 in Rudolf Tökés (ed.), *Eurocommunism and Detente* (New York University Press); parts of chapter 4 in Heinz Timmermann (ed.), *Die kommunistischen Parteien Sud-Europas* (Nomos Verlag); chapter 6 in David Albright (ed.), *Communism and Western European Party Systems* (Westview Press); and, an expanded version of chapter 7 in Howard Penniman (ed.), *Spain at the Polls: The Parliamentary Elections of 1977 and 1979* (American Enterprise Institute).

Finally, I should like to express my deepest thanks to my family. Words cannot express the gratitude and love I feel for them and for their contribution to this book. My parents have been constant examples, while Maria, Maria N., Julia, and Elizabeth have helped me begin to understand what is truly joyous about life. To all of them and to Guillermina Bisset, I owe this book and much else.

Communism and Political Change in Spain

Introduction

WITH THE DEATH of Francisco Franco in November 1975 and the subsequent democratization of Spain's political structure undertaken by his successor, King Juan Carlos de Borbón, and directed by Premier Adolfo Suárez, a new era opened in Spanish politics. Elections paving the way for the adoption of a Western-European-style parliamentary democracy were held in June 1977 and March 1979, and Spaniards approved a new constitution to replace the outdated and fascist-inspired Fundamental Laws.

After nearly four decades of authoritarian rule, hitherto repressed political and social groups demanded a place in that new democracy—none more insistently than the *Partido Comunista de España* (PCE). Operating illegally from the end of the Civil War in March 1939 until the party's legalization in April 1977, the PCE functioned during much of that time as the best-organized and most effective opposition force in the country. In the years after 1956, under the leadership of Secretary General Santiago Carrillo, the party shifted policy in many areas, adopting rather flexible postures toward developments in Spanish society. The Spanish Communists not only tried to shed their traditional anticlericalism and rigid adherence to Leninist precepts but, taking advantage of regime-sponsored syndical elections, built a political base around the illegal trade union known as the *Comisiones Obreras*.

The political significance of Spanish Communism has extended beyond the borders of Spain in recent years. To some extent before, but particularly after, the invasion of Czechoslovakia in August 1968, the PCE altered its international posture, abandoning its

1

unconditional support of the Soviet Union and becoming a prominent critic of Soviet domestic and foreign policies. Rejecting the
Soviet model for Spanish and other Western European societies,
the PCE also moved away from the classical Leninist view of so-
called bourgeois liberties and toward the idea that political and
civil liberties were fundamental rights in any system. The articulation of these views reached its climax with the publication in
early 1977 of *"Eurocommunism" and the State* by Santiago Carrillo. With this book, for the first time, the secretary general of a
Western European Communist party dared to deny the "socialist"
nature of the Soviet Union, insisting profound transformations
were necessary there before it could be considered a "democratic
workers' state."[1] Just a year later, at its April 1978 Ninth Congress,
the PCE formally dropped the reference to Leninism from its political program, describing itself simply as a "revolutionary and
democratic, Marxist organization." Although, as we shall see in the
course of this book, there have been important limits and ambiguities in the Spanish Communist evolution away from
Leninism, the adoption of such positions made Carrillo and the
PCE *causes célèbres* on the European Left.

That the Communists were the best-organized and most effective political group in Spain toward the end of the Franco era is
not surprising. Communist parties have usually been able to cope
more successfully with the rigors of clandestinity than other
groups. The traditional organizations of the Spanish Left—the
Anarchist and the Socialist ones—remained steadfast in their opposition to the Franco regime, but had difficulty adapting to clandestinity. The anarchist organizations were destroyed by repression; the Socialists also felt its effects, and their organization atrophied in exile, until a dynamic young leadership sparked its resurgence in the early 1970s. Their absence was evident during the
1960s and created a vacuum on the Left which the PCE, with the
unwitting help of a regime that assumed the slightest evidence of
dissent was the product of Communist infiltrators, tried with some
success to fill. Moreover, an authoritarian regime like the Francoist one characteristically faced no serious challenge from moderate or liberal elements, most of whom were neutralized or
coopted. The regime weakened centrist elements by discouraging
political involvement and periodically undertaking feeble and ultimately cosmetic efforts at reform.

More difficult to explain is why the PCE developed independent
international policies and moderate domestic ones. Much of the

social science research on the question of adaptation and change in Western European Communist parties insisted that substantial changes had taken place in these parties, that they could no longer be simply dismissed as foreign-inspired, and that the domestic context in which these parties operated and the opportunities afforded them were quite important in impelling changes in party policies. But implicit in much of the literature was the notion that only legal, mass-based parties felt pressure to moderate their positions and the question of whether similar characteristics could be ascribed to or studied in clandestine parties like the Spanish was never very seriously addressed. The dramatic differences under which legal and illegal parties operated, it cannot be denied, affected the way clandestine parties maintained and developed their organizations, searched for allies, and related to the Soviet Union and other members of the international Communist movement. However, the image of a clandestine party as necessarily small and sectarian, with a feeble implantation in society and no prospect for expanding its clientele beyond a narrow segment of the working class, and primarily or almost exclusively responsive to the wishes of the Soviet Union did not entirely fit the reality of the PCE.

The Communist role in Spanish opposition politics and the shift toward more accommodating, pluralistic, and consensual policies (more in line with the post-World War II initiatives of the Italian Communists, for example) became of special importance as politics in Spain entered a period of flux with the assassination of head of state Admiral Luis Carrero Blanco by Basque terrorists in December 1973. Dashing all realistic hopes for the survival of Franco's authoritarian system, Carrero's death opened the battle for the shape of politics in the post-Franco era.

Piqued by academic curiosity about the political relevance of Communism in mid-1970s Spain, I began my research into what caused the change in Spanish Communist perspectives. My investigations have led me to identify both the Spanish Communist desire to establish a national base and the party's attempt to legitimize their presence among broad sectors of the population as the moving forces behind the transformation of the PCE in the last two decades. The role of Santiago Carrillo in this process has been decisive, and the lessons he gleaned from the Civil War and its aftermath, I argue in chapter 1, made the PCE increasingly responsive to what it perceived as decisive shifts in Spanish social structure and attitudes.

Chapters 2 through 5 assess the policies Communist leaders

pursued with respect to specific social sectors, like the labor movement and the Catholic Church, and analyze the changes party leaders made in the PCE's ideological/organizational matrix and in the party's international frame of reference in an effort to maximize the Communist presence in Spanish society and insure for their party an important role in the post-Franco era. In this context, we shall pay close attention to how far the PCE moved away from its Leninist-Stalinist roots and attitudes, as well as to the limits of that evolution.

Many observers of the Spanish political scene, myself included, expected that the Communist ability to survive Francoist repression, their adoption of flexible and moderate domestic policies as well as of independent international ones, would allow the PCE to assume a key place in the politics of a democratic Spain. The Communists did play an important role during the transition to the post-Franco era; their moderation gave reformists in the opposition and within the regime additional room to maneuver and thereby frustrated the plans of those extremists (on the right and the left) who wanted to torpedo the democratization process. But since the death of Franco, Communist influence in Spanish politics has declined markedly. First, as I discuss in chapter 6, the PCE failed to seize the political initiative in the waning months of the ancien regime. Then, its performance in the June 1977 and March 1979 parliamentary elections (1.7 million votes and 9.2 percent of the total in the first contest, 1.9 million and 10.6 percent in the second) showed the Communists trailing the Socialists badly but hopeful still of shortening the distance between them and the PSOE. Chapter 7 explores the strategy and policies the PCE followed through early 1979 as it tried to cut into the three-to-one Socialist electoral advantage. Having failed to accomplish that objective in the March 1979 elections, the Communists then began to confront serious internal problems which had heretofore lain dormant. Chapter 8 will analyze the nature and the depth of the crises confronting the PCE after 1979. The turmoil within the Communist party coincided with two other major political developments: the disintegration of the UCD and the growth in the popularity of the Socialist party. By winning an absolute majority in the October 1982 parliamentary elections, the PSOE decisively established itself as the dominant force not only on the left but in the country as a whole. The Conclusion addresses the implications of the Socialist victory for the Communist party and speculates on the prospects for Communism in Spain.

Chapter One

The Past as Prelude

THE ROOTS OF CONTEMPORARY Spanish Communist policies and of the PCE's evolution over the last two decades lie tangled in a past replete with memorable and ignominious moments. During the Civil War and in the nearly forty-year struggle against Franco and his regime, the Communists demonstrated considerable heroism, but many of their actions also showed how deeply and corrosively the PCE had been affected by the cloaca of Stalinism. That legacy encouraged as well as limited the evolution of the PCE.[1]

I

Like other Communist parties, the PCE emerged in the wake of the Russian revolution and the ensuing upsurge of revolutionary fervor throughout Europe. However, unlike their French, German, or Czechoslovak counterparts, the Spanish Communists had only a precarious presence in their country during their first decade of activity; party membership never exceeded five thousand,[2] despite the enormous prestige and psychological influence exerted by the Bolshevik revolution.

The failure of Communism to catch on in Spain may be ascribed primarily to the hegemony enjoyed by the Anarchist and Socialist movements. Elsewhere in Western Europe, the Communists had been allowed to occupy the political space of the extreme Left. In

Spain, by contrast, Anarchism and Anarchosyndicalism—movements which had lost most of their vitality in France and Italy— still found fertile soil, especially among the Andalusian agricultural proletariat and the Catalan working class.[3] The *Confederación Nacional del Trabajo* (CNT), the Anarchist trade union organized in 1911, was a potent mass organization, numbering well over one million members just before the Civil War. The Anarchists, like the Communists, did not view the inception of the Second Republic in 1931 with favor; and, as the various strikes they called over the subsequent year or two demonstrated, it was they and not the PCE who were successful in getting workers out into the streets.

While Anarchism preempted an effective Communist presence on the extreme Left, the PCE also found its access to less radical sectors of the population blocked by the *Partido Socialista Obrero Español* (PSOE) and the influence that party exerted over the labor movement through its trade union affiliate, the *Unión General de Trabajadores* (UGT).[4] Founded in 1879, with a lineage tracing back to the proselytizing efforts of Karl Marx's son-in-law, the PSOE of the 1920s had, by and large, turned to the gradualist strategies and reliance on parliamentary method which characterized much of European social democracy. There was a discrepancy between that reformist practice and the party's continued reliance on revolutionary rhetoric. But, largely because Spain remained neutral during World War I, the PSOE avoided the organizational and ideological convulsions which shook other Socialist parties. To be sure, its left wing did grow after 1917, when rampant inflation brought on massive strikes throughout the country, but for some time, the various factions in the party maintained an uneasy coexistence.

The debate over whether or not to join the Third International resulted in extended arguments within the PSOE, and three congresses were required before a proposal supporting that option was definitively defeated by a small margin. Few of the fifty thousand PSOE members went over to the embryonic Communist movement, however. The stability of the membership was partially due to the calls for unity issued by prominent Socialist figures, including founder Pablo Iglesias who, though bedridden and wielding little formal power, was the symbolic masthead of Spanish Socialism. Also significant were the professions of revolutionary faith made by Socialists voting against entry into the nascent Comintern. Even a moderate like Julián Besteiro justified his position by saying that if "analogous circumstances were to develop in Spain, the Socialists should follow the Russian example with all its consequences."[5] Such phrases had a primarily rhetorical thrust for Besteiro, but that he felt compelled to use them was indicative of the radical undercurrent in the PSOE. Socialist ambivalence toward reform or revolution helped the PSOE in its competition with the Anarchists and Communists during the 1920s and early 1930s, but it also had less fortunate long-term consequences in that it contributed to the political incoherence of the PSOE prior to and during the Civil War.

While the political and social presence of the Anarchist and Socialist movements helps account for the weakness of the PCE in Spain, it is not the whole story. Also relevant were the acrimonious disputes going on within the Comintern. These conflicts, while not affecting only the PCE, became gnarled in the Spanish case by the influence various Comintern "advisors" exercised in party affairs. The list of Comintern leaders involved with the PCE reads like a "Who's Who" of the early international Communist movement: Borodin, Roy, Graziadei, Humbert-Droz, Duclos, Codevila and finally, during the Civil War, Togliatti. Most of these men had little or no knowledge of Spanish conditions and, in any case, they enforced the zigzagging tactics of the Third International with the zeal of the enlightened. The relative ease with which they obtained their influence indicates both the fledgling size of the PCE and its leaders' minimal ideological preparation.

Exacerbating these problems was the repression directed at the party during the Primo de Rivera dictatorship (1923–29). Most prominent party members were jailed during this phase, and the Spanish party, like its Italian counterpart, had to move its center of operations to Paris. From a highpoint of approximately five thousand in 1921–22, PCE membership dropped to fewer than five hundred by its Third Congress in August 1929.[6] The only relatively bright spot on its organizational ledger was the entry in May 1927 of several former Anarchosyndicalist militants from the city of Seville. What the party gained on one hand, however, it lost on the other. During the Comintern's sectarian, "third-period" phase, expulsions and purges became the order of the day. The most prominent losses came in 1932, when Andreu Nín and Joaquín Maurín, leaders of party federations in Cataluña and the Balearic Isles, were ousted because of their political and intellectual ties to Trotsky.

The Comintern was also instrumental in compelling the PCE to oppose the Second Spanish Republic, after its establishment in April 1931. Caught up in an extremist frenzy, the Third International ordered the Secretary General of the PCE, José Bullejos, to abandon his call for a "revolutionary defense of the republic" and instead to reiterate Communist opposition to any "pact or alliance with [an]other political force." Reflexively following orders from Moscow, the Spanish Communists also issued a call for the immediate establishment of "workers', peasants', and soldiers' soviets" which would supposedly carry Spain quickly toward socialism.[7]

The Communists remained locked into their role as a reduced, sectarian *groupuscule* until the shift to a Popular Front strategy in 1934 ended attacks on the Socialists and others on the Left. The change in Communist orientation became official in July 1935, but this was only the pro forma ratification of an initiative articulated in rough form more than a year before.[8] In Spain, the first formal steps toward unity of the Left came over the summer of 1934, and finally in September the Communists entered into the *Alianza Obrera* with the PSOE.[9]

The shift toward a Popular Front policy proved a watershed for the PCE and its fortunes, signaling the onset of a period during which Communist influence grew. Whatever the specific causes for the shift, the Communists increased their influence on the Left, once the new line had been adopted. The first major test of the antifascist bloc was the abortive Asturias revolt in October 1934. Although the PCE role was not nearly as great as the Communists subsequently claimed, the party emerged from that insurrection—which the government put down with much bloodshed—with a more visible profile, and a consolidated alliance with the Socialists. Equally important, so far as the PCE was concerned, the PSOE was far more radical after the Asturias revolt, and its left wing, rallying around Francisco Largo Caballero and the Socialist Youth, became dominant in internal party affairs.[10]

Largo Caballero, once considered a moderate, became the leader of the Socialist left wing after 1934. For some two-and-a-half years, the Communists lavished praise on him, helping build a personality cult around Caballero as a second Lenin. Members of the *caballerista* wing of the PSOE developed close ties with the PCE during this period. They played a leading role in the merger of the Socialist and Communist youth movements (April 1936) and encouraged talks aimed at unifying the PCE and PSOE. Although the Socialists retained a membership advantage over the Communists in the months preceding the Civil War,[11] the PCE gained an important psychological edge over the PSOE. To many left-wing Socialists, the PCE and the Russian revolution became points of reference, magnets toward which they were inexorably attracted.

The dynamic of Socialist-Communist unity led to the creation of the Popular Front bloc—composed of two Republican parties and the Catalan *Esquerra* in addition to the PSOE and PCE—which contested and won the February 1936 parliamentary election. In its aftermath, the Republicans formed a new government, but the climate of instability and polarization sweeping Spain numbered the days of constitutional rule. After several months, conservatives in the military made their move and Francisco Franco led a rebellion against the Second Republic. The fratricidal conflict would last for three years and involve three European powers—Italy, Germany, and the Soviet Union. It proved in many ways a dress rehearsal for World War II.

I I

Much has been written about the Spanish Communist role during the Civil War, and it is not our intention to add to that already extensive literature. We will focus instead on on the impact that role may have had on the PCE political style, on the perceptions the Communists developed of the other parties and groups, and on the way many of those on the non-Communist Left viewed the PCE after 1939.

During the Spanish Civil War, the PCE distinguished itself by advocating moderate policies and stretching out its hand to a beleaguered middle class. Against those Anarchists, left-wing Socialists, and Trotskyites who argued for social revolution in the short-term, the Communists counterposed the slogan: "First win the war, then proceed to revolutionary changes." Their approach struck a favorable chord among moderates and middle-of-the-roaders in the Republican camp, but those who stood to the Communists' Left became convinced that "the Communists were working . . . not to postpone the Spanish Revolution but to make sure it never happened."[12]

Such a judgment was harsh, but not without foundation. In the first place, the type of revolution the PCE favored was not the one envisioned by others on the Left. When the PCE talked about

Socialism, they meant change patterned after the Russian Revolution and accomplished under the aegis and direction of the Communist party. Because other groups would be relegated with lesser or greater dispatch to the dustbin of history, it is no wonder that the scenario found little favor among the Communists' erstwhile allies on the Left. The more moderate groups (and even the radical factions in the Socialist party) did not necessarily trust the PCE, but they obviously felt that, given the alternatives of revolution and terror now and revolution and death later, they preferred the latter. Such a fate did befall some leaders of the quasi-Trotskyite *Partido Obrero de Unificación Marxista* (POUM), as when the NKVD arrested Andreu Nín and subsequently assassinated him.[13] In the meantime, the Spanish Communists, whose role in the Nín affair is unclear,[14] sarcastically answered queries as to his whereabouts by insisting he was a Fascist agent and, as such, likely to be in Berlin or Rome.

During this period, the PCE never had more than two out of nine ministers in the cabinet, while its parliamentary representation was less than 7 percent of some 280 Popular Front deputies. And yet, the actions for which the Communists were responsible and the influence they exerted on the Republic side were not those of a weak party. What accounts for this heightened Communist influence during the Civil War?

Earlier, we noted that the Communists derived a psychological advantage from the fascination the Russian Revolution held for many PSOE left-wingers. Some of those individuals—Largo Caballero is a good example—had lost their enthusiasm for the Communist cause by early 1937; but others, particularly those more moderate politically, took their places as the Civil War wore on. Not only did they see the PCE as a bulwark of opposition to radicals on the Left, but they viewed the Soviet Union with increasing favor: it was the only major power openly willing to help the Republican government, sending military advisors to Spain and organizing the International Brigades.[15] These measures raised the prestige of the Soviet Union among broad sectors of the population and undoubtedly also worked to the benefit of the PCE. But the Spanish Communists received more than just a general psychological boost from all this. As Spanish agents of the Kremlin, they were the ones responsible for the distribution of Soviet arms-shipments and supplies. Accordingly, those the Soviet Union considered its enemies, like the Anarchists and the POUM, were persecuted and did not receive much in the way of assistance.[16]

The Soviet Union's role during the Civil War was important in helping the PCE expand its influence, but it was not the only factor in that process. The PCE displayed considerable political ability itself during the conflict. Obviously, there is much to criticize in the Communists' ruthlessness when disposing of no-longer-convenient allies and in their exploitation of fellow-travelers in the PSOE. Still, the PCE was the best-organized and most effective component on the Republican side.

At a time when most members of the Popular Front had fallen to quarreling among themselves and blaming each other for the war's failures, when bitter factional struggles rent the PSOE, and when the Anarchists seemed unable to resolve the contradictions between their utopian theories and Civil War realities, the Communists became the party of order and organization. They were, as one prominent analyst and critic said, the *partido militar* of the Republic.[17] The Communists spared no effort in organizing a command structure and reimposing discipline within the armed forces. They also came in on the ground floor when the government established the political commissariats for the armed forces in October 1936, and, as a result, gained control of perhaps 90 percent of the positions set up under that system.[18]

The expansion of Communist influence within the Popular Front bloc and the assistance the Soviet Union provided the Republican government did not avert the defeat of the Second Spanish Republic. The war ended in April 1939 amid recriminations and countercharges, with many on the Left blaming the PCE and Stalin for the loss. The party's detractors argued that, in frustrating the early efforts to link war and revolution in Spain, the Soviet Union and the PCE laid the groundwork for the Republican defeat. They insisted, moreover, that PCE compliance with Stalin's order to prolong the conflict as long as possible, only to strengthen the Soviet hand in negotiations with Hitler, led to unspeakable costs in human lives and suffering. These are serious charges, and although no clearcut judgment can be rendered on either of them, they are not groundless. Secret negotiations between Berlin and Moscow had begun perhaps as early as 1938, eventually leading to the German-Soviet Non-Aggression Pact in 1939.[19]

Perhaps the most important consequence of the Civil War for the PCE was its adverse effect on the Communist relationship with other parties on the Left. Some of the resentment these groups felt toward the PCE undoubtedly sprang from jealousy over the party's efficiency and organizational cohesion. But, as we noted, that

sentiment had a second dimension, relating to the complete identification between Spanish Communist and Russian interests. Outrage over the ruthlessness with which the Communists swept
away opposition led many on the Left—not to mention those on
the Franco side who saw Communism as an antinational virus and
the most hideous manifestation of all that was wrong with the
twentieth century—to ostracize the PCE. The Civil War rendered the
Communists suspect in the eyes of CNT and PSOE leaders and made
the PCE unwelcome as a political ally. The Communists participated
in the Republican government-in-exile from early 1946 until mid-
1947, but otherwise experienced the isolation perceptively described
as an *exilio dentro del exilio*.[20] This would not be formally overcome
until 1976, when the PCE finally joined most other opposition groups,
including the PSOE, in the *Plataforma de Convergencia*.

Anti-Communism thus became a matter of principle not only on
the Right but on the Left as well. The obstacles this disfavor
placed in the way of the Communists would begin to disappear
only when the torch of anti-Franco resistance passed from the
leaders in exile to those living in Spain who had not directly experienced the Civil War. However, this transition did not occur as
swiftly as the Communists would have liked.

Nevertheless, there was a more felicitious side to the PCE's isolation within the exile community: it compelled the party to eschew exile politics and to devote most of its efforts to clandestine
activity within Spain. The isolation of the Spanish Communists
with respect to other opposition groups and the virulently anti-
Communist line put forth by the Franco regime meant that, as the
PCE tried in the 1960s and 1970s to break out of the ghetto to
which it was relegated after the Civil War, some party leaders felt
compelled to move more vigorously than did their French and
Italian counterparts to break that isolation. The PCF and PCI were
hurt by popular anti-Communism, but they at least operated in a
relatively open environment and could thus more afford to let time
work its changes on the national scene.

The Civil War also gave direction to the Spanish Communist
political style. That style, emphasizing broad alliances and moderate policies, aimed at assuaging the fears of the Spanish middle
class. Obviously, the decision to adopt Popular Front policies after
1934 had a good deal to do with Stalin and the Comintern, but it is
equally true that the policy made excellent sense in its anti-fascist
dimension, particularly as the CNT and left-wing Socialists made

little effort to reassure the middle classes. Whatever other reasons there were for the adoption of those policies, they led to a growth in Communist influence and membership, demonstrating that the party did well when pursuing broad-front alliances.

The adoption of Popular Front policies also influenced Communist recruitment patterns along two distinct dimensions. First, during the tremendous expansion of the Communist organization in the Civil War years, many people of middle-class background entered the party.[21] The political implications of this *embourgeoisement* need not concern us here. But after 1939, when the Franco regime destroyed what remained of the Communist organization in Spain, the PCE—although placing great emphasis on developing its presence in the labor movement and among the proletariat more generally—never stopped trying to attract the middle class to its ranks.

The organizational expansion experienced by the PCE during the Civil War led to the recruitment of a new generation of leaders who saw the PCE as a rising star, the vehicle to lead the Spanish working class to socialism. A person of this persuasion might well have joined the CNT or PSOE in the 1920s or early 1930s. That he now turned to the Communist banner was indicative of burgeoning Communist influence. For example, many Socialist Youth leaders who joined the PCE in 1936, had been in their late teens or early twenties at the end of the Civil War and did not enter the highest PCE policy-making bodies until at least a decade later. By the mid-1950s, however, some from that generation became impatient with older leaders who believed the PCE, proudly isolated on the Left, should simply maintain its course and lambast its domestic and international adversaries for betraying the Republican cause after 1939. Reacting against such narrow-mindedness and taking advantage of the de-Stalinization experienced by the international Communist movement after 1953 as well as of the reappearance of worker and student strikes in Spain, Santiago Carrillo pushed for a more flexible and accommodating posture on the part of the PCE. Before analyzing the circumstances which led to that change, however, we must first focus on what happened to the PCE in the decade and a half following the Civil War. The isolation it experienced during that period and its failure to catalyze the overthrow of the Franco regime will explain why some PCE leaders felt bold steps were necessary in 1956 and subsequent years for the party to break out of its ghetto.

III

The PCE entered the post-Civil War era with its organization shattered and its leaders dispersed, first in France and then, because of the German occupation, throughout North and South America, the Soviet Union, and unoccupied Europe.[22] Party efforts in Spain during those years focused primarily on organizing in the prisons and camps of the regime; this was done almost instinctively and certainly without direction. Contact with those inside Spain was almost impossible. Through 1947 all Central Committee members sent to organize the party fell into the hands of the police, and most were executed. The exiles in France devoted their energies to setting up guerrilla contingents that fought as part of the French resistance movement.

As noted above, Spanish Communist relations with their erstwhile Popular Front partners were poor.[23] Leaders of the PCE continued to emphasize broad-front tactics, but important sectors of the Anarchist and Socialist movements refused to have anything to do with the PCE. The *Junta de Unión Nacional* (JUN), set up by the Communists in late 1943, was more or less a phantom organization, attracting slight support from non-Communist elements. Those Anarchists and Socialists who joined were a distinct minority within their respective organizations. Majority elements in the PSOE and CNT sponsored their own unitary coalitions, such as the *Junta Española de Liberación*, which was mostly a creation of the exile community in Mexico, and a more serious effort, the *Alianza Nacional de Fuerzas Democráticas* (ANFD), in late 1944. Having failed to rally support for the JUN and for its fighting arm, the *Agrupación de Guerrilleros Españoles*, the Communists eventually forsook both organizations. After negotiations with the Socialists, they entered the ANFD in July 1945.

The Communist decision to join the ANFD and subsequently the Republican government-in-exile, like Socialist acquiescence to these moves, was influenced by the euphoria among Republican exiles over the liberation of Europe.[24] Opponents of Franco became convinced that his regime was the most logical target for the victorious Allies. This did not prove to be the case. Events, among them the division of the Allied coalition along ideological lines and the consolidation of the Franco regime, frustrated the anti-Franco opposition. In the wake of that failure and with the escalation of the Cold War, the latent quarrels between Communists and non-Communist elements surfaced once again. The Communist minister left the Republican government-in-exile in August 1947.

Spanish Communist isolation, which became virtually total after 1947, had a profound impact on the party. Withdrawing more and more, it became a small, almost incestuous organization whose leaders conducted periodic purges to uncover various (mostly imagined) traitors. No sooner had party leaders returned to France in 1944 and 1945 than they took measures to root out "fascist agents of the POUM" and "Falangist provocateurs."[25] This paranoia led to the creation of commissions (reminiscent not only of those set up after World War II in the Soviet Union to process prisoners of war, but of the later show-trials in Eastern Europe against veterans of the International Brigades) which investigated the behavior and loyalties of those who had survived the concentration camps.[26]

Internal conflicts occupied much of the time of the party leadership after 1939. The exile community had been bitterly divided by the struggle between Jesús Hernández and Dolores Ibárruri for succession to the post of secretary general following the death of José Díaz in 1942. Hernández lost and subsequently broke with the party; his book *La Grande Trahison* presents a most unattractive view of life in the Spanish Communist exile-community.[27] Though his objectivity is open to question, we cite him in absence of more direct evidence about the excesses of this period. Party leaders prefer not to discuss the matter—yet it can scarcely be doubted that such things took place. Thus, Dolores Ibárruri in April 1956 noted:

> Our "war communism" led [to] a selective, policy-oriented criterion, which was not only his but of the entire party leadership, to hateful arbitrarinesses, to massive expulsion of those who were not considered faithful. . . . If, during that period, we did not lose the party, it was because, despite the poorness of our work, the base was healthy.[28]

It was not simply among the exiles that Antón and others acted with impunity. Party leaders also used heavy-handed methods, occasionally resorting to assassinations and turning people in to the Francoist police, in their struggle to reassert control over the Communist organization. For several years after 1939, contact between the exile-leadership and the members operating in Spain or even in France had been difficult, giving domestic leaders like Heriberto Quiñones and Jesús Monzón a relatively free hand in fashioning party policies. Until the end of World War II, there was little the exiled leaders could do about such attitudes, but after the invasion of Normandy, representatives of the Political Bureau returned to France and reasserted control. *Quiñonismo* and *monzonismo* (Quiñones had been executed in 1942) became heresies to be extirpated. Even more outrageous were the "physical eliminations" ordered by the PCE Secretariat against dissident Communists such as Gabriel León Trilla or Joan Comorera. Few escaped the tarring brush. Even the erstwhile war hero Enrique Líster, who left the party in 1970 to create a pro-Soviet faction, weathered a charge that he participated in a late 1940s plot to murder Dolores Ibárruri.

Reduced to squabbling among themselves, the Spanish Communists were also victims of the machinations of Soviet espionage and intelligence services. This phenomenon affected almost all exile communities, but Stalinism and the cooperation Soviet agencies had from individual PCE members (if not the entire leadership) during the Civil War aggravated the situation. Former Executive Committee member Jorge Semprún alluded to this penetration when he accused Eduardo García, who subsequently became organizational secretary, of being an agent of the KGB.[29] Blackmail and the settling of old political and personal accounts, which Líster detailed in his book *Basta!*,[30] undoubtedly made this one of the most harrowing periods in Spanish Communist history. Little has been written about it, but one can speculate that the experiences some had with the Soviet system helped lay the groundwork for their subsequent break with Stalinism. For others, like Carrillo, whose ideological evolution was more gradual, the background may have spurred the development of a nationalist resentment against the Soviet Union.

Throughout this period, the Spanish Communists did their best to put a brave face forward, and their public statements never lost the bravado characteristic of small exile groups. They exuded a false and misplaced *triunfalismo,* since many of the strikes or actions for which the party took credit either were led by other groups or were spontaneous phenomena for which no one group could claim responsibility. Important strikes did take place during this period in the Basque country (1947) and Barcelona (1951), but the former was really the last gasp of the Civil War, while the latter was only a first step toward opening new possibilities for organization and participation by opposition groups.

Eventually, the Communists also had to recognize the failure of their efforts to galvanize a guerrilla movement capable of over-throwing the Franco regime. Armed bands had been active in Spain since 1939 and estimates of two hundred thousand deaths in the first few years after the Civil War suggest a state of war still existed in many parts of the country.[31] Initially quite disorganized, the guerrilla movement did not assume major dimensions until the close of World War II, when the Communists (and others in the opposition) sent veterans from the anti-Nazi Resistance move-ments into Spain. Although internal divisions—such as the split which developed between Communist leaders operating within Spain and the exiled leadership—caused serious internal prob-lems for the PCE, the party remained firm in the view that the guerrillas would play the decisive role in leading the overthrow of the regime. Convinced that it was only a matter of time before the Franco regime followed its German and Italian counterparts, the Communists called for an armed insurrection against the regime. The PCE would subsequently criticize the Socialists for believing the anti-Franco rhetoric of the Western powers.

But if the Communists emphasized the decisive role of the guerrilla movement more than other groups did in 1945, this had less to do with their prescience than with the realization that, were the Allies to play a major part in the ouster of Franco, the Communist chances for influence and power would be drastically minimized. Although the Communists were certainly not the only ones active in the guerrilla movement—the PCE was especially visible in the Levante and in the Aragon-Catalan region, whereas CNT and PSOE elements were prominent in Andalucía and Asturias respectively—they exercised greater coordinated influence in a movement which numbered perhaps fifteen thousand men.[32] Guerrilla activity was most vigorous between 1945 and 1947, when the international isolation of the regime was at its height.[33] Thereafter, as the Cold War gathered momentum, the regime gained breathing space, effectively exploiting the divisions in the opposition camp and rallying national sentiment against foreign interference in Spanish affairs. As the consolidation of the regime became more apparent and a tide of exhaustion ran over the coun-try, the guerrilla movement declined. By the late 1940s, all that remained were scattered groups, many of whose actions now were hardly distinguishable from banditry. In the meantime, by mid-1947, Stalin had lost whatever interest he might have had in fomenting revolution in Western Europe, deciding instead to consolidate control over those areas contiguous to the Soviet Union. It was this message which Stalin gave a visiting high-level Spanish Communist delegation headed by Dolores Ibárruri in October 1948.[34] The PCE, he indicated, should take a page from the Bolshevik example, abandon the guerrilla struggle and concentrate on political activity to penetrate the mass organizations being established by the regime. This would allow the party to develop a Communist presence among various popular strata. The PCE leadership transmitted this message to its cadres, and there followed a sometimes-troubled phased withdrawal of the remaining Communist guerrillas: the last left Spain in June 1951.[35] With their departure the PCE accepted the survival of the regime as political reality.

I V

The fortunes of the PCE stood at their lowest ebb in the early 1950s. Under these circumstances, it would not have been surprising if the Spanish Communists had retreated further into their shell, reveling in their martyrdom and isolation. That this did not happen is in large measure due to a confluence of events and circumstances that resulted in a change of leadership and a shift toward less sectarian and more flexible policies.

Competition among the ruling oligarchs of Spanish Communism had been going on since the end of the Civil War and particularly after the death of Secretary General José Díaz in 1942. There was in this sense nothing new about the struggles in the early 1950s. Ranged on one side was the old guard in the party, people like Dolores Ibárruri, Vicente Uribe, and Francisco Antón who had been important figures in the PCE during the Civil War and owed their positions to the roles they had played at the time. Lined up on the other side was another member of the Political Bureau, Santiago Carrillo, increasingly a spokesman for change. On his return to liberated France in 1944, he had established a *comisión del interior* as a means to reassert exile control over the party organization in Spain.

As Secretary General of the Socialist Youth, Carrillo had engineered the group's merger with its Communist counterpart and joined the PCE in 1936. Shortly thereafter, he became a member of its Central Committee. Carrillo had been part of that activist wave filling the ranks of the Communist party, impelled by the conviction that the PCE was the most efficient and effective political instrument in Spain. To prove his loyalty to the party, Carrillo had written a public letter to his Socialist father in 1939 severing all ties to him because his father supported the *Junta* that seized control of Madrid in the last days of the war and negotiated the surrender of the capital with Franco.[36] Despite such a demonstration of party loyalty—whether done out of conviction, opportunism, or both—Carrillo remained an outsider among the party oligarchs.[37] Older members doubtless resented his relative youth, his Trotskyite leanings prior to entry in the PCE (he had at one point in 1935 proposed to Andreu Nín and Joaquín Maurín that they join the PSOE and help the Socialist Youth "bolshevize" the PSOE from within),[38] and perhaps even his role during the 1933 parliamentary campaign, when he coined or encouraged widespread use of the slogan "If you want to liberate Spain from Marxism, vote Communist."[39]

Carrillo spent only a few months early in World War II in the Soviet Union, then left that country, traveling to Latin America, the United States, and Portugal. In late 1944, he returned to France as the representative of the Political Bureau, where he established the aforementioned *comisión del interior* and began to develop his own power base.

By the late 1940s, Carrillo had overcome his earlier handicap and had become one of the four or five most important leaders of Spanish Communism, participating as such in the October 1948 meeting with Stalin. He undoubtedly had a hand in some of the excesses of the period, and it is unlikely that it was remorse over them that led him toward open conflict with fellow party oligarchs. More probably, personal rivalry was responsible. Antón, for example, was not the most engaging of individuals, and resentment against his imperiousness in the party was strong.[40] Shrewdly, Carrillo couched his support for disciplining Antón (he was first reprimanded in 1952, and ousted from the Political Bureau in July 1953) in general terms, arguing that his removal would restore party confidence in its leaders.

With Antón eliminated from the inner councils, a *troika* composed of Ibárruri, Uribe, and Carrillo ran the party. The last two did not square off against each other until the mid-1950s. Meanwhile, the death of Stalin in March 1953 injected a new element into the debates in the leadership. What had been essentially a conflict between personalities became a struggle between contending political approaches and attitudes, between those who thought things were just fine and others who felt the party and the anti-Franco opposition were slipping. A partial renovation of the Spanish Communist leadership had taken place at the Fifth Congress in 1954 with the entry of some activists from within Spain and the revision of party statutes. As yet, however, Carrillo did not present an open challenge to the existing leadership.

He moved in that direction after an internal controversy sparked by Spanish admission to the United Nations in late 1955. The reaction of the Political Bureau was to issue a statement over *Radio España Independiente* condemning the move.[41] They wanted to launch a massive international campaign condemning the event as yet another betrayal of the anti-Fascist and Republican cause by the West. In the meantime, and apparently not aware of the Bureau's attitude, Carrillo and three members of the Political Bureau who had stayed in Paris instead penned an article for *Mundo Obrero* praising the entry as "a logical continuation of the policy of co-existence" and "a new blow against the Francoist war policy."[42] The article reflected Carrillo's growing conviction that circumstances had changed internationally and in Spain since 1939, and that this change necessitated, at the very least, an adjustment in the policies and strategies of the PCE. But when Ibárruri learned of this document—which had in the meantime been sent to the printers—she was livid and threatened to have Carrillo immediately expelled for factional activity and indiscipline. In an effort to smooth matters, Carrillo sent Jorge Semprún to *La Pasionaria* in Bucharest to argue that the position adopted by her and the majority made little sense since any international campaign against Franco would fail.[43] Semprún did not persuade Ibárruri to accept Carrillo's position on the United Nations, but he did manage to convince her not to take any measures against Carrillo until the Political Bureau met in April 1956. In the meantime, however, she and others in the majority tried to mobilize opposition to Carrillo. To this end, they invited Fernando Claudín, one of the Political Bureau members who had joined Carrillo in drafting the *Mundo Obrero* article, to join the Spanish Communist delegation to the Twentieth CPSU Congress in February.[44]

Carrillo thus stood on the verge of expulsion from the PCE in early 1956. The fortuitous coincidence of two events saved him: Khrushchev's condemnation of Stalin at the CPSU Congress, and the first widespread political strikes since the end of the Civil War. Dolores Ibárruri now saw which way the wind was blowing in the international Communist movement and, probably still resentful of Vicente Uribe's acquiescence several years earlier to the ouster of Antón, she shifted her support to Carrillo. The official change came at a tumultuous, marathon Political Bureau meeting lasting from early April into the second week of May. Carrillo consolidated his position at a Central Committee plenum in August, coopting six new members into the Political Bureau. There, he delivered a report on "The Situation in the Leadership of the Party and the Problems of Reinforcing It." Using the revelations about Stalin as a foil to attack his opponents, he accused them of succumbing to the cult of personality and other deviations. Ibárruri herself did not become the target of significant criticism. Neither did the already disgraced Antón, whom Carrillo attacked largely in passing. It was Uribe, heretofore charged with responsibility for day-to-day operation of party affairs, who felt the brunt of the criticism. Carrillo described him sweepingly as one who "opposed collective leadership, did not accept criticism and self-criticism, was prone to self-satisfaction, tended to rely on personalist methods, inclined toward *practicismo,* and underestimated the importance of ideological work."[45]

Carrillo obviously profited politically from Khrushchev's condemnation of Stalin at the Twentieth CPSU Congress, but his victory should not be understood simply in those terms. Although he used the issue, Carrillo had not really analyzed Stalinism or its consequences. He agreed with Khrushchev that it was an aberration in an otherwise healthy system. This was in contrast to the argument of Togliatti in *Nuovi Argumenti* or of Fernando Claudín privately within the PCE, that Stalinism had in fact an institutional root.[46] Carrillo otherwise distinguished himself by loyally following the Soviet line after the invasion of Hungary. Furthermore, when in the early 1960s, Claudín and Semprún presented a global critique of Spanish policies—anticipating many "Eurocommunist" tenets—Carrillo engineered their expulsion.

More important than the de-Stalinization issue in Carrillo's victory within the party, therefore, were his proposals for revitalizing Communist strategy and organization. What began as a largely personal quarrel with Uribe, Antón, and others in the old guard was transformed over time into a political argument about what should be done to increase the influence of the Spanish Communist party. It may be surmised that the older members of the leadership were more satisfied with the existing state of affairs than was this young Turk, who saw his political talents wasted in what was rapidly becoming a restricted, sectarian nucleus that was out of touch with the situation in Spain. In an effort to inject an activist thrust into party policies (and probably also to outflank the older leaders), Carrillo argued for including Communists living in Spain in the Political Bureau and Central Committee. In 1956, he seized on student and worker strikes to argue that the party could now decisively break out of its isolation and lead the overthrow of Franco. Others in the leadership had always talked about the inevitability of change in Spain, about how Franco could not survive much longer, but they seemed reluctant to find ways of forcing matters to a head. There was an activist dimension to the arguments presented by Carrillo and an optimism implicit in them that rallied supporters to his side. His opposition to the majority's position on the issue of Spanish entry into the United Nations reflected the conviction that if change were to come, it would have to be accomplished by closely observing and adapting to changes in the situation in Spain.

Under Carrillo's direction, the Political Bureau approved a June 1956 call for National Reconciliation. Although the appeal was certainly in the tradition of previous PCE efforts to galvanize broad fronts against the Franco regime, it nevertheless represented an important break with the past. Coming on the twentieth anniversary of the outbreak of the Civil War, this move represented the first step toward bridging the two camps dividing Spain. Convinced that the regime had an extremely narrow base of domestic support and would soon fall under the weight of its economic and social contradictions, Carrillo persuaded others in the leadership to call for street demonstrations, as in May 1958 and June 1959, to mobilize broad strata of the Spanish population. Accordingly, the PCE exhorted Communist militants and sympathizers throughout Spain to prepare for an imminent national strike to overthrow the regime.

Life, as Marxists are fond of saying, rendered its judgment on this matter. The regime did not fall and, in retrospect, it is evident that Carrillo seriously misjudged the depth of the economic and social crisis of the late 1950s and early 1960s and the extent to which the 1959 Stabilization Plan could overcome it. He never admitted that his assessment was erroneous, however, insisting that the regime could not reform itself, that its fall would come through a general strike. As a result of that miscalculation, the party leadership and Carrillo had to spend a great deal of time and effort over the next decade explaining why its over-optimistic predictions had not materialized and fending off the attacks of assorted leftists—supporters of the various Popular Liberation Fronts, Maoists, and Castroists—who rejected the idea of peaceful transformation and the notions of extended interclass collaboration espoused by the party so insistently after 1956.

Underestimating the crisis facing the Franco regime only exacerbated tension in the highest ranks of the PCE. Carrillo and several other members of the Political Bureau journeyed to Eastern Europe in midsummer 1959 to convince Ibárruri that the *Huelga Nacional Pacífica* called the previous June had been an enormous success, confirming the correctness of those policies Carrillo had formulated since 1956.[47] Ibárruri, who remained the nominal Secretary General of the PCE until the Sixth Congress in December 1959, when Carrillo took her place, may not have been particularly satisfied with the explanation but, cast increasingly into the role of spectator and *grande dame,* she could muster little opposition to the new course.

A more significant challenge to Carrillo came from Fernando Claudín and Jorge Semprún. Beginning in 1963, the two men openly criticized the "subjectivism" of party policies and called for an end to all the talk about an imminent national strike. From an analytical point of view, Claudín and Semprún were close to the mark in predicting and explaining the failure of Communist efforts in this regard, but they did not understand the psychology of a clandestine party as well as Carrillo. He admitted that mistakes had been made but, comparing himself and the PCE to Lenin and the Bolsheviks, wondered whether "[mistakes] harm[ed] the revolutionary workers' movement or [whether] . . . on the contrary, [they] served to stimulate its faith, its confidence, its decision to fight, its inclination to make sacrifices which [were] sometimes great and which [were] required by the revolutionary struggle."[48] The Communist cadre, operating under hazardous conditions in Spain and sacrificing so much for party and cause, reacted favorably to the way Carrillo phrased the problem. The average militant had swallowed the unsavory revelations about Stalin not too long before and was not yet ready for another admission of defeat.

This same activist vision that first helped Carrillo take control of the PCE and later allowed him to maintain his power in the face of the Claudín/Semprún challenge was also responsible for encouraging change within the Spanish Communist party and in its policies. The belief in the inability of the Franco regime to reform its structures and the conviction that its downfall was imminent combined to force the PCE leadership (and particularly Santiago Carrillo) to address the issue of how to develop a broad base of support for the Communist party in a post-Franco democratic Spain. Over the next decade and a half, as Spanish Communist leaders realized the extent of the social and economic transformation Spain experienced, they saw an opportunity for their party to establish a presence among social groups which had heretofore been out of the Communist reach. This realization led the PCE to adjust and moderate its policies in many areas. In the next four chapters, we will analyze PCE efforts to achieve a preponderance on the Left and a major role in Spanish politics. We will focus on PCE policies toward the Catholic Church and its subculture and toward the labor movement, and on the revisions the Spanish Communist leadership made in the ideological, organizational, and foreign-policy spheres.

Chapter Two

The PCE and
Spanish Catholicism

CATHOLICISM HAS PLAYED a vital role in the formation and development of Spain. From the time of the *reconquista* to the Civil War, it has been a reference point in many, if not most, Spanish political choices and disputes. After the Franco victory in 1939, the church recovered much of the ground it had lost in the previous century, assuming once again a privileged position. It wielded enormous power, and church-state ties became so close that one had to look back to the union of throne and altar in the sixteenth and seventeenth centuries for a comparable situation. Moreover, despite the diminished influence of religion among the working class, Catholicism in Spain still exerted a profound influence on politics.

Eager to insure for itself a national presence in the post-Franco era, the Communist party had to acknowledge the reality of the church's power and devise an appropriate strategy toward Catholicism. Communist leaders could approach the Catholic question in either of two ways. One option, reflecting the anticlerical tradition of the European and Spanish Left, was to call for a frontal assault on the church *qua* ideological pillar of the conservative coalition ruling Spain. The Franco regime and church prelates had spared no effort to identify Catholicism with anti-Communism and the status quo; it would not have been surprising, therefore, for the PCE to have accepted battle on those terms. But such an approach, although consistent with Spanish tradition, would have reinforced

25

the illegitimacy of the party in the eyes of many Spaniards and would not have helped the party shed the political straightjacket it had been forced into in 1939.

The other, less dramatic alternative, while also intending to break the symbiotic relationship between church and state in Spain, would not allow the Right the opportunity to exploit religion as an issue. This strategy was the basis of the call for National Reconciliation issued in 1956. In subsequent years, as the party pursued the twin goals of developing and legitimizing its national presence, it was inclined to take an even more flexible posture with respect to the Catholic church and its subculture. Thus, the PCE adopted policies it hoped would help divorce Catholicism from social/political conservatism, and prevent the emergence of a strong, anti-Communist Christian Democratic party in Spain.

This chapter will analyze the policies followed by the PCE with respect to the Spanish church and Catholicism. A first section will explore the role of the church and its subculture in Franco Spain. The second section will focus on the Communist analysis of and response to that phenomenon, along with a consideration of the impact this had on the ideological and organizational matrices of the party. The final section will assess the efficacy of Communist policies toward Spanish Catholicism.

I

Catholicism has consistently been one of the principal bulwarks of opposition to change in nineteenth and twentieth century Spain. Struggling, as elsewhere in Latin Europe, against the secularizing trends of Liberalism and Socialism, Spanish Catholicism was a reservoir of moral and political support for conservative forces. As the cement from which the first Castilian monarchs and their successors built the Spanish nation, Catholicism became indissolubly part of the national identity.[1]

At the same time, cleavages along religious lines deepened in Spanish society, especially during the first decades of the twentieth century. The battle was begun after 1931 with the establishment of the Second Spanish Republic. Profoundly monarchist, most members of the Catholic hierarchy never more than grudgingly accepted the Republic. The few chances for an accommodation evaporated when the Republican Constitution approved in late 1931 adopted an openly anticlerical tone. Although Catholic hostility to the Republic contributed heavily to the polarization of Spain, an equal share of the responsibility for that development belongs in the Republican camp. Anarchists and Socialists, drawing on a lengthy anticlerical tradition which had led to the burning of convents and churches and attacks on the clergy, did little to temper this volatile situation. The Communists, whose political presence was not particularly notable in the years prior to the Civil War, shared those sentiments for the most part, but their anticlericalism appeared mild in comparison to the virulence of some Republicans and others on the Left.[2]

The moderation of the PCE on the Catholic question was relative and eminently tactical. Certainly, the tone of Communist speeches and writings during this period could hardly be described as sympathetic to the church. On more than one occasion the party justified attacks on churches and religious houses, and in fact (although the party subsequently toned down its statements on this matter) in 1935 the PCE demanded the expropriation without compensation of all church properties.[3] These attitudes were shared by others on the Left. Churches and religious beliefs, PCE leaders felt, would inevitably disappear as Spanish Catholics were shown the error of their ways. The PCE nevertheless showed a more sophisticated sense of political realism than others on the Left, distinguishing between Catholics supporting the Republic and those opposing it. The Communists went further, differentiating the reflexive anti-Republican stance of most Spanish Catholics from the reasoned political/social opposition of the hierarchy. The church enthusiastically greeted the Nationalist uprising Franco led in July 1936, and most members of the hierarchy signed a collective pastoral letter a year later, in which they lamented the "great national catastrophe" Spain had suffered but endorsed without hesitation the battle against the "enemies of God."[4] As a reward for lending the Civil War the overtones of a crusade in support of Western civilization and for insuring Vatican support for him, Franco granted the church a privileged institutional position with respect to the state after 1939, subsequently codifying that relationship with the August 1953 Concordat.

Catholic support for Franco during and after the Civil War was decisive, both in consolidating the regime domestically and in breaching its international isolation after the tide of World War II turned against the Axis powers and the threat of Allied intervention in Spain became real.

Nevertheless, the church was not entirely at ease in Franco's coalition. It had sided with the Nationalist insurgents because it was conservative and antimodern. Its ideological convictions were profoundly reactionary in the classical political sense and had none of the revolutionary qualities associated with Fascism or its Spanish variant, Falangism. The Catholic hierarchy hoped for the restoration of the sixteenth century theocratic, "National Catholic" state and thereby of its influence over Spanish society. Franco offered that prospect, but the church was nevertheless deeply apprehensive about the intentions and influence of the Falange. Full implementation of its statist ideology would lead to the curtailment of church privileges, particularly as these related to education and the spiritual formation of youth. The verdict of World War II and the unwillingness of Franco to permit the Falange to develop into a real state party helped settle the argument. In exchange for becoming the ideological pillar of the regime, the Catholic church was granted a series of privileges by Franco.[5]

Especially important in this respect was the Concordat Spain signed with the Vatican. That document established the confessionality of the state, exempting church publications from the official censorship, and giving the hierarchy the right to supervise doctrinal instruction in public schools. Another article in the agreement related to aspostolic labor organizations like the *Hermandades Obreras de Acción Católica* (HOAC) and *Juventud Obrera de Acción Católica* (JOAC), which were permitted to function independently of (though presumably parallel to) the official syndical structures. In exchange for these privileges, the church made express its commitment to the Franco regime and put the considerable weight of its prestige behind the government. Breaking a tradition it had observed since the late nineteenth century, the Vatican also agreed to allow the Spanish state indirectly to fill vacant bishoprics.[6]

The Concordat—which some bishops feared left too much room for state intervention in church affairs—marked the highpoint of church-state collaboration in Franco Spain. Restoring Catholicism to a position it had last enjoyed four centuries earlier, and decisively bolstering the legitimacy of the regime, the agreement appeared to usher in a new era. That expectation proved illusory. Profound changes in Spanish social structure, associated with industrialization, along with international events like the Second Vatican Council and some easing of the Cold War caused the

Spanish church to begin extricating itself from the embrace of the state over the next two decades.

Nowhere was this process more evident than with respect to apostolic labor organizations like the HOAC and JOAC. The apostolic groups involved in labor, it should be noted at the outset, were not formally syndical organizations. Like the *Associazioni Cristiani dei Lavoratori Italiani* in Italy and Catholic Action movements in Europe, the Spanish apostolic labor organizations started out as service-oriented movements whose objective was the "recuperation of the working world for Christ."[7] The church hierarchy saw these organizations as giving Catholicism an opportunity to penetrate the working class milieu where Socialist and Anarchosyndicalist ideas had always been preponderant. Founded in the late 1940s at a time of economic prostration, these organizations also provided a vehicle for Catholics with a social concern.

From their vantage point in the labor world, the HOAC and JOAC (the latter changed its name to JOC in 1956) became key actors in the struggle for influence between the Falange and the church. Although not intended to work at cross-purposes with the *Organización Sindical* (OS) run by the Falange, those organizations nevertheless were the only ones allowed by the terms of the August 1953 Concordat to break the labor monopoly of the *sindicato vertical.* Armed with their own newspapers, bulletins, and independent financial backing, the HOAC and JOC slowly shifted away from their original service orientation and began competing with the government.

The radicalization of the apostolic labor organization or, to be more precise, of some of their most active members, placed the Spanish Catholic hierarchy in an awkward position. Clearly, it opposed politicization of the apostolic labor organizations and the growing competition between them and the OS, but the bishops also had very strong reasons to defend these organizations against critics within the regime. For one thing, in expressing a social concern, Catholic labor activists were simply picking up on a refrain found in various episcopal statements of the period.[8] The bishops were likewise sensitive to the ever-present need of insuring Catholic influence in Spanish society as a whole and especially in the working class.

Episcopal concern with the Falangist doctrine and with the control that group had over the OS had been evident already in the

early 1950s, and, in response, the hierarchy stepped up its support
for Catholic Action. By 1960, an argument over just how representative the *sindicatos verticales* were culminated in an exchange of
letters between the HOAC leadership and the Minister of the
Movimiento José Solís.[9] The HOAC leaders complained about ir-
regularities in syndical elections and about obstacles placed in the
way of some activists, and Solís harshly rebutted the charges and
criticized the HOAC.

The various Catholic Action movements exerted the greatest
influence in the decade after 1956. Their growing estrangement
from the Franco regime caused problems for the Spanish hierarchy, leading most of the bishops eventually to move away from
their close identification with the regime. At the same time relations between the hierarchy and the apostolic labor organizations
became increasingly tense.

We have focused our attention on the apostolic labor organizations and the friction they caused between church and state in
Franco's Spain. Another source of friction was the radicalization
experienced by priests and clergy who worked either in
working-class areas or where regionalist sentiment ran high, as in
the Basque country or Cataluña.

The phenomenon of worker-priests had been imported from
France in the 1950s. Not surprisingly, sharing the lives of workers
and observing the extent to which they were repressed by the regime or by factory owners in collusion with the government was
an experience that radicalized many priests in the industrial belt
around Madrid, Barcelona and other large and growing cities. Beginning in the early 1960s, the involvement of individuals from
religious orders in opposition activities became a serious problem
for church and civil authorities. At first, the problem related simply to the use of parish halls and buildings as meeting places for
organizations where opposition influence was predominant: entry
into church properties was formally possible only with the permission of the priest or the bishop of the diocese.[10] Eventually,
priests and other members of religious orders lent more than
logistical support to groups in opposition; they finally became
members of these organizations. By 1968, arrested clergy were
sent to a special ecclesiastical prison.

The radicalization of clergy and Catholic Action militants was
evident throughout Spain, but it became particularly virulent in
the Basque country and Cataluña, where regional or separatist

sentiment overlapped with more general anti-Franco sentiment.[11]
The resurgence of opposition activity in the Basque country during the 1950s and 1960s was helped by its identification with
Basque Catholicism. Significantly, the myriad *Euzkadi ta Askatasuna* (ETA) groups active in the 1960s traced their origins to a
radicalization of the youth branch of the *Partido Nacionalista
Vasco.* Nor was it simple coincidence that one of the first signs of
open opposition to Franco came in 1960, when 339 Basque priests
issued a public statement demanding liberties in the region and
charging that the *Fuero de los Españoles*, the charter approved by
referendum in 1947, was a dead letter.[12]

The politicization of priests and clergy—their alienation aggravated by the presence of non-Basque, extremely conservative
bishops—achieved dramatic proportions in the Basque country. A
number of the religious became actively involved in one or another of the ETA groups, while many others helped hide and
otherwise protect the activists of the extreme Left. The situation
worsened as the government responded to acts of terror and political demonstrations by declaring martial law and treating Euzkadi
more and more as an occupied territory. This led not only to the
radicalization of many Catholics, but to greater tension between
national church and state.

Committed opposition among activist Catholics assumed a far
less virulent political dimension in Cataluña than in the Basque
country. The differences are related to the general question of the
contrast between regional or national styles; but it is noteworthy
that the politics of opposition practiced by those Catalan Catholics, clergy, and labor activists who grew disaffected with the
Franco regime was more traditional and had a unique cultural
component which was missing in the Basque country. As in other
parts of Spain, churches and parish halls, particularly in the towns
composing the industrial belt around Barcelona, became meeting
places for the *Comisiones Obreras*, among others.[13] Again, with
many Catholics leaning toward opposition politics, the national
hierarchy and the bishops of Cataluña had to defend those
privileges the church had been granted, which meant protecting
those people who fell under the Catholic umbrella, while avoiding
direct confrontation with the state.

Defending these privileges led to significant friction between
church and state in the ensuing decades. The Catholic hierarchy
gradually lost control and influence over many of the institutions it

fostered as well as over important segments of Catholic opinion. What were some of the reasons for this change in the Catholic mentality in Spain?

Of major importance were the profound social and economic changes taking place in Spain, beginning in the late 1950s. Spain went from a predominantly agrarian and rural country to one in which (by 1973) three-quarters of the active labor force was employed in the industrial or service sectors. This process of economic development (discussed in detail in the chapter on labor) led to dramatic shifts in demographic patterns and to the inevitable tensions and psychological changes associated with modernization. Millions of people migrated from the country to cities in Spain and throughout Europe, with a significant decline in religious patterns of behavior. The church failed to maintain or develop an effective presence in many of the working-class *barrios* which sprang up around the major cities.

Those venturing into these areas, whether clergy or members of the apostolic labor organizations, were soon drawn into the vortex of social struggle. For them, the evident contradiction between church social doctrine and the political/social reality of the Franco regime fueled a profound sense of shame which gradually led to a commitment to opposition politics. Feeling their church had betrayed the poor and working class, many Catholic activitists at some time or another joined one of the myriad Left and extreme Left groups which appeared in Spain during the 1960s.

If the church and its related organizations could not help but be affected by the development and transformation of Spanish society, the process was nevertheless aggravated by the role it played and the privileges it enjoyed under Franco. Considered a "perfect" society, that is, one which functioned independent of the state, under the terms of the Concordat, the church enjoyed great freedom under the regime. This autonomy posed no real threat so long as the groups covered by that institutional umbrella were loyal to the state erected after 1939. Over time, of course, not only did individual members of these groups move away from the regime, but the hierarchy lost control and influence over entities like the apostolic labor organization or the movement known as *Justicia y Paz*. The church and the organizational network it had developed after 1939 became a place where otherwise repressed social and political ideas could be raised and defended.[14] Sitting at the apex of a pyramid that was a microcosm of Spanish society, the hierarchy was caught in an irresolvable quandary over whether to defend organizations under its aegis which identified less and less with the Franco regime or to reaffirm loyalty to the government as required under the terms of the Concordat.

Further impetus for change came from the Second Vatican Council which completed its work in 1964. Launched by John XXIII and concluded by his successor Paul VI, Vatican II represented a clear break on the part of the international church with what Avery Dulles has called its "institutional model." The shift away from identification with conservative social and political systems and toward the reassertion of church independence from even the most "Catholic" of states had a most profound impact on Spanish Catholicism. Spanish bishops had seen their support for the Francoist cause during and after the Civil War as an opportunity to enshrine in the mid-twentieth century the principles proclaimed centuries earlier by Rome, which principles had also been the core of what had been not so coincidentally a Spanish-led Counter-Reformation. The doctrines emanating from the Council and the various encyclicals issued by John XXIII and Paul VI undermined the authority of the Spanish hierarchy, giving critics within the church authoritative sources on which to base their attacks on the existing state of affairs.

II

In an effort to win the benevolent tolerance of the church hierarchy and the support of Catholics in the society at large, the PCE had adopted a relatively moderate attitude toward the Catholic world during the Civil War. Whatever the reasons for that moderation (undoubtedly it was little more than a tactical maneuver imposed by the weakness of the Communist movement in Spain and internationally), in the aftermath of that conflict, the PCE did not abandon its broad-front orientation and calls for collaboration with Catholics. Fundamentally hostile to Catholicism, the Spanish Communists nevertheless looked for points of contact with representatives of the *sector católico* in their search for anti-Fascist unity during World War II. In this, of course, they were doing nothing particularly innovative or unique. Collaboration between Communists and Catholics was very much the order of the day among the Latin European Communist parties.[15]

But to call for unity with "[those] Catholics who wished to liquidate fascism"[16] was wishful thinking in the Spain of the late 1940s. Few Spaniards wanted to have anything to do with that Leninist tolerance extolled by the Spanish Communists. Despite all its efforts, the PCE could not escape the dichotomy so deeply ingrained in the Spanish mind that the Civil War had been a conflict in which the forces of Catholicism had fought against and defeated those of irreligion, materialism, and Communism. More favorable circumstances would emerge only in the wake of the definitive consolidation of the Franco regime. The PCE first had to concede failure when it abandoned in 1948 its guerrilla effort against Franco. It stood by powerless while Franco achieved the consolidation of the regime by signing a Concordat with the Vatican in August 1953 and a Base Agreement with the United States one month later.

The death of Josef Stalin in 1953 coincided with and helped deepen the crisis brought on by the failure to overthrow Franco. We have discussed de-Stalinization in the PCE, and there is no need to repeat the analysis here. What is important to note is that along with a general reevaluation of the social and political alliance-strategies of the PCE came a new emphasis on reassuring Spanish Catholics of the moderate intentions of the party.

The first uncertain steps in this direction came at the Fifth PCE Congress in November 1954, when delegates approved inclusion in the party program of a reference to the effect that "given the religious sentiment of a great part of the population," the party promised its support for a continuation of the state subsidy to the church in the post-Franco era.[17] With this step, the PCE hoped to reassure Catholics that the Communists, if victorious in their efforts to oust Franco, would not move against one of the most important privileges accorded the church. Coming at a time when the Falange and the Catholic hierarchy were battling for influence within the councils of the regime, the pronouncement supposedly gave Catholics less reason to support Franco and would also make it more difficult for the hierarchy to rally Catholic support around a separate political party, as had been done in Italy. It probably did neither. Anyone who took the trouble (were they to have found a copy) to read the report Dolores Ibárruri delivered in the name of the Central Committee would have noticed that, although at a formal level the PCE distinguished between religion as a permissible personal option and the church as an institution that necessarily defended the political and social status quo, in practice this had little effect. Thus, Ibárruri stressed that the party was not and could not be neutral on the question of religion. "We make and will make propaganda against religious prejudices," she said to the assembled delegates, "because religion goes against science and against progress and because the ruling classes have used religious beliefs to keep the workers and the popular masses under their domination."[18]

The Spanish Communist call for National Reconciliation issued in June 1956 signaled an important change in Communist policies toward Catholicism and the church. Little in the document referred specifically to the church, and the call was very much in line with previous Communist initiatives to galvanize a broad front against the Franco regime. Yet the *Declaración del PCE por la Reconciliación Nacional* was, as we have argued earlier, a very important document. It was the first salvo fired by a newly dominant faction associated with Santiago Carrillo, the first real step taken by the Spanish Communist party to put the past behind and concentrate on building its presence in the post-Franco era. Its emphasis on overcoming the divisions of the Civil War eventually struck a responsive chord in the more liberal religious circles and among Catholics who desired the restoration of poltical liberties.

The Communists, it is fair to say, did not greet the incorporation of Catholics into the opposition with unrestrained enthusiasm. They viewed the emergence of the more moderate Christian Democratic groups (such as the *Unión Democrática Cristiana,* founded in Madrid in October 1956) and figures like the former Minister of Education Joaquín Ruíz Giménez and the Seville lawyer Manuel Jiménez Fernández with a mixture of approval, concern, and disdain. The PCE interpreted such developments as signs of advanced decomposition in the Franco coalition, but Communist leaders remained certain that this commitment to the anti-Franco opposition was shallow indeed, that those individuals and their followers would just as soon settle for cosmetic changes in the system, so long as these included their groups' legalizations. Leaders of the PCE viewed more radical groups, like the *Frente de Liberación Popular* (FLP) in a similar way. They welcomed its participation in the anti-Franco struggle as further evidence that church support for the regime was wavering. But the PCE, perhaps stung by criticism from the FLP that the Communist party was not revolutionary enough, warned the working class not to be fooled by radical rhetoric. Those active, noted a writer in the Communist

journal *Nuestras Ideas*, were for the most part "sincere and decided" opponents of the Franco regime, but their participation in
the struggle also had important limits. "As members of the church
[*sic*]," he went on, "they become, even if they do not intend to,
vehicles for the penetration of religious ideas in the ranks of
workers and peasants . . . [and thereby] retard the necessary raising of consciousness on the part of the popular masses."[19]

This sort of language appeared in PCE publications as the Communists were extending their hands to both moderate and radical
Catholic groups, urging these and other groups to join them in the
Jornada de Reconciliación Nacional of May 1958 and the demonstration in favor of the *Huelga Nacional Pacífica* of June 1959.
Neither initiative had great success, and no Catholic group, except
the FLP, overcame its reticence about joint action with the Communists. This outcome is not particularly surprising given the history of Catholic-Communist relations in Spain and the less than
appealing image the PCE projected. Granted the new leadership
under Santiago Carrillo had been deliberate in voicing a more
conciliatory line, but whatever evolution was to take place in the
Communist perception of the Catholic world had just begun. Not
only were most Communist leaders still profoundly Stalinized in
their perception of the world, but it would have been exceedingly
difficult to overcome in the space of a few short years the resistance of party militants (some of whose membership dated back to
the Civil War) and others to such overtures, in light of the repression they endured at the hands of a regime so strongly supported
by the Catholic church. The process would have to wait until
memories of the Stalinist period had faded and until Communist
leaders had become convinced that new and more significant concessions were necessary before the party could wean Catholics
from Francoism.[20]

Members of the apostolic labor organizations had played an important role in spurring the changes which affected the Spanish
church and subculture in the late 1950s and early 1960s. They
were also important in the formation and subsequent organizational expansion of the *Comisiones Obreras*. As we shall see in
chapter 3, it was in the *Comisiones* and while fighting for greater
representation of Spanish workers that many Catholic labor activists became exposed to Marxist ideas and, more specifically, to
the Communist party.

The convergence was not easy to accomplish, but in its search for contact with Catholics the PCE did not hesitate to take advantage of what Santiago Carrillo called the *complexe de culpabilité* many Catholics had about the church's identification with the regime.[21] The Communist party was the *coco* (a Spanish expression signifying the forbidden fruit or a taboo subject), and all Spaniards were warned about it as soon as they began to reach political maturity. The Franco regime lost no opportunity to brand all opposition within the country, as well as outside, as the product of a Communist conspiracy. Though effective in some ways, this approach contributed at the same time to giving the public a certain fascination with the Communists; because of the supposed omnipresence of the PCE, the party became for many the symbol of opposition to the regime. Just as anti-Communism helped define those who supported Franco, so pro-Communism or at least a sense of sympathy for the PCE often characterized those Catholics who eventually moved into the ranks of the opposition. Indeed, as time went by, many of those Catholics who were particularly anxious to purge themselves for the support their church had lent Franco felt there was no better way of demonstrating their antiregime convictions than by joining, supporting, or collaborating with the PCE.

Collaboration between Catholics and Communists in the labor movement was important to the PCE for two reasons. It allowed the party to develop an organizational structure and presence in a crucial sector of Spanish society, encouraging also a more flexible posture vis-à-vis the Catholic world as a whole. Members of the leadership or party intellectuals could publish articles in *Cuadernos para el Diálogo* edited by Joaquín Ruíz Giménez, or have prominent Catholic lawyers defend them at their trials, but what really had an impact on otherwise sectarian working-class militants were the visible successes achieved through cooperation in the nascent *Comisiones Obreras*. While militants might not be particularly happy about dealing with Catholic labor activists, as good Leninists and therefore as realists, they could hardly deny the benefits the party was accruing. However grudging that admission, it allowed people like Santiago Carrillo, whose role in the development and evolution of PCE policy was vitally important, to press further in their quest for alliance with the Catholic sector.

Also important, as mentioned above, was the Second Vatican Council and the papacy of John XXIII. The ferocious anticlericalism of the Latin European Left had always been matched

by the virulent hostility toward Communism on the part of the
Catholic church. The Vatican Council marked an important shift in
this regard. Not only did some bishops talk openly in the sessions
about dialogue with Marxists, but in the encyclical *Pacem in Terris*
issued in 1963 while the Council was in session, John XXIII essentially supported collaboration, drawing a distinction between a
theory that is false and in contradiction with Catholic doctrine
(i.e., Marxism) and a practice which, although flowing from such
theory, has elements which are "good and worthy of approba-
tion."[22]

As might be expected, the Spanish Communist leadership
greeted this turnabout in official church attitudes with enthusiasm.
Party newspapers and journals carried numerous articles emphasizing the significance of the shifts and published documents
by prominent Catholic theologians. The journal *Realidad* included, in 1964, the text of an address delivered at the Vatican
Council by a Spanish bishop, Guerra Campos, discussing at some
length the issues on which Christians and Marxists agreed and
disagreed, to which PCE ideologist Manuel Azcárate appended a
commentary emphasizing the convergence.[23] In line with efforts
to encourage a greater interaction with the new breed of Spanish
theologians, the magazine also published articles by those who rejected Catholic traditionalism in doctrine and politics.[24] Although
no Spanish Communists leader attained the prominence of men
like Lucio Lombardo Radice or Roger Garaudy in the Christian-
Marxist dialogue, party ideologues were also active in the
"dialogue" sponsored by the *Paulusgesellschaft* and the Institute
of Sociology of the Czech Academy of Sciences in the mid-1960s.

The clearest exposition of the Communist argument may be
found in *Después de Franco, Qué?* and *Nuevos Enfoques a Problemas de Hoy,* two books Carrillo published in the mid-1960s.
These provide a sense both of the substance and the limits
(whether these result from his personal beliefs, from constraints
imposed on him by the party he led, or some combination of the
two) of his evolution on the Catholic question. In the first work,[25]
the Secretary General of the PCE presented what was by now the
rather traditional Communist analysis of the church in Spain. He
noted that the church no longer identified itself with the regime,
but warned that this did not mean it "had passed, in its entirety, to
democratic positions." The Communist, he went on, had much in
common with "a democratic and progressive Catholicism," and

there was no reason why, despite the obvious differences in ideology, Marxists and Catholics could not collaborate in the construction of a more just society.

Carrillo focused a good deal of attention in *Después de Franco, Qué?* on the various Christian Democratic movements then developing in Spain, both within and outside the regime. In what was perhaps his most interesting point about Catholics and Christian Democracy, Carrillo noted the presence in Spain of left-wing Christian Democrats and urged them not to participate in any efforts to create an Italian-style Christian Democratic party. Such a party would inevitably become, Carrillo stressed, "the organization of the Spanish neo-Right and an instrument of the financial landowning oligarchies." This argument was significant because from it developed the Spanish variant of the "historic compromise" formula. Carrillo subsequently became convinced that preventing the emergence of a Christian Democratic party was one of the keys to securing the *ruptura* from Francoism and that success in that venture would mean that the PCE alone among the Western European Communist parties had been successful in moving their country into the more advanced phase of "political and social democracy."

In *Nuevos Enfoques a Problemas de Hoy,*[26] by contrast, Carrillo had to explain away why the *Huelga General Pacífica* had failed to materialize, and consequently, his analyses were much more detailed and emphasized the complexity of bringing about radical change. But, while his assessment of the prospects for change in the Catholic world was more guarded, Carrillo also took the opportunity to inject some changes into the Communist scheme of analysis. Once again, Carrillo spoke favorably of the trends at work in the Catholic world since the death of Pius XII in 1958, but he was more emphatic in his criticism of the Spanish hierarchy. Time had showed the bishops to have no independence "in the face of the fascist temporal power," he said. They allowed the church to be little more than "an instrument of State policy." Against this church that defended conservative political and social positions, there now stood another, the so-called church of the poor, Carrillo stressed. For the latter (this represented a change in the Communist analysis), religion was no longer what Marx had called the opium of the people, having become, instead, a "factor for progress." This was, of course, not quite the same as calling religion a factor for revolution, as some radical Catholics or Catholic radicals would have liked, but it was a step in that direction and, in any case, Carrillo insisted that the overcoming of all alienation was an issue which could be put on the historical backburner, that differences between materialism and Christianity should not prevent collaboration against Franco in the construction of socialism. Such an offer of alliance and cooperation in the phase of developing socialism had never before been extended by the PCE.

The ambiguities inherent in Carrillo's formula made his defense of democracy less than satisfactory. Thus, the Catholics could not have been overly reassured by his cryptic remarks that Communist parties had to find less "primitive" ways for dealing with religion than had been found in Eastern Europe.[27]

The concessions Carrillo appeared to make on one hand, he took back with the other, but we should not underestimate the significance of some positions implicitly or explicitly sketched in *Nuevos Enfoques*. One such vital notion concerned the importance of the battle of ideas in the revolutionary process in Spain. *Nuevos Enfoques* was an important political document because it underscored a growing awareness on the part of Spanish Communist leaders of the complexities of leading a revolution in advanced industrial societies, an awareness that led to the adoption of Gramscian notions about the importance of the struggle over ideas in those societies where a rapid thrust to power had been precluded. The church would be a key battleground in the "war of position" with the class enemy.

This was not the only notable point in *Nuevos Enfoques*, however. Despite its limits, the offer of long-term collaboration also was significant in that it meant that the PCE had moved beyond considering alliance with Catholics in the labor movement, the university, or elsewhere from an essentially defensive point of view whose principal objective was detaching the Catholic sector from the regime. That persisted, of course, but now the PCE went on record as expressing a belief in the possibility of an active Catholic presence on the side of those who favored socialism. Carrillo clearly articulated this view when he declared in an interview with *Le Monde* that socialism would come to Spain with a crucifix in one hand and a hammer and sickle in the other.[28] Implicit in that formulation was a change in the alliance patterns and strategies of the PCE: the party had begun to develop a vision of politics which in some ways tried to transcend the classical formula of polarization.

In the decade or so following Santiago Carrillo's ascendancy in the PCE, the Spanish Communist view of Catholics as political allies changed. Most of those changes were modifications of tactics and style, and consequently of limited significance. Yet once the PCE and its leaders had decided that they not only needed but could cultivate good relations with Catholics in Spain, the party engaged in a dynamic process which, despite protestations to the contrary, party leaders did not entirely understand and could not in any case control. As they sought to take advantage of the fissures and cleavages developing within the Catholic church and subculture, Carrillo and the PCE found themselves forced to make important concessions in the heretofore sacred areas of ideology and organizational structure and practice.

The connection between those dimensions and their relationship to the Catholic issue in Spain is illustrated through an analysis of the role played in the Catholic policy of the PCE by Alfonso Carlos Comín, a prominent Catholic radical, member of the PCE and PSUC Executive Committees and of the movement known as *Cristianos por el Socialismo* (CpS). Our analysis will consist of three parts. The first will be a description of the nature and policies of the CpS, with particular attention to the marriage of Marxism and Christianity it proposes; the second, a discussion of Comín's participation in that movement and of the reasons for his subsequent entry into the Communist Party. Finally, we will analyze the impact he and others like him have had on the policies of the PCE as these pertained to the Catholic question.

Cristianos por el Socialismo is an international organization founded in April 1971 by radical Catholics who wanted to give organizational expression to their support for Salvador Allende and the Popular Unity coalition which had elected him president in Chile. It arrived formally on the Spanish political scene in January 1973, holding its first national meeting in Calafall, a town on the outskirts of Barcelona.[29] The inaugural document emphasized a dual commitment to faith in Christ and to revolutionary politics. Distinguishing between the church as an institution and religion as a phenomenon, the document stressed that the latter was not an obstacle to revolutionary political action. Because the true Christian could not be on the side of the oppressing classes or even feign neutrality in the class battle, he was by definition anti-capitalist and prosocialist.[30]

The movement's effort to marry Marxism and Christianity was

no inconsiderable task, given the profound differences between the two, not only on the causes and nature of alienation but also on the prospects for ending it. Theoreticians in the CPS stressed the divergence between Marx and Engels in their approach to religion and demonstrated that the views of the latter had influenced Plekhanov, Lenin, and subsequently the entire international Communist movement.[31] Those CPS members who wrote on the question insisted that Marx had a much less virulent outlook than Engels. The author of *Das Kapital*, they argued, saw the extinciton of religion coming about as the result of changes in social structure under socialism. Engels, by contrast, adopted the more rationalist position that the elimination of religion would result from its defeat by science. He suggested, in the words of one commentator, that "the fight against religion [was] a precondition for the transformation of circumstances."[32] Lenin inherited and deepened this antireligious element in Engel's thought by stressing that physical matter was the only reality and that Marxism had to be atheistic because religion was the ideology of oppression.

The political implications of this view for the believer who wanted to participate in the construction of a new society were rather clear. The Leninist might be more than willing—assuming he was neither overly sectarian nor dogmatic—to enter into a political alliance with a group of believers or even to allow their participation in the Communist party, but only as an eminently tactical move. And believers, according to this view, would enter not because of religion but despite it; eventually, as their political maturity deepened, they would drop religious beliefs altogether.

Theoreticians in the CPS (probably a significant proportion of the membership, given the composition of the movement) rejected the Leninist view of religion and recognized the limits beyond which a revision of his thought could not go and still remain true to its core values. Their posture with respect to Marxism was different, even if controversial. Marxism, stressed one authoritative spokesman for the group, did not represent "an unappealable negation of faith in Christ," and atheism was not a fundamental element in Marxism.[33] He accepted the Marxist critique of the church as a historical institution, of Christianity as a specific religion, and of magical religion, but rejected the notion that Marxism could make any definitive judgment today about the essence and future of religion. A Marxist who considered himself a Christian would have one view on that problem, and a Marxist with no religious commitment another. There should be no discrimination toward the believers on this score in any party defining itself as Marxist. As to the question of the contradictions confronting the individual who professed to be both a Marxist and Christian, CPS defended itself by insisting that a much graver conflict existed between "faith" and "capitalist materialism."[34] Although some CPS members claimed a specific, political role for their organization alongside the parties of the Left in the construction of a socialist society, most of them saw the movement as essentially ideological, with a special emphasis on the battle for socialist ideas within the Catholic church and community. Placing itself firmly on the side of the anti-Franco opposition, *Cristianos por el Socialismo* nevertheless emphasized its political ecumenism and independence of all parties.[35]

These individuals and ideas were an important part of the Spanish Catholic counterculture that developed in the later years of the Franco regime. Obviously, many people could and did disagree with the Christian-Marxist or Christian-Socialist synthesis they proposed; but what cannot be denied was the power these ideas exerted over an increasingly significant number of Catholics in Spain. The Anarchists and the Socialist PSOE had not really known how to respond to the radicalization of Catholics and were probably in as much of a quandary about the phenomenon as were the Francoists and the church hierarchy on the other side. The Anarchist movement never recovered from this lapse, and the PSOE only began to do so after a new group of leaders, some of Catholic background, successfully challenged the exile-leadership for control of the party in the early 1970s.

Of the traditional organizations of the Left, the PCE showed the greatest flexibility in dealing with Catholic radicals and devoted the most attention to the Catholic question. However, this policy did not pay off as quickly among Spanish workers as many Communist leaders had expected. In the early stages, most radicalized Catholics rejected the Communist alternative as too moderate, searching for other groups that would live up to the ideal of revolutionary militance and action with which they had been inculcated by Francoist education and propaganda. While they lambasted the PCE, however, these individuals still used the Communist party as their point of reference. In the late 1960s and early 1970s, when the inevitable disillusion with Maoism, Castroism, or Trotskyism set in and the much-touted prospects for armed revolution did not materialize, many of these people began to reconsider their position vis-à-vis the Communist party.

One person in this category was Alfonso Carlos Comín. A long-time radical political activist (who also happened to bear an uncanny resemblance to Jesus Christ as depicted in the West), Comín had been a member of the *Frente de Liberación Popular* (founded in 1958, it was the precursor of the radical Christian movements in Franco Spain). Then in the early 1960s he joined the Maoist Catalan splinter group known as *Bandera Roja*. Along with his more strictly political activisin, Comín developed quite a reputation as a theoretician of Christian radicalism.

Perhaps his most significant work was a book entitled *Fe en la Tierra* (1975). In it, Comín explored in quasiautobiographical form his personal evolution from traditional to radical Catholicism and called for a "reinterpretation of faith from [a] socialist option."[36] Directing the brunt of his criticism at the institutional church, he emphasized its role as ideological apparatus at the service of the capitalist state and expressed dismay at what he considered its perpetual betrayal of the working class. But, although many pages in that book were taken up with a vigorous critique of Spanish Catholicism, Comín also directed some very pointed barbs at Communism as well. He dealt with the Communist question in the Aesopic language required to evade the Francoist censor. Thus, when he called upon Communist parties to realize the revolutionary potential "which exists in some Christian sectors," he used the French Communists as his foil, blasting their doctrinal narrowness and unwillingness to do more than tolerate the participation of Catholics in their ranks.[37]

Comín wrote *Fe en la Tierra* in 1973–74, at a time when he and *Bandera Roja* had toned down their radical and anti-PCE rhetoric considerably. Communist leaders, for their part, anxious to strengthen their hand for what promised to be a tumultuous transition to the post-Franco era, had been working to narrow their differences with Catholic radicals in *Bandera Roja* and other groups. They had greeted the formation of *Cristianos por el Socialismo* in Spain with enthusiasm: in a report to the September 1973 Central Committee, PSUC Secretary General Gregorio López Raimundo paid the members of the radical Catholic opposition a handsome compliment by referring to them as "our most consistent allies."[38] Such words were not uttered without purpose and they bore fruit. Discussions with Comín and his associates apparently helped allay fears about the role "believers" would be allowed to play in party affairs, and, in November 1974, approximately five hundred members of *Bandera Roja* entered the Catalan filial of the PCE, the PSUC.

From a numerical point of view, the fusion was only mildly significant, and then primarily in Cataluña where BR was active, but from a broader perspective it represented a significant step for the Communist party, bolstering the credibility of the PCE with the Christian-Marxist sector, many of whom now saw the Communists as ready to make important ideological and organizational concessions. Significantly, Carrillo personally negotiated the entry of BR, and Comín, besides being coopted into the PSUC Executive Committee with three of his companions, also entered the PCE Executive where he became the Spanish Communist spokesman on the Catholic question.

It is quite likely that most Communists welcomed the entry of Comín and his associates into PCE ranks as an important step toward overcoming anti-Communist sentiment in the Spanish population. Had they known the price exacted by Comín for joining, they might have been less pleased. A first sign came in February 1975, when the Executive Committee issued a statement on the membership of Christians in the PCE.[39] Although the communiqué was short and made its points lightly, there was no mistaking the thrust. Admitting that the evolution of the church in Spain and the role Christians had played in the battles defending the interests of the working class "had not always been valued and understood" by the party, the Executive Committee promised to "assume and impel forward" the Socialist option chosen by Christians. Turning to the more sensitive question of what the "Christian Communist" could expect once he joined the party, it promised the "believer" access to any and all positions of responsibility, "without any type of discrimination, with the same rights and duties as any other militant."

To soothe the tempers of those ruffled by the text, the PCE theoretical journal *Nuestra Bandera* published an explanatory article.[40] In it, Federico Melchor of the Executive Committee sought to make palatable the new announced policy about Christian faith no longer precluding full membership in the PCE. Previously, the party had admitted "believers" to its ranks, but, in keeping with the traditional Leninist posture on the issue, it did so grudgingly, emphasizing the profound contradiction between faith and the militance entailed in a Marxist, revolutionary organization. Melchor admitted that a "philosophical contradiction" made it difficult to reconcile faith in religious phenomena and belief in historical and dialectical materialism, but he now stressed that this contradiction was, to borrow the Maoist phrase, "nonantagonistic" in nature. In the final analysis, Melchor asserted, what mattered, what was "the definitive essential criterion of the Communist," was the struggle against the capitalist system, and on that issue there was plenary agreement with the Christians who had already entered and those who would join the party in the future.

The February 1975 statement and a commitment to equality for Catholics in the party were undoubtedly the price Comín exacted for his support of the *Bandera Roja* merging with the PCE. Carrillo and others in the Executive Committee may have found this a rather unobjectionable demand, but it appears that not everyone in the Committee was so favorably disposed in this matter. Melchor, for example, appeared at times less than spirited in his defense of the communiqué, and one has the sense after reading the article closely that, for all the openmindedness he projected on the issue, he apparently believed that Catholics who joined the PCE did so despite their religious faith and by no means—as Comín sometimes intimated—because of it.

Another member of the Executive Committee, Ignacio Gallego, did not come out in direct opposition to the statement, but he made his reservations clear nevertheless and suggested that limits should be imposed on organizational/ideological concessions. Gallego devoted an entire chapter in his organizational manual, *Desarrollo del Partido Comunista,* to the question of Christians in the Communist party.[41] He praised the revolutionary instincts of those Catholics who had joined the PCE, calling for "reciprocal trust" between them and other members. But—in pointed contrast to Carrillo—he downplayed the significance of their entry into Communist ranks, insisting it represented a minoritarian phenomenon in the Catholic world. The February 1975 document had adopted a rather undogmatic approach toward the contradiction between Marxism and Christianity, but Gallego emphasized once again that the party had its own underlying philosophy which Catholic members were free to accept or reject. Implicit in his argument, of course, was the notion that a member could not be fully in tune with the party so long as he clung to his religious convictions.[42]

Such manifestations of opposition or recalcitrance in its highest ranks represented only the most visible signs of discontent on these questions in the PCE. As he made clear in a speech at the Second PCE Conference in July 1975, however, Comín had a potent ally in these matters, namely Carrillo, and with his support Comín pushed for more explicit statements about the rights and duties of Catholic Communists. It was in Cataluña where Comín had at once the most success and fostered the greatest antagonism. Shortly after his entry into the party, he encouraged the PSUC Executive Committee to promote a discussion in the organization with a view to reinforcing the February 1975 statement. It was a year and a half later, at the third plenum of the PSUC Central Committee in September 1976, that the Catalan party finally issued its own substantially stronger statement on the question.[43] Stressing that the party was "confessionally neither atheist nor believer," the communiqué argued that those Catholics who joined the party had overcome "the confusion between faith and politics." The PSUC, the statement declared, should accept these people along with their faith, because through their participation in the organization its lay character would be reinforced. The identification of Communism with atheism, it went on, was "metaphysical" in nature and had supposed "a reduction in the political-ideological horizon of Marxism." Lest anyone miss the point, the penultimate paragraph in the declaration stated: "What we have expressed here about the militance of Christians is the *policy of the entire party*, a new policy which in some aspects demands a greater knowledge of the evolution of the church by the Party."(Emphasis in the original)

Opposition to this statement had been strong in some sectors of the Catalan party, with the issues of "Christian Communists" becoming linked to what critics perceived as the lack of ideological clarity, cohesion, and principle in the leadership's position. The discontent, inchoate for the most part, was articulated in an article written by PSUC Central Committee member Manuel Sacristán and published in the journal *Materiales*.[44] A long-time member of the PSUC/PCE, he was perhaps the party's most eminent theoretician, but had become increasingly disenchanted with the excessive tacticism displayed by Carrillo on this and other issues. He viewed many of the changes the PCE Secretary General had engineered as little more than a capitulation to bourgeois ideas and as tending toward the progressive elimination of democracy within the party.

Carrillo's efforts to strengthen the Communist presence among

Catholics and vice versa were vulnerable on both those counts. Sacristán said he did not object to the presence of Catholics in the Communist party. The party was lay in character, and as such its statutes did not make any philosophical declaration. And yet, he insisted, it was lay in a profoundly Marxist way, something which all who entered it should understand. It only added to the danger of ideological confusion, Sacristán declared, to see atheism and the Marxist critique of religion as only indirectly linked to the core of Marxist values. They were central to it. Sacristán then went on to berate the Communist leadership—or, in his words, "that fraction of it which is dominant on the Christian issue"—for its *entreguismo* in the ideological struggle. He insisted that the notion, broached in some party publications after the Comín entry, of an absolutely private zone each individual possessed which no one, not even the party, should penetrate was "a quintessential part of bourgeois culture" and as such, alien to Communism.

Despite Sacristán's intellectual weight, Comín prevailed. The support Carrillo gave Comín and the investment the party leadership made by inviting him into the PCE with *Bandera Roja* carried the day in Cataluña and elsewhere. Whatever Carrillo's intentions—whether he had genuinely changed since 1967 and now looked to Catholics (and the Socialists as well) to be equal partners with the PCE in the struggle for socialism—is, of course, impossbile to determine and may be irrelevant. What is important from a political point of view is the fact that the views defended by Comín became official party policy and their adoption represented quite a shift in the Communist approach. What effect these changes may have had on Spaniards' attitudes toward the PCE is a question we shall now address.

III

Despite the great attention the Communists devoted to the Catholic question and the vigorous efforts of the party in the 1960s and 1970s to overcome the almost reflexive anti-Communism of the Catholic hierarchy and subculture, they did not reap the immediate rewards their leaders had expected. The Communists made two important political mistakes with respect to the Catholic world. They underestimated the adaptability of the church hierarchy and its capacity to distance itself from the state and still remain an influential force in the country. The second miscalculation concerned the political consequences the absence of a strong Christian Democratic party would have in Spain.

The Communists had thought that if the hierarchy had lost its position as the "center of gravity"[45] for the Catholic world, there would be broad-based Catholic support for the *ruptura* with Francoism. They may have been correct in that first assessment, but the church, and more important, the hierarchy weathered Vatican II, through a combination of skill and luck. Paul VI and the Vatican played an important role in this development, judiciously using procedures adopted at the Second Vatican Council to help loosen church-state ties and shift the balance of power within the hierarchy in favor of "conciliar" bishops.

Underestimating the room for maneuver at the disposal of the reformist faction in the Church hierarchy was one of the errors committed by the Spanish Communists. They also miscalculated the necessary place and role of a Christian Democratic party in Spain. Reasoning that, as in post-World War II Italy, a Christian Democratic party would serve as a bulwark of opposition to the Left, Spanish Communist leaders had worked hard to prevent a strong, anti-Communist Christian Democratic movement from getting off the ground. This had been one of the principal reasons for the toning down of their anticlericalism. Communist efforts to prevent the emergence of such a party had been helped by the ideological diversity among the various Christian Democratic groups,[46] as well as by the personal differences separating the most prominent of those individuals.

Carrillo and the PCE assiduously courted Joaquín Ruíz Giménez in the hope that he and his associates might perhaps decide to go it alone and create a "progressive" Christian Democratic party allied with Socialists and Communists. Ruíz Giménez anguished over this option for some time, trying in the year after Franco's death to serve as a bridge within Christian Democracy and between the opposition and moderates in the regime. In the end he failed, and so did Christian Democracy. It did not lay claim successfully to the political and social Center: this feat was accomplished by Adolfo Suárez and his political vehicle, the *Unión de Centro Democrático*, in which more conservative Christian Democrats participated.

Under other circumstances, the failure of a Christian Democratic party to materialize in Spain would have been a first-rate political victory for the Spanish Communists. But PCE leaders mis-

judged when they saw Christian Democracy as the only movement or organization capable of filling the political and social Center. Many Communists were perhaps too fixed on parallels with
past developments in Italy and were convinced by a dogmatic
theory of social change that a reformist faction from within the
regime could not capture the political initiative during the transition to the post-Franco era. They refused to believe until it was
too late that such a faction, if it had mass support, would perform
admirably as the functional equivalent of Christian Democracy in
Spain.

Chapter Three

The PCE and Labor

THE DEVELOPMENT OF A presence in the labor movement was of
critical importance to the Spanish Communist leadership's efforts
to secure an important role for their party in the post-Franco era.
Traditionally, the PCE had not had much influence among the
working class in Spain: the Socialist *Unión General de Trabajadores* (UGT) and the Anarchosyndicalist *Confederación Nacional
del Trabajo* (CNT) had dominated Spanish labor prior to the Civil
War and, although perceptibly weakened after several decades of
Francoist rule, both groups retained a presence there. The working class was obviously influential in Spanish society because of
its size. Nearly 32 percent of the active population in 1960 could
be classified as belonging to the industrial proletariat and, as good
Marxist-Leninists,[1] PCE leaders could look forward to the day
when workers would constitute the overwhelming proportion of
the population. In fact, it had always been something of a sore
point with the Communists in Spain that their party had developed a reputation during the Civil War for being an organization
composed of alarmed middle-class citizens seeking protection in
the face of Socialist and Anarchist radicalism. The Civil War, it
could certainly be argued, represented an exceptional episode in
Spanish and PCE history, but if the Communists failed to develop a
base in the labor movement, this would jeopardize the political
future of a party whose historical raison d'être lay in its claim to
represent the working class and its interests.

This chapter will explore PCE efforts in the years after 1956 to develop a base in the labor movement. Our analysis will focus first on the impact of the Civil War on labor and how the UGT and CNT lost their hold on that sector. A second section will analyze the changes in Spanish society since the early 1950s and their impact on the growth of working-class dissent in the country. Next, we shall explore the origins and development of the *Comisiones Obreras,* discussing the growth of Communist influence in that movement. Finally, we shall assess the successes and failures of Communist syndical strategy and their relation to the more narrow political fortunes of the PCE.

I

Traditional, conservative forces had supported Franco during the Civil War in order to retain their hegemony over Spanish society. They preferred to deal with an emerging working class not by coopting it, but by brutally repressing it. Beginning in 1936, the insurgent Nationalist forces issued a spate of decrees outlawing independent trade unions like the UGT and CNT, expropriating their properties, and setting up a vertically organized *sindicato* to function as an integral part of the state.[2] The *Fuero del Trabajo,* issued in March 1938 and clearly patterned after the Italian and Portuguese Fascist examples, was a programmatic document announcing the creation of National-Syndicalist Centers and forbidding "all individual or collective acts which in any way disturb[ed] the normality of production." These and other laws (such as Article 222 of the Penal Code which equated strikes with acts of sedition, and the *Ley de Reglamentaciones* issued in 1942) presented the corporatist organization of society as an original and altogether felicitous way of side-stepping the problem of class conflict and of bringing about national unity. In practice, of course, nothing could have been farther from the truth: the structures were simply imposed on the working class, and the *sindicatos* functioned essentially as an instrument of state policy under the control and supervision of the only political organization permitted a legal presence, the *Falange Española Tradicionalista y de las JONS.*

Earlier, we saw that in the years after 1939 the Franco regime unleashed an extremely harsh repression on those who had supported the Popular Front. The UGT and CNT, each of which attained peak memberships of approximately 1,800,000 workers in 1937, bore an important part of this repression. Both organizations and the Communists participated in a guerrilla struggle against Franco, playing some role in the May 1947 and March 1951 strikes.[3] These were impressive demonstrations of a continuing popular resistance to the Franco regime, but with the change in the international climate and, specifically, the end of Russo-American collaboration as a result of the Cold War, any hopes the anti-Franco opposition might have had of reversing the Civil War verdict vanished. Intervention by the victorious Allies had become out of the question, and, as a result, the regime redoubled its efforts to eradicate what remained of the underground opposition network. The guerrilla movement withered away by the late 1940s, as did the UGT and CNT organizations operating in Spain. The damage each suffered is reflected in the fact that from 1943 to 1954 fifteen National Committees of the CNT and seven UGT Executive Committees fell into the hands of the police.[4]

Repression and the gradual easing of the international isolation of the Franco regime produced an atmosphere of psychological and political exhaustion in the opposition labor movement and also exacerbated tensions within the UGT and CNT organizations. Personal disputes, rooted in the period prior to 1939, had become aggravated in the wake of the Civil War and assumed an even more virulent character when the anticipated Allied intervention did not materialize and Franco remained in power. At a time when unity was of the utmost importance, various factions in the CNT, for example, revived an old quarrel over whether or not to collaborate with other opposition forces.[5] Maximalists in the organization called for abstention, while others argued in favor of cooperating with anti-Franco groups in the Republican government-in-exile. What started out as a rather Byzantine squabble among exiles had devastating consequences within Spain, where the CNT organization was deeply affected. Similar quarrels victimized the UGT. Its exile organization divided into pro-Communist and anti-Communist factions and, even after a formal reunification in 1945, tension between the two wings continued unabated for several years.

A decade and a half after the end of the Civil War, the Franco regime had a solid hold over Spanish labor. The CNT and UGT had been reduced to a precarious existence within the country (nuclei of the CNT were still somewhat active in Cataluña and those of the UGT in Asturias and the Basque country), and their leaderships had been forced into exile. The decision to shift the focus of organization from Spain to France was a natural consequence of the repression aimed at both organizations. This dislocation made it more difficult, however, for Socialists and Anarchosyndicalist leaders to remain sensitive to changes taking place in Spain, aggravating tension between exiled leaders and those living inside the country.

This was to have important consequences, for, beginning in the 1950s, Spanish society would experience a process of modernization and industrialization that dramatically transformed the face of the country, opening up new opportunities and challenges for those groups contending for influence among the working class.

I I

Isolated internationally, the Franco regime had made a virtue out of necessity in the years immediately following the Civil War, following a policy of autarchy or self-sufficiency. Unavoidable as it might have been under the circumstances, that policy was not very successful in putting Spain back on its feet after the devastation it had suffered. Indeed, the most notable accomplishment of the period appears to have been further state intervention in economic affairs. Not until 1956 did wage levels in the country attain pre-1936 levels.[6]

A change in economic policy, replacing autarky and opening most economic areas to private initiative and the play of market forces, came in the early 1950s, when the government made a commitment to rapid economic growth and industrialization. The new policy suffered from some serious shortcomings—among them the Spanish market's inability to handle the increased production resulting from industrial expansion. This contributed to a short-term crisis in 1955–56, when a rapid inflationary spiral reduced the value of the *peseta* and caused a rapid depletion of currency reserves. But in the longer run, the change would contribute to a deep transformation of the sociostructural bases of the country. In a little over two decades, Spain developed from an agrarian, rural country with over 49 percent of its active population engaged in agriculture into a largely industrialized, urban one, in which (in 1975) that percentage had dropped to approximately 26.[7] Economic expansion led millions of Spaniards to emigrate during those years to urban centers like Madrid and Barcelona and to cities in the Basque country.[8] This not only effected profound changes in the habits and thinking of many people, but also set the structural conditions for new manifestations of labor conflict and dissent.

The economic policies initiated in 1951 promoted rapid economic growth but, as we indicated earlier, also had some less favorable consequences. They triggered an inflation rate averaging 10 percent annually for a period of five years. Wages did not keep pace, and labor discontent grew in many parts of the country.[9] As noted earlier, there had been strikes in May 1947 and in March 1951 (as well as in Bilbao in December 1953), but the strike movement that began in the spring of 1956 in Pamplona and subsequently spread to Barcelona and Asturias was of much greater importance. These strikes mobilized large numbers of people, and the government acceded to many of the demands, granting significant wage increases in April and November of that year. More important, the strikes sparked the first overt manifestations in Spanish cities and universities of political opposition to the regime.

We have already discussed the importance of the year 1956 as a turning point in recent Spanish history. It is important to note here only that the wage raises decreed that year aggravated rather than resolved the economic crisis, stimulating consumption and inflation. The February 1957 ministerial reshuffle introduced a group of technocrats, affiliated with the secular religious organization known as *Opus Dei*, into the Cabinet and adjunct administrative organs. Charged with the key economic ministries, that group instituted important changes in the economic policies of the regime. Their objective was to promote growth and productivity by streamlining the economy and integrating it into the international economic system without jeopardizing Spanish authoritarian political structures.

Changes in the economic policies of the regime affected industrial relations as well. In April 1958, the new Cabinet revamped the existing collective bargaining law.[10] Previously, the official *Organización Sindical* (OS) negotiated wages under guidelines set by the Ministry of Labor. The system had been made more flexible in June 1956, but it was not until nearly two years later that the government finally allowed employers and employees to negotiate contracts in those factories with fifty or more employees. The decision—taken primarily in an effort to increase productivity and defuse the political volatility of labor-management conflict—also energized the roles of *enlaces sindicales* (shop stewards) and *jurados de empresa* (collective-bargaining negotiating committees) which formed part of the official syndical structure.[11]

The labor situation began to change under the new system. A potent strike movement began in Asturias and the Basque country in 1957 and 1958, picking up once again in late 1961 and 1962 and spreading to Madrid, Barcelona, and Valencia as well. Many in the opposition inaccurately thought the movement presaged the imminent downfall of the Franco regime. This did not happen, and it eventually became clear that the strikes had a predominantly economic character. Those in 1961–62 coincided with the end of a wage freeze imposed by the March 1959 Stabilization Plan. Moreover, the massive migration to Europe (particularly France and Germany) which began in the late 1950s also alleviated the crisis.[12] Not only was a potentially volatile labor surplus exported, but these same emigrants became a prime source of revenue for the Spanish economy through the remittances they sent home. However, the effort to revitalize the official syndical structure and to make it a functional channel for worker demands and discontent brought the government mixed results. Statistics reveal that the changes in the collective bargaining structures had quite an impact on the number of contracts negotiated directly by employers and employees,[13] but the decision also weakened the *Organización Sindical* at the factory level, giving the syndical opposition an opening it could exploit.

III

Generally speaking, the syndical opposition of the late 1950s and early 1960s fell into three broad categories.

There were, first, the vestiges of the UGT and CNT in Spain. Both organizations had suffered heavily in the first decades of the Franco regime and saw in the strike movements of the late 1950s and early 1960s an opportunity to revitalize their organizations. In early 1960, they joined forces with the Basque trade union *Solidaridad de Trabajadores Vascos* to found the *Alianza Sindical* (AS). Created largely through the efforts of the exiled UGT and CNT leaderships, the AS was not long lived, falling victim to a growing rift between the exile community and militants working in Spain.

The latter soon left, establishing their own *Alianza Sindical Obrera* (ASO). It received financial and organizational support from the International Confederation of Free Trade Unions and the International Federation of Metallurgical Workers, its members participating in the nascent *Comisiones Obreras* until 1963–64. At that point, they withdrew, arguing the need for a specifically separate and clandestine trade union organization.[14]

The second important component of the syndical opposition developed out of the Catholic Action movement. Under the terms of the August 1953 Concordat signed with the Vatican, apostolic organizations like the *Hermandades Obreras de Acción Católica* (HOAC) and the *Juventud Obrera Católica* (JOC) could organize among the working class, functioning independent of (although in theory certainly not at cross-purposes with) the official vertical syndical structure. Strictly speaking, the Concordat did not grant them official recognition as a separate union, but it did give the HOAC and JOC great flexibility and latitude in fulfilling their apostolate. As a result, Catholic Action militants were well placed to profit from the organizational vacuum created by the failure of the regime-sponsored structures to respond to the demands of an expanding working class. They played an important role in the strikes of the late 1950s and early 1960s, and, on one notable occasion, the government even fined the HOAC national president for supporting the Asturias mineworkers' strike of 1962.[15]

In the course of those years, as HOAC and JOC activists sought to resolve the contradiction between Church social teaching and the unequivocal alignment of the Catholic hierarchy with an oppressive political regime, the apostolic labor organizations underwent a secularization (closely resembling the experience of ACLI in Italy), with the more radical elements playing an important role in the growth and development of the *Comisiones Obreras*. Many groups emerged from Catholic Action and joined the ranks of the opposition. The most important of these were the *Unión Sindical Obrera* (USO), many of whose leading cadres came from the JOC and the *Acción Sindical de Trabajadores* (AST), whose first members came from the Madrid-based and Jesuit-sponsored *Vanguardia Obrera Juvenil*. Both organizations soon transcended their Catholic origins, but it was the AST whose evolution was most marked. Adopting a Marxist-Leninist philosophy in the late 1960s, it also changed names, becoming the *Organización Revolucionaria de Trabajadores* (ORT).

The Communist party was the third important component of this syndical opposition. The PCE had no significant labor presence in Spain prior to the Civil War. It had made some headway in the UGT after 1934 when Communist militants joined the Socialist-led union, and had expanded that influence during the Civil War. Nevertheless, except in Cataluña where the UGT had fallen for the most part under the control of the Catalan Communist organization, the PCE was still far from challenging the hegemony the UGT and CNT exercised over the Spanish working class. After the Franco victory, the Communists suffered a repression no less virulent than that aimed at the Socialists or Anarchosyndicalists: indeed, as it was presumed to be an agent of Moscow, the PCE may have been treated more harshly. Because it had fewer labor activists, however, the repression was probably less extensive numerically.

Earlier, we noted the decision of Spanish and Catalan Communist leaders in October 1948 to abandon the guerrilla struggle against Franco and the illusion of a possible national insurrection against his rule. At this same meeting, they decided to infiltrate organizations like the *sindicatos verticales* and the *Sindicato Español Universitario* with access to mass audiences and whose structures permitted Communists to develop contacts among the general population. Longstanding revolutionary practice suggested PCE members active in the labor movement combine, insofar as they could, legal and illegal activities,[16] but such a policy also had sources in Spanish tradition. The PSOE and UGT had collaborated in the government of Spanish dictator Primo de Rivera (1923–30) in an effort to outflank the CNT in the labor movement.

Communist leaders saw the decision to work within the *Organización Sindical* and to participate in the periodic syndical elections as allowing the PCE to break the traditional Socialist/Anarchosyndicalist hold on labor. Nonetheless, the decision did not meet with universal approval. First put into practice in 1950, the policy had detractors who felt it only reinforced the vertical structures, and for several years, the Communists had a difficult time convincing workers that, despite a justified repugnance toward the *Organización Sindical*, penetrating its structures would in the longer run work to Communist advantage.[17] Polemics on this issue became rather heated in the 1960s and early 1970s, but the April 1958 changes in the collective-bargaining scheme appeared to make the Communist decision particularly prescient.

Not only did this approach permit the Communists to develop a presence among the new generations of Spanish workers then flooding the major cities, and offer a pool from which to recruit new cadres, but, by encouraging interaction with Catholic Action militants at the factory level, it also effected a rapprochement with important sectors of the Catholic Church.

Anarchists and Socialists, Communists, Catholics and even some disenchanted Falangists were active in the first *comisiones obreras* which developed in Spain in the latter part of the 1950s. For most observers of the Spanish political and syndical scene, the words *comisiones obreras* today define a trade union characterized by its close ties to the Communist party and political line. But this was by no means the case in 1957–58 when the first *comisión obrera* negotiated grievances and wages with representatives of the *La Camocha* mine in Asturias. That *comisión obrera* and those appearing later were spontaneous, dissolving once the conflict that spawned them subsided. During this early phase, they acted as workers' councils formed to handle grievances that the *Organización Sindical* avoided. Ironically, it was the government decision in 1958 to stimulate economic recovery by changing the collective-bargaining system that gave the movement a shot in the arm. *Comisiones* formed by *enlaces, jurados* and/or other activists, all designated by their fellow workers, carried on negotiations at the factory level and—where the movement was strong—reported back to general worker assemblies.[18] During this phase, the *comisiones obreras* was a broad movement bringing together those resisting Franco's imposed structures as well as the many who simply found that the official structures did not adequately represent their interests.

The *comisiones obreras* benefitted initially from an uncertain juridical status: at first, the regime entertained the notion that it could channel dissent through them. This explains in part the relative tolerance exhibited by the regime as the *comisiones obreras* began to put down organizational roots after the 1962–63 strikes. The next two or three years saw an expansion of the *comisiones* as they developed provincial and regional structures.

It was during this organizational expansion and transformation of the *comisiones* that the Communists distinguished themselves. They had initially created a vehicle known as the *Oposición Sindical Obrera* (OSO), through which they hoped to harness the *comisiones obreras* to the party.[19] This effort was unsuccessful: the oso consisted of little more than the PCE worker cells, and after a few years Communist leaders dissolved the organization. They ordered militants to work exclusively within the nascent organization being built up around the workers' commissions. Communist labor activists played important roles in fleshing out provincial, regional, and eventually national infrastructures, developing a substantial Communist influence in the organization.

Another reason the regime tolerated the *comisiones obreras* movement involved the struggle for influence being waged by the Falange and the *Opus Dei* at the government level and by the Falange and groups within Catholic Action at the syndical level. The Falange, though it had lost influence after the 1957 Cabinet reshuffle, still had an important voice in syndical affairs through the administrative apparatus of the *Movimiento,* with which it tried to reinforce its position in the government and in its competition with Catholic labor activists. The ambivalence some Falangists felt toward the regime now manifested itself with the participation of individuals like José Hernándo and Ceferino Maestú Barrio in the *Comisiones Obreras.* Concerned over what they perceived to be the incipient Communist control over the *Comisiones* organization, however, they soon left the cc.oo., and in 1967 participated in an abortive effort with the uso, the ugt, and a Christian-oriented *Federación Solidaria de Trabajadores* to create a *Frente Democrático Sindical.*[20]

With the departure of the Falangist elements from *comisiones* and the earlier withdrawal of those Anarchosyndicalists and Socialists still affiliated with the CNT and UGT, Communists and Catholic Action activists became the animating spirit in the cc.oo. The great majority of those participating in the *comisiones obreras* had no political affiliation and had been attracted to the movement either by its success in forcing the renegotiation of higher wages or—and this was important in light of the Anarchosyndicalist tradition—by its syndicalist thrust in calling for autonomy from all political parties and for class unity. These reasons remained valid for many who joined in strike movements and demonstrations through the end of the Franco era and during the transition to democracy. As we move from *movimiento* to *organización,* from *comisiones* to *Comisiones,* people of this persuasion were less in evidence, however. Instead, Communists and radicalized Catholic labor activists had the greater influence.

The mid-1960s were a time of exhilaration for those who supported or were active in the *Comisiones Obreras*. It was not that other organizations had vanished completely from the Spanish syndical map; rather that the CC.OO., claiming factory assemblies as its source of legitimacy but using the posts of *enlaces* and *jurados* for protection, continued to expand their organization.[21] This was the context for the *Comisiones Obreras'* first national documents—*Ante el Futuro del Sindicalismo*, appearing in March 1966, and *Qué Son las Comisiones Obreras?* issued in June of that year—in which they openly rejected the existing syndical organization and criticized capitalist society as fundamentally unjust.[22]

The notion that *Comisiones* would soon enough step into the vacuum left by a disintegrating *Organización Sindical* found fertile ground in the minds of many activists, not least among Communists who saw the Franco regime and the economic oligrachy it represented as more isolated than ever and in its final phase of decomposition. They saw in the various liberalization measures announced in the years after 1962[23] ample proof of the regime's diminished will to resist. For example, with the modification of Article 222 of the penal code, all strikes were still illegal, but the new law distinguished between political and economic strikes and did not equate the latter with military sedition.

This was the situation when the Franco regime announced the convocation of syndical elections for September 1966. Calling for a heavy turnout, the minister secretary general of the *Movimiento*, José Solís, went on national television to tell Spaniards that "the [offical] syndicalism was not at the service of any political group." The regime cranked up its propaganda apparatus and proclaimed the slogan, "Vote for the best!" The decision to encourage participation contrasted sharply with the downplaying of these elections when they were first introduced, but the new policy was readily understandable in 1966. It fit with the image of moderation and openness the government tried to project as it pursued entry into the European Economic Community. The syndical elections had been also designed to affect the municipal races scheduled for November. More important, the regime hoped to influence the December 1966 referendum for the *Ley Orgánica* which would insure the institutional continuity of the regime. These demonstrations of popular participation were designed to convince foreign, primarily European observers that, despite much that was dubious about the regime, Spain was not, after all, so different from its neighbors.

The *Comisiones Obreras* also called for a heavy turnout but, as might be expected, for quite different reasons from the government. Syndical elections had last been held in 1963. This time around, in the language used at the time, the *Comisiones* leaders hoped to capture the vertical syndicate. They wanted a clear electoral victory at the first step toward unleashing a general strike which would oust Franco and his collaborators.

Participation in the 1966 syndical elections was quite high, with over 80 percent turning out; abstentions occurred to a significant degree only in the Basque country and Cataluña. The *Comisiones* claimed an enormous success in the elections and its leaders became convinced that the end of Francoism was imminent. The Communists, to take the predictions of a group whose influence was becoming more and more preponderant within the CC.OO., concluded in the aftermath that the situation facing the government and the opposition was very similar to that preceding the massive victory by antimonarchical groups in the April 1931 municipal elections forcing the abdication of Alfonso XIII and the establishment of a parliamentary republic. It is now evident their optimism and that of groups to their Left (with which they were in radical disagreement regarding the role of the middle classes in opposing Franco) was not well founded. Political and syndical activists of most opposition groups underestimated the regime's resolution in the face of growing dissent as well as its capacity for repression. The CC.OO. call for public protest against the 1966 referendum, and the refusal of labor activists associated with the Communist party to eschew public meetings of the *Comisiones,* on the grounds that it was neither a clandestine or an illegal organization, had harsh repercussions. As one member of the *Brigada Político-Social* told one arrested activist: "We might not be able any longer to stop the working class, but we are going to screw you, the leaders."[24]

The government's decision to crack down on the *Comisiones Obreras* began to be carried out before the December 1966 referendum but intensified perceptibly after nationwide demonstrations organized by the CC.OO. in January 1967 drew thousands of people. In response, the government ordered the arrest of hundreds of *Comisiones* and other labor activists. The *Tribunal Supremo,* for its part, declared the CC.OO. to be organizationally dependent on the Communist party and an illegal political association in violation of the Penal Code.[25] The repression decimated many provincial and regional organizations: within months, *Comisiones* organizations in Vizcaya, Barcelona, Madrid, and elsewhere had been dismembered. The climax came in 1969, when the government declared martial law throughout Spain. Coinciding as it did with a downturn in the national economy, the repression put *Comisiones* at a considerable disadvantage. An increase in unemployment made strike actions difficult and dangerous, and a wage freeze decreed in November 1967 set a ceiling of 5.9 percent on raises included in any renegotiated contract.[26] Many employers, looking for an excuse to get rid of troublesome workers, provoked strikes and then fired people.

Communist influence in the *Comisiones* organization—already strong before 1966—increased markedly with the government decision to break the CC.OO. The PCE, the one organization with a real national network, put itself at the disposal of the *Comisiones* and tightened its control over the policy-making bodies of the movement. Another important and related element in the expansion of Communist influence in the CC.OO. was the party's role in coordinating and distributing solidarity funds from outside Spain. The PCE funneled money and organizational assistance to the *Comisiones* from Communist-controlled or -influenced unions like the *Confédération Générale du Travail* and *Confederazione Generale Italiana del Lavoro* and from the Soviet-backed World Federation of Trade Unions.[27]

The repression and the tense political atmosphere exacerbated the problems between *Comisiones* and other groups. Some organizations like the USO, a participant in the first *comisiones obreras,* and whose syndicalist orientation was well known, withdrew from the *Comisiones* during this period, charging that it had become a mere "transmission belt" for the PCE.[28] The UGT had disavowed any connection with the *comisiones obreras,* once their organizational transformation was underway, and accused the Communist party of seizing control of the organization despite its much-touted suprapartisan nature. The UGT likewise criticized the decision to participate in the syndical elections as falling for a well-laid government trap.

Other groups—sprouting from the Sino-Soviet split—ripped into the PCE for controlling the *Comisiones* but reserved their most acid epithets for the politics of National Reconciliation, seeing its emphasis on peaceful change and broad-alliance politics as a capitulation to the Spanish bourgeoisie. Their outrage became particularly intense in the wake of the May 1968 events in France and the "hot autumn" Italy experienced a year later.[29]

The debate within the *Comisiones Obreras* between the Communists and those to their Left focused on several issues. One was what response the CC.OO. should adopt with respect to the repression unleashed by the government. We have already seen that the PCE urged its activists in the *Comisiones* to mobilize the working class and go on the offensive. The June 1967 *Asamblea General* of the CC.OO. took up this call, directing its activists to resist the *clandestinización* of the organization.[30] The extreme Left groups agreed with the Communist thesis that "the abyss between the political system and the *fuerzas vivas* of the country" had never been greater, but they concluded that in the face of the government offensive, the CC.OO. should forsake their public character and go underground. The danger in such a response, as the Communists did not hesitate to indicate, lay in having *Comisiones* become little more than a sect, losing what mass audience it had developed.[31]

Another issue dividing *Comisiones* was the relationship the working class and the CC.OO. should have with other classes or forces in the struggle against Franco. The Communists hoped to negotiate a joint platform between the working class, middle-class forces, and even the so-called evolutionist current within the regime. In this process, they envisaged the *Comisiones* as elaborating an economic program capable at once of galvanizing the working class and reassuring the middle classes by having as its only political dimension the attainment of democratic liberties.[32] The various extreme Left groups in *Comisiones* espoused radically different views. Unlike the PCE, they saw no chance for a bourgeois-democratic revolution in Spain: the socioeconomic system there was a state-monopoly capitalist one, and from that phase the only possible advance was to a socialist one. Accordingly, the parties of the Left and those active in the CC.OO. should not waste their time trying to attract the middle classes to their banner. Instead, they should defend an openly anticapitalist orientation.[33]

A final but related point of disagreement concerned the role of the *Comisiones Obreras*. The Spanish Communist party had described *Comisiones* as the prototype of the *sindicato de nuevo tipo*. It would not function along classical trade-union lines, but act instead as a *movimiento sociopolítico* drawing no distinction between *afiliados* and *no afiliados*. Concurrently, there ran an effort to set up permanent structures for the organization of *Comisiones*. The expanded Communist influence after 1963 led to serious internal difficulties in *Comisiones,* with the extreme leftists charging the PCE had betrayed the original ideals of the movement. The charge may have been just, for the Communists certainly had not hesitated to use the CC.OO. to further their political objectives. However the most vociferous of their accusers would have proceeded likewise had they had the opportunity, hence, their demands that *comisiones* function as a nascent organ of working-class power or as the embryo of a new proletarian party must be viewed with some skepticism.[34]

The arguments between the Communists and the ultra-Left became particularly vehement in Cataluña and had a very deleterious effect on the working-class movement there. The opposition to the PCE/PSUC focused on the *Front Obrer de Catalunya.* The FOC was the Catalan branch of the FLP (or "Felipes"). The founders of the FLP/FOC had been much impressed by the example of the Algerian FLN and the 26th of July Movement in Cuba, and presented their organization as a radical and revolutionary alternative to the reformist practice of the Communist and Socialist parties. At once disdainful and admiring of the PCE, FOC activists collaborated with the party in the May 1958 national strike and, more generally, played a role in the demonstrations of the period. Relations between the FLP/FOC and the Catalan Communists deteriorated sharply in the mid-1960s, as the former used its influence among metallurgical workers to take control of the *Comisión Obrera Local de Barcelona* (COLB). In an effort to preempt further FOC efforts to disrupt Communist control over the nascent national *Comisiones* organization, PSUC labor activists created their own vehicle, the *Coordinadora Nacional de Catalunya* (CONC).[35]

The two organizations waged a bitter internecine battle and proved unable to put their rivalries aside in the interest of unity against Franco. While the CONC organized itself around textile, construction, and metal industries, the COLB called for the organization of *Comisiones* by geographical zones, hoping to combine the workers commissions with neighborhood associations. When the government decreed its wage freeze in November 1967 and the PSUC indicated it did not necessarily oppose worker participation in the negotiation of new wage agreements, the FOC predictably called for the boycott of all negotiations. The disputes probably did little to earn either organization the respect of the unaffiliated worker, who had little inkling about the reasons for all the fuss.[36]

The repression aimed at *Comisiones* and other labor organizations in the late 1960s and early 1970s did not diminish labor conflict in Spain. Strikes and work stoppages, which had earlier focused primarily on economic demands, changed in character. They became shorter in duration, but were increasingly demonstrations of worker solidarity. *Conflictividad laboral,* as the government euphemistically described the still-illegal strikes, did not decline. Meanwhile, labor militance became more widespread.[37] After 1970, hardly a year went by without an important strike and in some cases violent confrontations with the police.[38]

The harsh repression suffered by *Comisiones* activists at the hands of the regime damaged but did not eradicate the clandestine organization of the movement. The government, aided on occasion by employers eager to rid themselves of troublesome employees, forced the dismissal of thousands of activists and the arrest of many others.[39]

Ironically enough, the repression unleashed on the *Comisiones Obreras* helped establish that organization as the single national symbol of labor opposition to the dictatorship. This preeminence, together with the undoubted political and organizational abilities CC.OO. activists displayed in the fight for higher salaries and benefits, was to have important consequences in the post-Franco era. It helped the *Comisiones* hold its own against a revitalized UGT in the months after Franco's death in November 1975. The repression also formed a core of dedicated labor activists upon which the Communists could build a mass-based party, and their presence on PCE lists in the June 1977 and March 1979 elections attracted worker votes to the party.

The negative consequences of the Communist insistence that *Comisiones* activists function openly (*salir a la superficie,* in the jargon of the period) were manifest. The "catastrophist analysis of the correlation of forces"—a term used by a PCE Central Committee member to describe the Communist assessment in the late 1960s and early 1970s—is apparent from even a cursory glance at the numerous communiqués issued by various *Reuniones Generales* of the *Comisiones* from 1967 to 1972.[40] Many people paid a price, either being dismissed from their jobs or arrested, for what in retrospect must be considered a serious political error on the part of the Communist leadership. That the party and the

Comisiones Obreras were not more heavily damaged by the experience is in large measure due to the failure of the opponents to capitalize on those mistakes. However unwise the decisions adopted by the PCE, the policies of the extreme Left were even more so. Communist calls for and predictions of a general strike were clearly off the mark, but ultra-Left claims that Spain was on the verge of a socialist revolution and one that would come on the heels of a violent uprising bordered on the lunatic.

Outside the *Comisiones* and the various factions operating within it, only two organizations had influence in the labor movement. One was the *Unión Sindical Obrera,* with some strength in Cataluña, Madrid, and the Basque country. The other was the UGT, which retained influence only in the Basque country and Asturias. We know that repression had heavily damaged the UGT in the decades after the Civil War. Its decision to boycott the regime-sponsored syndical election hurt the UGT as well, cutting the organization off from the new sources of working-class activism. The USO had withdrawn from the CC.OO., but, unlike the UGT, its militants continued to favor electoral participation. Both organizations placed themselves at a marked disadvantage with respect to the *Comisiones* by trying to maintain classical trade union structures under the Franco dictatorship. All three were clandestine, but the CC.OO. claimed factory assemblies as the source of their legitimacy and also had a greater flexibility.

One of the most divisive issues facing the labor movement in the 1960s and 1970s concerned political infiltration of the *Organización Sindical.* The Communist party favored such participation from the outset. Only after the *Comisiones* organizational expansion during the mid-1960s (and particularly in the context of the 1966 syndical elections) did the matter assume a real importance, however. It was at this point that the Communists began to consider seriously the possibility of capturing the existing syndical structure from within. Thereafter, the PCE became the most assiduous supporter of participation. Those organizations refusing to endorse such a course of action would become, Communist leaders believed, meaningless anachronisms in the syndical panorama.

So convinced were they of the shrewdness of their strategy that in 1971, when the government followed up suspension of *habeas corpus* throughout the country with a decision permitting the renovation of only 50 percent of the *enlaces,* the Communists still urged workers to vote and denounced those who favored abstention.[41] Over 80 percent of the eligible working population voted, but abstentions were again high in the Basque country (recall that the trials of *Euzkadi ta Askatasuna* terrorists had been held less than a year before) and in some of the most strife-torn factories in the country.

Four years later, when the next elections were celebrated, the situation was less tense, with supporters and opponents of the regime generally waiting for the death of the aged *caudillo*. Participation was greater than in 1971, with USO, ORT, and the *Partido del Trabajo* joining the PCE in fielding candidates. Despite the relatively high turnout, the elections still did not establish the utility of infiltrating the *sindicato vertical*. While sources close to *Comisiones* claimed that its candidates had won 70 to 80 percent of the *enlace* and *jurado* posts, the *Organización Sindical* insisted that the opposition had captured only 3 or 4 percent of the total.[42] The real figure probably lies somewhere in the middle: perhaps 25 to 30 percent of the *enlaces* elected in the larger factories of the larger cities were members of the *candidatura democrática unitaria*, as the opposition was called. In any case, many who supported *Comisiones* were more economically than politically motivated.

The argument over what proportion of *enlaces/jurados* belonged to the labor opposition underscores one difficulty we face in measuring the success of the tactics of *Comisiones* and other organizations. Determining how close the Communists came to fulfilling the objectives set years before is also difficult. Were a verdict to be based on the results in the syndical elections of early 1978,[43] and if our judgment took into account the virtual absence of Communists in the syndical field prior to the Civil War, we would have to pronounce that tactic as a complete success. If, on the other hand, we use as our measure the objectives the PCE originally set for itself, namely, one day to step in and take control of the *Organización Sindical*, then a less favorable judgment must be made.

Election to the post of *enlace* or *jurado* gave a member of the labor opposition ample latitude and access to worker assemblies and the like. Yet in some factories, election to such posts and genuine representation of workers' interests was tantamount to asking for dismissal or arrest. There were cities and regions, as well as industrial branches, where penetration of the syndical structures was effective,[44] but these were exceptional cases. By and large, the pyramidal structure of the OS acted as a barrier against infiltrators. Procedural rules limited the eligible candidates to employees who had worked at a factory for two years, in most cases, and who had never resigned or been ousted from the syndical organization. The method of indirect election had workers electing *enlaces* at the first level, but the electorate narrowed through each of the seven successive steps.[45]

Most of the polemics about the efficacy of efforts to penetrate the *Organización Sindical* in the 1960s and 1970s pitted the Communists, the *Comisiones Obreras,* and several other groups against either the more traditional syndical organizations like the UGT and CNT or against various extreme Left parties. Debate spread in the wake of the June 1975 syndical elections, with the apparent success of *Comisiones* candidates. Strong arguments erupted within the Communist party about the implications of the showing and, more indirectly, about what had been accomplished by participating in the syndical elections over the previous ten or fifteen years.

One group in the Spanish Communist leadership, whose most visible spokesman was Isidor Boix, at the time a member of the *Partit Socialista Unificat de Catalunya* Secretariat with responsibility for labor affairs and of the PCE Executive Committee, insisted that the *Comisiones* performance in June 1975 had made possible the takeover of the *Organización Sindical.* Basing their arguments primarily on the experience of the Baix Llobregat (where, labor activists affiliated with *Comisiones* had taken over provincial and branch unions and had formed an *Intersindical* to coordinate strikes in the region), Boix and others contended that the *ruptura sindical,* the syndical equivalent of the PCE demand for a break with all Francoist institutions, had already begun.[46] The time had come for leadership to pass from *Comisiones* to those individuals in elected posts in the vertical hierarchy who would be the architects of the future *confederación sindical unitaria.*

In voicing these views, Boix was simply elaborating a theme Communist leaders had always stressed: namely, that the way to achieve the *ruptura* was to penetrate the *sindicato vertical* and take it over, that a ready-made skeleton for organic labor unity was in place. His argument was perfectly consistent with the spirit of early *Comisiones* statements which suggested that the CC.OO. represented all of the working class and as such was the rightful heir of the *sindicato vertical*. Communist leaders had repeatedly emphasized their commitment to that ideal as well as to the suprapartisan nature of the *Comisiones* as movement and organization. What had begun as a necessity, imposed upon the labor movement because of its inchoate structure and its reliance on factory assemblies, the PCE sought to make a virtue. The Communists insisted, that *Comisiones* was the prototype of a *sindicato de nuevo tipo*, an original contribution to reunification at the national and international level of a labor movement split after 1917. If it could achieve the *ruptura* at the syndical level and thereby contribute decisively to the demise of the Franco regime, then the CC.OO. would become the hegemonic force in Spanish labor. *Comisones*, the Communists believed, would then have little difficulty implanting a factory-council system of industrial relations, particularly since the 1958 collective-bargaining law gave Spanish workers many rights that, at a formal level, went much beyond those existing in other European countries.

The Boix posture was perfectly consistent with previous Communist-party doctrine as well as with the syndicalist thrust of many *Comisiones* statements of the mid-1960s.[47] But such statements of ecumenical intention had been painless to make when *Comisiones* appeared to be the only candidate for labor influence in the country; in 1975 this was no longer the case. *Comisiones* now faced competition not only from the *Unión Sindical Obrera* but from the UGT, which had been dormant for much of the previous decade. Invigorated by the ouster of older leaders in 1971 by younger militants working within Spain and by the infusion of organizational/financial assistance from Western European unions like the *Deutsche Gesellschaftsbund* (DGB) after the April 1974 revolution in Portugal, the UGT had begun to enlist members of the younger generation of Spanish workers to its ranks.

The growth of these two unions, which opposed factory councils as defined by *Comisiones* on the grounds these served only to obfuscate the reality of Communist control of the organization, forced a change in PCE policy. Heretofore, the Communists had considered the PSOE-supported UGT (there was less hostility toward the USO since many Communist labor activists believed an accommodation with it would be easier) as a candidate for extinction and obscurity. Although PCE leaders certainly did not believe that either the UGT or the USO could pose a real challenge to *Comisiones* and to the incipient Communist hegemony over the labor movement, they could no longer ignore those organizations altogether and instead had to find ways of neutralizing that presence. Such an effort could only be successful if the PCE consolidated its own control over the *Comisiones*. Any premature move to occupy the *sindicato vertical* would be disastrous for the party.

Fear of just such an outcome caused a majority in the PCE leadership to look with disfavor on the Boix thesis. His analysis implied that *Comisiones* would act as a catalyst in the takeover of the *Organización Sindical*, but that, as a catalyst, its formal organization (where the party was firmly in control) would be consumed during the transformation. The majority wanted the reinforcement of *Comisiones* as a mass-based organization under the leadership of the Communist party. It regarded with horror suggestions such as those advanced by Boix because their implementation would jeopardize Communist influence and hegemony.[48] The PCE Second National Conference in September 1975 hotly debated the issues, and, a few weeks later at a meeting of Communist labor activists, the party rejected the proposal put forward by Boix.[49]

With the post-Franco era visibly around the corner, the PCE had to address forthrightly the task of bringing about the *ruptura sindical*. Boix and his supporters had presented the case for one possible course of action; as we have seen, it did not find much favor. Nicolás Sartorius, the leading ideologue of the *Comisiones* and already a prominent figure in the Communist party, publicly sketched another proposal.[50] In his article, Sartorius emphasized how *Comisiones* had to maintain its heritage as a movement incorporating all workers and perform as an organization with defined structures. Admitting that *Comisiones* might have to accept the continued presence of groups with more classical trade-union structures, he urged it to resist the temptation of becoming an organization based simply on *afiliados*. Such a course would denude the movement of its originality. As a *movimiento organizado sociopolítico*, the CC.OO. had to find the formula that would permit individual membership, while relying on general factory assemblies for legitimacy and support. Sartorius proposed (the idea had been floated by *Comisiones* on and off since 1967) that all the organizations making up the labor opposition to the regime join in sponsoring a *congreso sindical constituyente* from which the *confederación unitaria* would emerge.

Various documents published by the Comisiones in late 1975 and early 1976 picked up on this idea,[51] and CC.OO. leaders intensified their efforts to persuade the UGT and USO to participate. The only catch was that the proposed merger would not occur between equal partners: *Comisiones* would be the axis on which the new confederation would turn. As might be expected, the other organizations rejected the offer. While aware that the notion of syndical unity undoubtedly appealed to many Spanish workers, they saw the idea proposed by *Comisiones* and the Communists as a rather transparent effort to establish their own control over the entire labor movement.[52]

The dispute over Communist influence in the *Comisiones Obreras* became particularly heated in the wake of a July 1976 PCE Central Committee session held in Rome. It then became public knowledge that 21 of 27 members of the *Coordinadora General* belonged to the PCE and that Marcelino Camacho belonged to its Executive Committee. The report did much to reinforce the idea that *Comisiones*, despite its claims to autonomy and independence, was very much *the* Communist trade union in the country. While it had been more or less an open secret that Camacho and other prominent *Comisiones* leaders were members of the PCE, what surprised and disturbed many Spaniards was the extent of Communist influence in the highest policy-making body of the CC.OO. and the degree to which the PCE had tried to disguise that fact. The UGT too had very close ties to the PSOE, but this had always been rather openly acknowledged.

In the face of unfavorable UGT and USO responses to *Comisiones* overtures, the CC.OO. leadership decided at a gathering in May 1976 of seventy-nine national delegates to persist and hold the *congreso sindical* themselves.[53] *Comisiones* proposed that the election of delegates for this congress take place at factory assemblies open to all workers, and that a million cards be distributed and sold to its supporters. The problem, of course, was that *Comisiones* claimed the delegates elected would represent the entire factory and made no effort to clarify whether or not buying a card meant one was a member of the *Comisiones Obreras*. But CC.OO. leaders obviously overestimated how much they could capitalize on this intentional ambiguity. The proposal received such strong criticism—threatening moreover Communist efforts to effect a rapprochement with the PSOE and thus insure the Socialists did not accept legalization without demanding the same for the PCE—that less than a month later *Comisiones* leaders admitted they were not organizing the *congreso obrero*, but simply an *Asamblea General*. When it finally met in late June 1976, the delegates adopted the Communist proposal that *Comisiones* be transformed into something like a trade union with membership rolls, but preserving its flexible structures.[54]

The shift in policy had been forced upon the *Comisiones* by the reality of syndical pluralism and by the failure of the opposition to consummate the long-awaited *ruptura política*. Some Communist labor activists continued to speculate about such a *ruptura* and about the impossibility of reforming either the existing political or syndical structures because the perpetuation of such an illusion helped the party galvanize support within the CC.OO. for its organizational transformation. Thus, Sartorius in his report to the *Asamblea General* argued that such a reinforcement would facilitate the mobilizations necessary to accomplish the *ruptura*. Such verbal aggressiveness had little relation to practice, however, as the Communists had forsaken public demonstrations after March or April 1976, for fear that such policies would simply increase the hostility of the military toward the party. But the vitriolic language temporarily appeased the demands of a minority faction within the *Comisiones* that was associated with extreme Left groups, like the ORT and the PTE, which wanted the CC.OO. to brush aside the objections of other syndical organizations and create a *central unitaria*.[55] The so-called *unitarios* presented a proposal along those lines at the *Asamblea*, receiving the support of about 10 percent of the delegates for their motion. Several months later, however the PTE and ORT withdrew from *Comisones* to set up separate organizations.

So far we have emphasized the tactical side of Communist policy toward the *Comisiones Obreras* as it related to the *ruptura*. We should also stress that only the most cynical Communist labor activists bandied about the term *ruptura*; many had a deep emotional commitment to its realization, even as this stubbornness in the face of political developments retarded *Comisiones*'s organizational transformation.[56] Blinded in some ways by the desire to consummate a *ruptura* and to celebrate the *congreso obrero constituyente* (still talked about in September 1976), *Comisiones* leaders saw the unity-of-action pact it signed with the UGT and USO in late summer 1976 (known as the *Coordinadora de Organizaciones Sindicales*) as an important first step toward a not-too-distant organic unity. In fact, nothing could have been farther from the truth: the COS never really got off the ground and eventually

disbanded in March 1977 after the UGT demanded, as the condition for its continued participation, that all who held posts in the
sindicato vertical resign.

IV

By late summer 1976, the political initiative—in some senses up
for grabs since the previous November—had shifted decisively in
favor of the reformers within the government. The political opposition now functioned primarily as one more pressure-group
whose opinion the government considered but which was not decisive in the final analysis. While the shift in the political initiative
had been marked, it was much less pronounced in the syndical
field. Despite persistent government efforts, a *reforma sindical*
was never in the cards: various government proposals were caught
in the cross-fire between opposition labor organizations on the one
hand and the old stalwarts of the *sindicato vertical* (what some
called the *bunker sindical*) on the other. The existence of several
syndical organizations among the opposition—all ready to work at
cross-purposes from each other—increased the government's
margin for maneuver. Thus, over the course of the next year or
two, the government effectively played the UGT and *Comisiones*
off against each other, using differences between them on whether
collective bargaining at the plant level should be in the hands of a
comité de empresa (as CC.OO. insisted) or of the enterprise *sección
sindical* (as the UGT demanded) to undercut the position of both.

The proliferation of syndical organizations—by one count in
mid-1977 there were forty of them—represented a severe setback
for the *Comisiones Obreras*. Once confident of their future preeminence, they had to accept the reality of a growing UGT (its resurgence sparked by an upturn in PSOE fortunes), the presence of
the USO and of other labor organizations. With their organization
more closely identified than ever with the Communist party, many
Comisiones leaders now assumed a markedly defensive orientation whose dominant characteristics included a good deal of introspection and self-critical analysis.[57] Nevertheless, and perhaps
understandably since there had been no decisive defeat in the
syndical arena, few PCE labor activists were sharply critical of
their party's strategy and tactics in the labor movement. Most preferred to focus on the lost opportunities and the alleged anti-
unitary behavior of other organizations in the labor opposition.

Comisiones leaders continued to emphasize the role factory assemblies would play in the consolidation of a new type of industrial relations system in Spain, but we can wonder just how radically different their perspectives were in late 1976 and into 1977 (and later) from those animating the first *comisiones obreras*.

Chapter Four

Ideology and Organization in the PCE

THE PRECEDING TWO chapters have examined PCE efforts to exploit shifts in the traditional cleavages of Spanish society so as to lay the foundation for subsequent Communist political activity. The Communist leadership coupled these policies with concentrated efforts to overcome the image, reinforced by decades of regime propaganda, that the PCE was an essentially alien force, national only in a very formal and narrow sense, whose tactical moderation masked an insatiable lust for power that would be satisfied only with total control. Thus, Spanish Communist leaders extensively revised their party's ideological matrix by partially abandoning traditional Leninist values in favor of more accommodating, pluralistic, and consensual ones, as well as by modifying PCE organizational doctrine. Anxious to articulate a democratic model of socialism, the PCE disavowed any commitment to the violent overthrow of the existing economic and social system, and assiduously advocated what Santiago Carrillo called "revolutionary reformism."[1]

As in other areas, the changes in the organizational and ideological dimensions of Spanish Communism flowed from the reevaluation undertaken after 1956 by Carrillo and others in the PCE leadership. In one sense, they were responding to a profound domestic imperative, but other circumstances affected the transformations in ideology and organization as well. First, the crisis of confidence and leadership in the Soviet Union since the death of Stalin encouraged claims for national roads to socialism and for political and ideological independence from Moscow. In the case of West European parties like the PCE or the PCI, the movement away from Soviet tutelage and toward the assumption of democratic values was also powered by the failure of Leninism to provide a suitable model for the successful seizure of power on the Continent. Yet most, if not all, the issues raised and the doctrinal/organizational innovations proposed by the PCE and some of its Western European counterparts were not novel. That these issues were addressed again is tribute to the fact that after a long and sterile lapse those parties were returning to the mainstream of Western European Marxist thought.

I

During the Spanish Civil War, the PCE earned a reputation as a prominent advocate of moderation and restraint: its Popular Front experience made it the international Communist movement's premier exponent of broad-front tactics. The Communist policy of first winning the war, and only then moving to promote the social revolution, brought the PCE harsh criticism from left-wing Socialists and Anarchists who accused the party of betraying the Spanish Revolution to further the aims of Soviet foreign policy. The charge was not without foundation, as the PCE was only too willing, during the war years and after, to do Moscow's bidding.* Of greater enduring significance, however, was the decisive influence the Civil War had on the political style of Spanish Communism.

The PCE's emphasis on broad, multiclass alliances and on a gradualist strategy of social change was instrumental in attracting several hundred thousand Spaniards to the Communist banner in the years 1936–39. Most did not belong to the working class.[2] Explanations for this "embourgeoisement" suggest that the moderate line Moscow imposed on the Spanish party made it impossible for the PCE to compete effectively with the Anarchist CNT and the Socialist UGT in the labor movement. Over the next four decades, and despite the vicissitudes of clandestinity, the Spanish Communists acted as though their political space were preempted on the Left.

This orientation deepened perceptibly in the mid-1950s with Carrillo's ascendance. Under his stewardship, the Spanish party promulgated its now famous call for National Reconciliation; in subsequent years, the PCE spared little effort in its attempt to bridge the chasm separating it from the Spanish middle classes.

The call for National Reconciliation and subsequent appeals were inspired by the idea that the overthrow of the Franco regime and the establishment of political democracy could be a relatively peaceful process. Because the Franco dictatorship was, in the PCE's estimation, not the dictatorship of the bourgeois class but only of a "monopolist" stratum, it would be possible to rally a broad, heterogeneous front against the regime, around a minimum program calling for a provisional government, the establishment of fundamental political and civil liberties, amnesty, and elections to a constituent assembly. Such a broad coalition would preclude the need for a classic armed uprising.[3]

For a number of years, PCE leaders coupled this moderate approach with the view that Franco's downfall was imminent and would set the structural conditions for the elimination of the existing state-monopoly capitalist system.[4] The theoretical justification for this assessment lay in the Communist analysis that Spanish capitalism had developed unevenly. After 1939, Spanish capitalism had attained a degree of economic concentration which effectively established a state capitalist system. But, alongside this economic superstructure, characteristic of advanced industrial societies, there existed a backward society. The elimination of the feudal remnants in agriculture and the abolition of the autocratic, centralistic political structure (accomplished in most Western European countries by the "bourgeois-democratic" revolutions of the eighteenth and nineteenth centuries) remained the order of the day. This combination was, in the Spanish Communist view, explosive. The working class, which was harshly exploited, along with the peasantry, who wanted agrarian reform, and the "non-monopolist" sectors of the middle class, who saw the regime as having failed to complete the "bourgeois-democratic" revolution—all three could be galvanized to oppose that "financial oligarchy and the latifundist aristocracy" that had triumphed in the Civil War.

The PCE's scheme evidently had something in it for everyone. It could reassure the Spanish middle classes that with their participation the overthrow of the regime could be peaceful and that in the ensuing *democracia política y social* (akin to the *democratie avancée* of the French Communists), the constrictions on private property would be directed essentially at the "monopolies." The working class and its allies—destined by force of circumstance to lead this late-blooming "bourgeois-democratic" revolution—could be sustained in the struggle by the prospect of structural transformation. As a result, the workers could accept a gradual pace in return for middle-class support.[5]

In line with the adoption of this gradualist strategy for social change, the Communists also abandoned the classical Leninist thesis that monopoly capitalism, as the highest stage of capitalist development, could only be followed by socialism. Like most of its European coreligionists, the PCE conceived of an antimonopolist *democracia política y social* as a stage spanning several decades and serving as a relatively painless "transition to the transition." During this phase, social and private forms of property would coexist in relative harmony, the latter "play[ing] the same complementary role it has in the present system."[6] Government would control profits through tax measures, but would insure these were sufficient to stimulate private initiative. The principal economic measures were to include the nationalization of banking, credit facilities, and large industrial concerns, a reform of the fiscal system and the state planning apparatus, a reorientation of enterprises already under state control, a revision of the social security system, and the initiation of an agrarian reform. The projected reforms would be directed at the large, "monopolistic and latifundist" concerns.[7] In agriculture as in industry, the expropriation of property belonging to multinational concerns would only be undertaken if these could be replaced or managed by Spanish nationals. Commanding the heights of the economy, a ruling coalition of the Left could lead the country toward further socialization without risking undue or premature polarization of political life. The Allende experience in Chile showed the Spanish Communists that too precipitous a pace in social transformation would lead to the flight of capital and trained personnel and would only erode popular support for the new government.

II

The inability of the Anarchists and Socialists to adapt effectively to changes in Spanish social structure and syndical legislation permitted the Communists to develop an important presence among the working class. While stressing the decisive importance of that sector to the realization of Spanish Communist objectives, PCE leaders tried always to avoid (with varying success) that sectarian, *ouvriériste* orientation characteristic of their Portuguese counterparts. The Spanish Communist party may have relied on its working-class base for support during the most difficult moments of the anti-Franco struggle, but it also sought to expand its base beyond the confines of the proletariat and to court the middle classes.

As part of this effort, the Spanish Communist leadership decided to revamp the traditional Leninist scheme that the working class in alliance with the peasantry would play the leading role in the transition to socialism. The PCE argued that such a conception, while accurate in early twentieth-century Russia, did not fit contemporary Spain or, more broadly, Western Europe.[8] The declining importance of the agricultural sector in advanced industrial societies, along with the effects of the scientific-technical revolution,[9] made it impossible for the working class to lead in alliance with the peasantry alone. During the *democracia política y social*, as well as in the subsequent stage of socialist construction, that role would fall to what the party called the *alianza de las fuerzas del trabajo y de la cultura* ("alliance of the forces of labor and culture"—AFTC).

The term "Labor" included the working class and peasantry, relatively easy categories to define, whereas "forces of culture" was vague in the extreme. It did not refer to a specific class— Carrillo called it *une realité sociale de masse* in *Demain l'Espagne*[10]—but to professionals, like lawyers, physicians, scientists, and journalists; administrative personnel in industry and government; and members of the university community.[11] According to the new interpretation, those forces objectively interested in joining the working class as permanent allies on the road to socialism would constitute the overwhelming majority of the population in an advanced industrial society. As a consequence, socialism no longer had to be imposed by a tiny minority in the name of the people: the people, expressing themselves electorally, could gradually expand "bourgeois" democratic rights from the political to the economic sphere until socialism had been established. That process would take place over several decades and, although as Marxist-Leninists the Spanish Communists could never renounce the inevitability of the destruction of all forms of private property, the reduction in the numbers and the influence of the middle class would result more from atrophy than anything else. Under these circumstances and with vehement opposition only from the partisans of monopoly capital, the major task of the Left would be to find the appropriate issues and formulas to galvanize the broad currents interested in transforming society.

Acknowledging that socialism was not a near-term possibility, the PCE adopted the Gramscian notion that in advanced industrial societies the Left must not only destroy or radically transform those instruments of coercion and direct domination which make up the state, but also break the hold "bourgeois" ideology had over the state. For the Spanish Communists, then, the road to socialism was a long one. Only after the working class and its allies, united in the *alianza de las fuerzas del trabajo y de la cultura,* had first broken the spiritual and cultural dominance of the "ruling" class, could they assume plenary powers and definitively establish socialist relations of production.[12]

In line with this thinking, the Spanish Communists determined that the contemporary capitalist state could be exploited primarily by a strategy emphasizing reform over revolution. As Marxists, they continued to view the state as the instrument by which one class commits organized violence on another; its takeover was the core issue of the political process. Their approach to this issue differed from the traditional Leninist one. The Bolshevik leader had devised a rather simple and direct strategy, arguing that the bourgeois state had to be seized, violently destroyed, and a dictatorship of the proletariat established as a precondition for the construction of socialism. The Spanish Communists, by contrast, stressed the complex relationship between state and society in the latter part of the twentieth century. They insisted it was no longer simply a matter of "destroying the state, but rather of eliminating those sectors in the [state] machine which are the expression, the instrument of monopolistic rule [the political police, top administrators, reactionary sectors in the army, finance and so on] and neutralizing and even winning over one part of the state machine by a democratic and even socialist transformation."[13]

Spokesmen for the PCE rationalized their party's shift on how to transform the state by pointing to changes in the role of the Spanish state and in the structure of Spanish society. The modern state, the argument went, could no longer project the image of impartiality to other sectors of the middle class, but had become instead the "exclusive instrument" of monopoly capital. This change in the nature of the state or, more precisely, in how nonmonopoly sectors of the bourgeoisie perceived it, was symptomatic of the deep gulf between the interests of the monopolies and those of the rest of society. Because the monopolies represented such a small proportion of the national electorate, they could easily be defeated by an alliance between disgruntled sectors of the middle classes and the "forces of labor and culture."[14] Under these circumstances, the state was not as impregnable as it might have appeared at first glance.

The second proposition advanced by the PCE with respect to the state related to the transformation of Spanish society over the preceding four decades and particularly after the adoption of the Stabilization Plan in 1959. These changes—similar to those already experienced by other Western European countries—had had a significant impact on the state, causing it to assume many social-welfare functions.[15] Western European Communist ideologues refused for quite some time to accept the far-reaching nature of such changes. When they did—with the Italian Communists probably in the vanguard—it was primarily to justify their own failure to accomplish the revolution and maintain the morale of their militants. The Spanish Communists shifted their views on the nature of the welfare state beginning in the 1960s, arguing that with the state having assumed responsibilities for social security, education, and the like, it could no longer be defined solely as the instrument for "bourgeois" domination of the proletariat.[16] Increasing state intervention in the economy, and the consequent expansion of the public sector also suggested, in the Spanish Communist estimation, that the objective conditions for socialism were becoming ever more ripe. The change in the character and function of the state had also led to an increase in the number of government functionaries; and, since most of these employees supposedly came from the lower social classes, the PCE argued that a certain process of democratization had begun and would continue in the "mass of the state machine."[17]

On occasion PCE spokesmen appeared ready to embrace the notions about the evolutionary transition to socialism earlier advanced by such revisionist *bêtes noires* as Karl Kautsky and Eduard Bernstein: thus, Carrillo at one point insisted that the advance toward socialism "would not be the consequence of coercive measures but rather of the development of productive forces."[18] For the most part, however, the PCE warned that it would be illusory to assume such a transformation would come about through purely cultural and ideological action. Even during the most peaceful of processes, a rupture of the existing order must take place. Qualitative changes in the political and economic structures would result from coincident mass pressure outside the government and transformation of the state apparatus *from* within. At this point, the working class and its allies would assume complete power within society, but, since popular support would be so overwhelming, they need not exercise that power through the classical dictatorship of the proletariat. More moderate, sophisticated, and less drastic measures would suffice, measures that could be perfectly compatible with the continuation of parliamentary democracy.[19]

The change in the Spanish Communist perception of the state and of the party's own strategy for bringing about societal change also led to a revision of its notions about the role trade unions might play in that process. A revolutionary strategy premised on reforms, the PCE concluded, meant that the labor movement could no longer rely on narrow trade union membership.[20] Communists active in the labor movement should create a *sindicato de nuevo tipo* which would be based on factory councils and which would thus break down the barrier between members and non-members. These organizations would be better suited than the primarily *defensive* trade unions to break down capitalist control of the organization of production and to relate problems at the factory level to those more broadly afflicting the working class. Actively cooperating with the political parties of the Left (but avowedly suprapartisan), the *Comisiones Obreras* could create elements of socialism at the enterprise level.[21]

III

Having shifted away from the traditional Leninist emphasis on the quick and violent seizure of political power and opted instead for a slow and measured advance toward socialism, the PCE could also abandon Lenin's assessment of "bourgeois" liberties as counters simply to be manipulated and exploited by those forces intending to overthrow the existing order.[22] Thus, the Political Resolution of the Eighth PCE Congress spoke of a socialist society as one that would respect fundamental political liberties, freedom of information and criticism, freedom of artistic and intellectual creation, and political pluralism.[23]

Promises of fidelity to fundamental liberties appeared in the

communiqués signed by the PCE with the French and Italian
Communists in 1975 and 1977 and in the constituional draft presented to the Spanish people before the June 1977 election.[24] Furthermore, it was the Communists who proposed including a bill of
rights in the new constitution that would guarantee personal
liberties, freedom of assembly, the inviolability of the home and
correspondence, freedom of religion and expression, and the right
to travel freely within and outside Spain. These principles, they
insisted, were not to be merely declarative: the state and the
judiciary would be under a legal obligation actively to defend
them.

As the Spanish Communists were well aware, the vision of a
society both socialist and democratic was attractive to many
Spainards active in the opposition, particularly when contrasted to
the realities of the Soviet and East European regimes. Although
assuming by the late 1960s and early 1970s a more permanent and
strategic dimension, Spanish Communist ideological revisions did
not erase doubts as to their ultimate intentions.

One question related to the role the Communist party expected
to play in the revolutionary process in Spain and to its future relationship with other political and social forces. The contemporary
Spanish Communist view emphasized that all parties engaged in
the construction of socialism would be on an equal footing. Agreed
on the fundamentals, they would be free to carry on a lively
ideological debate as to the best specific measures to adopt at a
given moment. At one level, then, the PCE put aside the Leninist
notion of the vanguard role belonging *ipso facto* to the Communists, with other organizations, if allowed to exist as in the
German Democratic Republic or in Czechoslovakia, conceded
only a clearly subordinate role. The Spanish Communists opted
instead for the more flexible, though perhaps no less substantively
elitist, notion that the Communist party must earn its leading role
and should, in any case, aspire to function as a directing rather
than a dominating force.[25]

Another doctrinal innovation, this one unique to the PCE, concerned how the "alliance of the forces of labor and culture" would
exercise its future hegemony in Spanish society. The standard
Leninist view emphasized the Communist party role in that
enterprise. The PCE did likewise, but it insisted that the vanguard
role in the revolutionary process in Spain belonged not to any
single party but to the coalition of forces—parties, trade unions,

neighborhood and housewife associations, even organizations like *Cristianos por el Socialismo*—all of which were grouped in something called the "new political formation (NFP)."[26] The NFP would lead and, in some senses, coincide with the new historic bloc whose objective was the construction of socialism. It would elaborate a minimum program and establish joint deliberative organs, but individual groups or parties would retain organizational autonomy.

Rhetorically, then, the Spanish Communists moved away from the notion that the Communist party was the vanguard of the working class, having a scientific method rooted in Marxist-Leninist ideology which gave it exclusive power to understand and, in some ways, to control the historical process. Yet the change was not replete with inconsistencies. Carrillo and his associates continued to insist on a special role for the PCE.[27] Moreover, one finds in official PCE publications repeated use of phrases identifying the party as "the vanguard of the working class," as "the political representative of the proletariat," or as "the most conscious part of those masses organized for the political struggle."[28] That such claims were still made despite the passage of time and the innumerable errors committed in the name of historical clairvoyance suggests that the PCE had not entirely moved beyond the old dogmas.

The Communist attitude toward the labor movement provided ample evidence in this respect. Contemporary PCE doctrine rejected the classical Leninist "transmission belt" formulation of party/trade union relations, insisting that mass movements must be independent of and autonomous from all political parties. But the Spanish Communists had a peculiar understanding of what "independence and autonomy" meant,[29] and their practice in the labor movement showed the PCE to have had a largely instrumental approach toward the working class. For example, the *Comisiones Obreras* emerged in the early 1960s as a movement based on factory assemblies whose militants took advantage of regime-sponsored syndical elections to infiltrate the official *Organización Sindical.* This mixture of legal and illegal work, which, on the Left, only the Communists encouraged, helped the movement deal with the rigors of repression. By the latter part of the decade, the CC.OO. had emerged as the principal labor organization in the country. At that time, the Communists argued that the *Comisiones,* as a "sociopolitical movement," above political parties, could eschew traditional labor union structures with their bureaucracies and membership rolls. They continued to make this argument until mid-1976, when it became apparent that the CC.OO. would not be able, as the Communists had hoped, to force the dismantling of the vertical syndical structures or take over the *Organización Sindical*.

It was in this context that the General Assembly of the *Comisiones* met in July 1976. During that session, the Communists abandoned a decade-long policy and pushed through a motion calling for the transformation of *Comisiones* structures and the creation of a *confederación sindical* along more traditional lines. This change in policy, they stressed, came in response to continued Socialist opposition to the *Comisiones* and to the fact that Franco's heirs were giving preferential treatment to the Socialist UGT in an effort to diminish Communist strength. These objections or explanations do have a basis in fact. But the fundamental reason for the change in policy was that PCE leaders, seeing their drive for syndical and political dominance on the Left thwarted by the rival trade union organizations like the UGT and USO, believed the transformation of *Comisiones* to be the only way the party could effectively compete with its rivals.

Another place where the ambiguities of the Spanish Communist evolution were visible was in the PCE's analysis of the character and origins of the Soviet state. This issue may appear at first to have been a red herring; but nothing could be further from the truth. The Spanish Communist response to such issues reflected its own priorities and its vision of socialist society. Globally speaking, there are, in the Marxist scheme of things, five alternative ways of analyzing and describing the character of Soviet society. In shorthand fashion, these are: state capitalist; neither capitalist nor socialist (a new, entirely unique model of property relations); a transitional society between capitalism and socialism; a primary socialist society; and finally, a fully developed or "real" socialism. Advocates of the last three postures could be found in the PCE. Dolores Ibárruri and older cadres consider Soviet society an example of mature socialism. A second group—including several members of the Executive Committee, like Ignacio Gallego or even Simón Sánchez Montero—view the Soviet Union, despite its errors and shortcomings, as a country where great advances have been made and socialism is being built.[30]

The most critical comments came—whether out of nationalist

pique, democratic conviction, for public relations purposes, or some combination of the three—from PCE Secretary General Santiago Carrillo and from Manuel Azcárate, the principal party theoretician and ideologue. In *"Eurocomunismo" y Estado,* Carrillo argued that the Soviet Union finds itself in an intermediate phase between capitalism and socialism, in a situation analogous to that of the absolute monarchies during the transition from feudalism to modern parliamentary democratic practice.[31] As a consequence, both party and society in that country need "a serious and profound transformation in order for the country to become an authentic workers' democracy."[32] However, Carrillo was ambivalent about the nature of transformations required there. At one point in the book, he declared that the material conditions for passage to a "evolved socialism" had been fulfilled; at another, that fundamentally important political and economic problems were still to be remedied.[33] Azcárate, for his part, argued that while "primitive socialist" relations of production existed in the Soviet Union, an authoritarian state preserved many features of capitalism and repression.[34] Neither Carrillo nor Azcárate rejected the premise that the Soviet state created in the wake of the October 1917 revolution was not only of historical importance but, despite its subsequent shortcomings, well worth the price.

Despite everything they have written, Spanish Communist idealization of the Bolshevik seizure of power is readily understandable, particularly if we remember how the origins and identity of the PCE are closely tied to the October revolution. For whatever reason, Carrillo, the international Communist movement's most legitimate Martin Luther, demonstrated himself unwilling to renounce that patrimony. But when he continued to insist that Lenin and the Bolsheviks should have seized power, he and his party implicitly asserted that socialism, at least in its lesser forms, does not require political liberties. They were, in effect, holding to the view that socialism and democracy do not necessarily go hand in hand, that "when a revolutionary moment develops, one has to take advantage of it and seize power."[35]

Such an attitude led the Spanish Communists to adopt some very ambiguous positions with respect to political liberties and human rights. Communist leaders went on record as favoring unrestricted political debate, not only before reaching socialism, but once the construction of socialism had begun; and yet, it was less than a decade ago (and after the invasion of Czechoslovakia) that the PCE declared that an opposition would be tolerated by socialism only "under certain circumstances" and, then, if it "presented itself openly without trying to dissimulate either its nature or its program."[36] In any case, when the Communist party asserted its intention to build a pluralist socialist society, it is important to remember that the Communist conception of pluralism was significantly different from the traditional Western one, which considers that fresh energies and unexpected ideas may spring at any moment from any point or group in society. The fact is that, in the PCE's interpretation of socialist society, the vestiges of class society—such as "bourgeois" political parties—will have to disappear.

Further questions arise with respect to the Spanish Communist position on human-rights violations in the Eastern bloc. Beginning in the 1960s, the PCE repeatedly criticized what it termed violations of "socialist legality" there. The first thrust in that direction came in 1966 with the publication of an article by Carrillo decrying the imprisonment of Soviet dissidents Daniel and Siniavsky.[37] It was followed up in 1974, when the Spanish Communists objected to the measures adopted by the Soviet regime against Alexander Solzhenitsyn and, in 1977, when they protested the jailing of the signatories of Charter 1977 in Czechoslovakia.[38]

We might conclude at first glance that little more could justifiably have been asked of the PCE on these occasions. Upon closer inspection, however, there were peculiar distinctions the Spanish party made before deciding whether to criticize human-rights violations and political repression in a "socialist" country. The PCE invariably distinguished between situations where "socialism" was in danger and where it is not. One particularly demonstrative example of this sort of reasoning may be found in the Carrillo book/interview *Demain l'Espagne*.[39] There, the Spanish Communist leader criticized the campaign directed at Solzhenitsyn but expressed his support for the Castro regime's no less abhorrent treatment of the dissident Cuban poet Heberto Padilla. The distinction between the two cases turned, in Carrillo's opinion, on the issue of how "dangerous" each writer was to his native social and political system. A similar pattern of reasoning was evident in an article Azcárate wrote in 1970 entitled "Political Liberties and Socialism,"[40] in which he criticized the invasion of Czechoslovakia in August 1968 but defended that of Hungary in October 1956. Once again, the distinctions made between the two situations were very revealing. In Budapest, "the enemies of socialism who were trying to take advantage of existing liberties" were a danger to the existing order; in Prague, they were not.

The unwillingness of Carrillo (and we may safely presume his party) to assert that political repression was beyond "class" and should be forthrightly condemned regardless of circumstance was of deep political significance. Either liberty was acknowledged as consubstantial with socialism or it was not. Either democracy is the only guarantee of socialism or it is not. If the Spanish Communists did not believe it to be so, the depth of their conviction about democratic socialism must be questioned.

I V

So far in this chapter, we have focused on the changes brought about in the Spanish Communist ideological matrix by shifts in the strategic vision of the party. The adoption (at least for the short and medium term) of a revolutionary reformism and the shelving of plans for a quick assault on the citadels of power also had an important impact on the structure and the functioning of the PCE.

Organizational practice and ideological belief have always been closely linked in the Communist scheme of things, an interdependence that contributes to the distinctiveness of Communist parties. The vanguard doctrine and the claim to historical omniscience it engenders are the ideological justification for the maintenance of a highly centralized, quasimilitaristic party apparatus. Equipped with the weapon of democratic centralism, the leaders of that apparatus have been able not only to shift policies radically at times but to stifle dissent.

Most Communist parties did not live up to the "combat-party" ideal sketched in the famous Twenty One Conditions adopted by the first Comintern Congress, but in the 1920s and 1930s they came close enough to fan a virulent anti-Communist reaction in many countries. The last three or four decades, as the Communist movement in Western Europe has been forced to concede its inability to attain power by means of traditional Leninist methods, have witnessed a certain softening of organizational doctrine and practice in most of the Continental parties. The first steps away from the Leninist cadre party were taken during the Popular Front era, when parties like the French and the Spanish attained memberships numbering in the hundreds of thousands. A coherent, alternative organizational doctrine did not really begin to develop, however, until after World War II. The PCI, and preeminently Palmiro Togliatti, was faced with a tremendous expansion in membership as a result of the Communist role in the anti-Fascist Resistance, but became increasingly conscious of the unlikelihood that any revolutionary explosion would occur. This period laid the foundations for the *partito nuovo*, a party structured along democratic centralist lines but flexible enough to accommodate and manage a mass-based organization.[41]

The Spanish Communist party, whose development into a mass movement during the Civil War may have encouraged Togliatti, had by contrast experienced a harsh repression after the Franco victory in 1939, and many of its members either died or went into exile. What remained of the PCE organization in Spain was a nucleus of activists with little organic connection between them besides the *Radio España Indepediente* transmitter broadcasting from Moscow. The unsuccessful guerrilla struggle that the party helped wage in the 1940s further decimated it. By the latter part of that decade, the guerrillas had degenerated into bandit groups, active in remote rural areas but isolated from the general population.

The PCE turned inward in the late 1940s, but a change in the leadership midway through the next decade prevented the hardening of those narrow and dogmatic policies. The renovation began after the death of Stalin in March 1953 and picked up steam at the Fifth PCE Congress in 1954, with the entry into the Central Committee of new members who worked in Spain. Its first phase ended in 1956, when Carrillo and his supporters in the highest ranks of the party assumed control. This shift had important organizational consequences.

Carrillo wanted the PCE to begin laying the foundations for its transformation into a mass-based organization. Accordingly, he supported the modification of party statutes at the Sixth PCE Congress in December 1959, so as to permit membership without formal participation in cells.[42] Over the course of the next decade, the party broke organizational tradition further, taking advantage of the protection afforded Communist lawyers, engineers, doctors, economists, and the like by professional associations, and permitting the establishment of organizations along essentially corporatist lines. These changes were intended not only to protect party members from the hazards of clandestinity, but to facilitate the incorporation of intellectuals and professionals (representatives of the "forces of culture") into the party. Communist efforts to catalyze anti-Franco sentiment among intellectuals, in the universities, and among professional groups and to attract them to its ranks included the publication of underground journals like *Argumentos, Realidad, Revolución y Técnica*, and *Revolución, Ciencia y Técnica*. It is difficult to measure the success of those efforts; for, though many intellectuals and university-trained people were at some point either members of the PCE or under its influence, few remained in the party for extended periods. On the other hand, there were individuals like Ramón Tamames. He apparently entered the PCE in 1956 and became a member of its Executive Committee in the summer of 1976: in the interim, this prominent economist acted as consultant to various ministries and played a role in shaping national economic policies. Aside from the *Comisiones Obreras*, the PCE also used front organizations like the *Movimiento Democrático de Mujeres*, neighborhood and housewife associations, and various *Clubs de Amigos de la UNESCO* to develop contacts with various social strata.

During the years of clandestinity, the PCE effort to expand its membership led to one particularly interesting organizational innovation: the creation of regional Communist parties, first in Cataluña, the Basque country and Galicia and later in Asturias, Andalucía, Valenca, and in other parts of the country. This policy aimed to take advantage of the historical tensions between center and periphery in Spain that had been seriously aggravated by the autocratic centralism of the Franco regime. Results were mixed, however. The PCE was not overly successful with this strategy in the Basque country and Galicia. In the first, the *Partido Comunista de Euzkadi* had to deal with extreme nationalists within the various *Euzkadi ta Askatasuna* groups and with the distrust of the PCE among many young people in the region—not to mention their more conservative elders—who considered the party little more than a branch for the Madrid-based leadership. In Galicia, the *Partido Comunista de Galicia* depended on the *Comisiones Obreras* in the industrial centers like Vigo and El Ferrol, and had difficulty penetrating outside the large factories or among peasants in the country. Cataluña offered the Communists their most notable success. There, the *Partit Socialista Unificat de Catalunya* (PSUC), product of a fusion of four groups in July 1936, played a leading role in the constitution of several opposition fronts such as the *Assemblea de Catalunya* and the *Consell de Forces Politiques de Catalunya* and, despite the distrust of the most *catalanista* sectors of the population, became one of the most important groups in the region. Although the PSUC entered the Comintern in 1939—the only regional party ever to do so—and although in subsequent years its organization suffered periodically from recurring internal problems over how seriously to take its regional specificity, there can be little doubt that during the Franco era the PSUC functioned primarily as an instrument of the PCE's political strategy with severely limited organizational autonomy. In this latter respect, it is worth noting that the negotiations leading to the entry in 1974 of the leftist group called *Bandera Roja* into the PSUC were carried on by Carrillo, with the regional party leadership only asked to give pro forma approval to the results. As we shall see, however, this situation changed.

Although from the late 1960s official PCE spokesmen did not hesitate to claim for the party a membership in excess of 100,000 people, they substantially exaggerated the success of their efforts rather greatly. Even the 160,000 members claimed in April 1977 (or the target figure of 300,000 for the end of that year set by the Central Committee in July 1976) were far off the mark and exceeded Communist capabilities.[43] Only after Franco's death in November 1975 did the PCE begin to break out of the mold of a restricted cadre party. Even then, it faced difficulties in many areas that inhibited its transformation. The final step in laying the structural foundation for this shift did not in any case come until July 1976, when the Central Committee instructed Communist organizations to drop the traditional cell-structures and change to work and neighborhood *agrupaciones* which would hold public meetings.[44]

The implications of the shift from cell to *agrupación*, along with the expansion in the number of individuals in the leading bodies of the party and in the party more generally, were not altogether clear. On the one hand, the various efforts to create a mass-based party represented a clear break with Leninist tradition. On the other hand, a growth in the number of people in an organization does not necessarily make it more internally democratic or less antidemocratic in its approach to social and political problems. While the leadership's brusque policy shifts may become more difficult to accomplish during normal times, such changes hardly assure that during crisis conditions (when, after all, the challenges to democracy are greatest) the party might not opt for revolution. The expansion of the PCE Central Committee from 40 members in 1965 to 111 in 1970 and 134 in 1976 (its size rivaled that of parties with much greater memberships) does not in itself mean greater democracy exists within the party. Faced with a Central Committee rendered unwieldy by its numbers, the important decisions continued to be made by a reduced number of people either in the Secretariat or in the permanent committee of the Executive Committee.

Predictably, some provincial PCE organizations used the shift from cell to *agrupación*—known in Communist jargon as *territorialización*, it affected primarily service-sector employees organized by branches of production and professionals in quasicorporatist *agrupaciones*—to strip power from troublesome elements.[45] Those who thought the decision to "territorialize" would bring about radical changes in the attitudes and patterns of the PCE were to be disappointed: party leaders were quick to clarify that workplace *agrupaciones* were preferable to neighborhood ones and that the functions of the cell had not been abolished but rather shifted so as to become the responsibility of the *comité político* of the *agrupación*.

V

The decision to transform the PCE into a *partido de masas* went hand in hand with promises of greater internal democracy and freedom of discussion. Those promises may not have been entirely fulfilled, but it cannot be denied that, over the course of the last three decades, the Spanish Communist party became much more open and that discussion, although circumscribed, occurred in the 1970s to a degree unequaled in party history.

The extent of PCE progress in this regard should not be underestimated. In the 1940s and early 1950s, disagreement with or disobedience of the directives emanating from the Political Bureau (as the highest policy-making organ in the party was called until 1960) brought with it the very real threat of physical elimination. The decade and a half following the Civil War saw a rather sordid chapter in Spanish Communist history, and it is small wonder that those members of the present leadership who lived through the period make few references to it.[46] Most had emigrated in 1939 to the Soviet Union, and their personal squabbles and petty conspiracies became mired in the cloaca of Stalinism. The Communist exile community in the Soviet Union and Eastern Europe was a particular target of the KGB. Ibárruri herself was more than once rumored to have been arrested by the police in the late 1940s.[47] The exiles set their quarrels aside only when they felt challenged by those considered to be outsiders. For example, they expelled Jesús Monzón, accusing him of "deviationism and adventurist opportunism," after he resisted their efforts in 1944–45 to reassert control over the clandestine Communist organization in Spain.[48]

The search for and condemnation of "agents" in Spanish Communist ranks came to an end for the most part with the death of Stalin. Party leaders attributed their mistakes and crimes to the excesses of the Soviet leader and to Beria. Over the next few years, as in most other parties, the struggle between rival factions in the leadership, which had been going on for several years in relatively muted fashion, broke out more and more into the open. It was a generational struggle, more than anything else, pitting younger members of the leadership who had joined the party in most cases just prior to the Civil War—men like Santiago Carrillo, Fernando Claudín and Ignacio Gallego—against older stalwarts like Vicente Uribe, who directed clandestine party activities in Spain, and Francisco Antón, whose rise in the leadership had been due to his personal ties with Dolores Ibárruri. Because of her symbolic importance as Secretary General, she stood in many ways apart from the fray but could not have been very comfortable during her speeches to party cadres when she admitted to serious deficiencies and *sectarismo* in the work of the leadership.

Self-criticism was, in any case, entirely appropriate. The party stood in splendid domestic and international isolation. The Central Committee had not met in plenary session since the Civil War. And the exiled leaders were too busy enlarging their respective fiefs and plotting against each other to devote much time or effort to the anti-Franco struggle.

The inner-party jostling continued through the spring of 1956, when Carrillo assumed a dominant role in party affairs. The policy changes he subsequently effected went against the grain of many Communist militants and provoked serious internal strains. Real disillusionment did not set in until the early part of the next decade, however, when it became apparent that predictions about the imminent downfall of the regime were far off the mark. Earlier in this chapter, we discussed the exodus of many younger and some older militants and their decision to form a multiplicity of extreme Left groups. Repeatedly, and to some extent justifiably, alluding to the dangers of too open a discussion, Carrillo used his control of the party apparatus and the device of democratic centralism to silence those who refused to accept the new line.[49]

Even as influential a member of the PCE Executive Committee as Fernando Claudín could not break Carrillo's hold over the Spanish party. Claudín was thought by many to be second in influence only to Carrillo, and he had supported the renovation initiated by Carrillo. He and Jorge Semprún parted company with the PCE Secretary General in the early 1960s over what they perceived as the blind official insistence that the regime was increasingly isolated and would soon fall. The more theoretically inclined of the two, Claudín argued that behind the "voluntarist" and "subjectivist" view of the party leadership lay an incorrect analysis of the socioeconomic basis of the regime. Carrillo and the others had misjudged the profundity of the change which Spanish society and economy had experienced since the end of the Civil War. This prevented them from recognizing that political power in Spain could shift from a conservative faction to a more liberal one, with no change in the fundamental structure of the state-monopoly capitalist system and no social revolution. Such a liberalization could lead, Claudín argued, to the establishment of a Western European-style parliamentary democracy and even to the legalization of the Communist party, albeit under a temporary cover like that of the EDA in Greece a decade and a half before. At the same time, he insisted, because the economic system of Spain had developed to the highest stage of capitalism (namely, that of the state monopoly), it was inevitable that any revolution have a socialist character.[50]

By arguing in this fashion, Claudín sought to bridge the growing chasm between revolutionary rhetoric and reformist practice, the latter clearly manifested in the opposition's inability to force a change in the regime. He deplored, and history appears to have vindicated him, the unwillingness of Carrillo and others in the leadership to realize or accept that a revolutionary situation did not exist in Spain and would not for some time. He believed this denial would only exacerbate tensions within the party and between the party and various splinter groups which had been spawned in reaction to the failure of the policies and predictions of the PCE. Discussion over the various points Claudín raised (in-

cluding issues like greater internal democracy and independence
from the Soviet Union) lasted well over a year, but, at a March
1964 Executive Committee meeting, Carrillo and his supporters
refused to accede to Claudín's demands that a special Central
Committee meeting be called to debate the issues, and dismissed
the dissidents from their posts. Formal expulsion came a year
later.

Unlike so many other Communist dissidents, neither man took
the subsequent step of organizing a rival group, and thus the immediate organizational consequences of the affair were limited.
From a longer-range perspective, however, the PCE suffered from
the loss of some of its best and most incisive thinkers. Carrillo
subsequently incorporated many (although certainly not all) of
their ideas, but the belated perception of the possibility and viability of a reformist solution to the Franco problem would damage
the party and its credibility.

Carrillo was tolerant toward Claudín and toward more or less
open debate at the highest ranks of the party (that is, among the
members of the Executive Committee) both because Claudín and
his ally, Jorge Semprún, were known for their intellectual and
personal honesty and because neither looked for outside sources
of support or manipulated the issues to set up any rival organization. More importantly, however, the two men had been among
Carrillo's strongest supporters after 1956 and held important posts
within the party. While trying to avoid too sharp a clash, he also
had to take care not to appear too closely identified with them, lest
disgruntled older members of the leadership seize the occasion to
blame Carrillo for moving too fast since 1956 and not knowing
how to keep a handle on the situation. What brought Carrillo and
those older party leaders together was an aversion to seeing power
slip from the hands of the exiled leadership. The demand for a
plenary meeting of the Central Committee and subsequent full
debate in the Spanish Communist organization was unacceptable.
Whether Claudín and Semprún could have gained the support of a
cadre base whose members were tiring of constant exhortations to
bring about the illusory national strike is, of course, impossible to
ascertain. Whatever the merits of their arguments, it would probably have been exeedingly difficult from a psychological point of
view for many Communists operating in Spain to accept the failure of their longstanding efforts to overthrow Franco.[51]

Carrillo handled the challenge posed by pro-Soviet elements

after the Czech invasion with no less dexterity. Aware that most party members had pro-Soviet sympathies,[52] and unsure of how committed Moscow was to "normalizing" the situation in the PCE, Carrillo was at first cautious. Organizational Secretary Eduardo García and several other members of the Central Committee opposed the official line, yet the former retained his post for nearly nine months, being ousted only after circulating an open letter criticizing Carrillo. Through late 1968, Carrillo used the dissidents' increasingly open fractional activity to rally the leadership and the cadre base behind him. He did not yet voice the biting criticisms of the Soviet Union and its domestic and foreign policies that would become his trademark in subsequent years; instead he emphasized the negative consequences such fractional activity would have on effective anti-Franco action. Such arguments carried much weight, particularly as they were reinforced by a decades-long tradition of unthinking submission to orders emanating from above. Dolores Ibárruri played an important role in this affair. Known for her close ties to Moscow, she nevertheless opted at a critical moment to side with Carrillo, by and large settling the issue for the pro-Soviet groups. Carrillo, just to be on the safe side however, had the Secretariat coopt twenty-nine new members to the Central Committee prior to a September 1970 showdown.

Carrillo survived these threats to his leadership (as well as less important ones posed by Marxist-Leninist groups and the *Oposición de Izquierda al Partido Comunista* in 1973 and 1974) through judicious use of democratic centralism and the organizational instruments it supplied. Democratic centralist principles—like the submission of the minority to the majority will (that is, not simply accepting the decision but actively supporting it down the hierarchical line), and the interdiction of horizontal communications between potential or actual minorities in different cells or other party organs—gave the leadership great leeway in handling dissent. Party statutes—particularly Article 13, permitting unlimited cooptation into and by the Central Committee; Article 21, allowing that body to establish the norms for selection to the party congresses; and Article 26, permitting the designation of any members of lower party organizations by the Central Committee—also helped in that endeavor.[53]

When speaking of internal democracy, party leaders inevitably insisted that a strict centralism was imperative under conditions of clandestinity. Once the party were legalized and operating openly in the country, a much greater discussion would be encouraged, within limits, of course. Democratic centralism would still be the guiding organizational principle and, although it would function with a greater emphasis on the "democratic" than on the "centralism," currents of opinion would never be permitted to crystallize into factions.[54]

The leadership's rationales for the necessity for democratic centralism, despite changes in ideology and political strategy, varied, but generally revolved around two notions. One was that the existence of factions was tolerable or natural only in a multiclass party and not in the party of the working class whose political homogeneity had to be maintained. The other asserted that, as the fusion of revolutionary will and action, the PCE could not "permit itself, through an excess of *democratisme,* to lose the opportunity to act."[55]

Both of these ideas point up an essential ambiguity in the organizational and ideological evolution of the PCE. Centralization of functions and homogeneity in the party can hardly be said to deepen its democratic quality. Certainly, it is true, as Communist leaders repeatedly insisted, that in some respects other Spanish parties functioned as centralistically (or oligarchically) as the PCE. But the crucial difference between the Communist and most other parties resided, then as now, in the fact that the latter did not have totalist aspirations to effect radical and profound changes in society. The argument for separation and balance of powers within the party and outside it, as well as the idea that no class or party can claim to be the fountainhead of all worthwhile ideas may be profoundly liberal notions, but they are also deeply democratic ones. The way a group comes to power spills over into the way it exercises governmental responsibilities, hence there is no way to construct an artificial barrier between what is prized in terms of internal organization and what are considered correct political or administrative choices for the society at large. It has been rather incongruous, in fact, for PCE leaders to insist with such vehemence on the value of diversity and the propriety of "national" paths with respect to the international Communist movement and then to turn and praise a model of internal organization enshrining quite the opposite ideals of homogeneity and centralism.

In only one Spanish Communist organization—the *Partit Socialista Unificat de Catalunya*—was democratic centralism sufficiently watered down so that authentic political debates and a lively competition among different groups could take place. The internal democratization of the PSUC accelerated in the twilight of the Franco era, and divergences within its seventy-five member Central Committee became intense. They forced the postpone-ment, first of a Barcelona provincial conference, and later of the party's Fourth Congress, originally scheduled for the spring of 1977 and finally held in November of that year.

The struggle for power within the PSUC pitted several groups against each other.[56] One group within the PSUC included many individuals who had been in the ultraleftist *Bandera Roja* ("Red Flag") group. Although this group had been radical in the late 1960s and early 1970s, most of its members who joined the PSUC became quite moderate in their politics, with wags referring to them derisively as *banderas blancas* ("white flags"). The most prominent representatives of this current were intellectuals like Jordi Borja, Alfonso Carlos Comín (now deceased), and Jordi Solé Tura, and labor leaders from the Baix Llobregat area like Carlos Navales and Agustí Prats. One might characterize their views as "right Eurocommunist": they did not put much stress on the class struggle or on polarization politics. Borja, for example, wrote an article in the journal *Taula de Canvi* in which he virtually said that the working class has no greater right to demand socialism than many other sectors of society. "Today," he argued in late 1976,

> the ideals of socialism can be renewed, in the context of a democratic State, through joint action by the great traditions which have had a progressive impact in the Western world: Christianity, liberal Socialism and Communism.[57]

A second PSUC group, rallying around Organizational Secretary Josep Serradell and Margarida Abril, both in the Catalan Exec-utive Committee, received the nickname *históricos*. As the name suggests, its most distinguished exponents had been in the PSUC for some time and had a vision marked to some extent by their lengthy membership and clandestine experience. The *históricos* were what might be termed recalcitrant or partial "Eurocom-munists," accepting what had become PCE and PSUC policy more out of a sense of discipline than as a matter of conviction. They did their best to retain as much of the Leninist ideological baggage and *Weltanschauung* as possible, even while the party developed a mass membership and electoral base. The *históricos* saw the

PSUC (and PCE) relationship with the labor movement, neighbor-hood associations, and other mass organizations from an undiluted Leninist perspective, viewing these groups as inferior and subject to control by the party. As later became apparent, moreover, their foreign policy reflex was to justify Soviet actions and to emphasize solidarity with the so-called socialist bloc.

Between the *banderas blancas* and the *históricos* stood a third group, dubbed the "Eurocommunist" faction. The bulk of the Catalan leadership—Antonio Gutiérrez Díaz, José López Bulla, José Rodríguez Rovira, Joaquim Sempere, Rafael Ribó, and Antoni Lucchetti—belonged to this group. By 1980, it would divide into "Leninist" and "Eurocommunist" components, but initially this group represented a centrist and synthetic position. By and large, these individuals supported the renovation Carrillo had impelled beginning in 1956, and they wished to purge the party of "Stalinist" political and organizational residues and to introduce democratic norms to the PCE/PSUC. Yet their support for "Eurocommunism" had a different tone from that of the *banderas blancas*. They insisted on the continued vitality of the revolution-ary tradition of the Third International (its constitution marked, they believe, a definite and necessary rupture with the reformism of international social democracy), and they warned against losing identity through an excessive tactical flexibility. They thought more in terms of Left alternatives (even when in the context of broader alliances with middle-class parties) and saw no necessary contradiction between "Eurocommunism" properly understood and "real" Leninism.

No other Spanish Communist organization contained such well-defined groups in competition with each other. It would take the Ninth PCE Congress in April 1978, and particularly the now-famous Thesis 15 dropping the appellation "Leninist" and de-fining the party simply as a "Marxist, revolutionary and democratic organization," to spark similar debate in other PCE organizations and to show how far the party as a whole had to go before claiming it functioned along democratic lines internally.

VI

Any global assessment of the changes wrought by Santiago Car-rillo and his associates in the Spanish Communist leadership in the spheres of ideology and organization prior to 1977 must first stress the distance traveled by the PCE. From total ideological/ political subservience to the Soviet Union and strict reliance on the Leninist model, the Spanish party became, over two decades, one of the most outspoken advocates of socialism with a human face. And yet, the Spanish Communist evolution was not without significant ambiguities, as shown in our analysis of authoritative party statements. These ambivalences grew stronger down the organizational ladder. Unfortunately, there have been no empirical data available to give us a clearer picture of what the ordinary Communist militant or sympathizer thought about the changes impelled by party leaders during the Franco era, but certainly talk of civil liberties and emphasis on individual rights found little echo in the lower ranks of the party. Efforts to effect a change in attitude there encountered well-entrenched *ouvriériste* and sectarian orientations. The influence of individuals imbued with these attitudes had been minimized during the 1960s and early 1970s, as the PCE concentrated its efforts on recruiting intellectuals and university activists; but it grew markedly in 1975 and 1976, as the leadership leaned on its labor activists for help in transforming the PCE from a cadre- to a mass-based organization.

Although of an obvious, intrinsic political significance, the ambiguities in the Spanish Communist ideological/organizational evolution also influenced the party's political ambitions. Popular suspicion made it even more difficult for the PCE to cast off its Stalinist past and image, especially with the legacy of the virulently anti-Communist propaganda propounded by the Franco regime, and this suspicion undermined the Communist drive for legitimacy, presence, and influence in the post-Franco era. So long as the PCE retained its organizational advantage over other opposition groups, its image was not a particularly relevant problem. It would become so, however, if the other groups, and particularly the Socialists on the Left, were given the opportunity to flesh out their structures and develop a mass audience. Under these circumstances, the Communist organizational superiority would dwindle, and the ambiguities in its evolution would become more the focus of attention. In this sense, it was the Socialist PSOE that posed the clearest challenge to the Communists. We discuss the political decline and subsequent rise of the PSOE in chapters 6 and 7. Here, we can simply note that in the early 1970s, control of the party passed to a new generation of Socialist leaders operating within Spain. Battling the Communists for the political space of democratic socialism, the PSOE had no Stalinist past or previous embarrassing ties to the Soviet Union to explain away. Its lemma of "socialism is liberty" stood subtly but unmistakably against the Communist one of "socialism in liberty." Given the opportunity to strengthen and develop their organization, the PSOE could take advantage of Communist ambiguities and use them as an effective public relations foil.

Chapter Five

The Foreign Policy
of the PCE

THERE WERE CLEARLY favorable consequences of the Spanish Communist defense of broad coalition politics in the struggle against the Franco regime and of its emphasis on the value of democracy and pluralism in the construction of a socialist society. However, it became clear to Santiago Carrillo and others in the PCE leadership that, in order to establish and enhance its credibility as a profoundly national party, the PCE needed to adopt as well an independent posture toward the Soviet Union. Such a course might not be met with favor by militants operating under the difficult conditions in Spain or even by a majority of those outside the country. Nevertheless, Communist leaders understood that unless the PCE were convincing on this score—particularly given the reputation the party had earned by its former ties to the Soviet Union and its role during the Popular Front era—it would not achieve a broad, multiclass presence in the post-Franco era.

At first, in the early and mid-1960s, all the Spanish Communists expected of their Russian counterparts was to be allowed a certain freedom of action and perhaps to be consulted on important issues having to do either with the international Communist movement or with state-to-state relations with the Franco regime. After the Warsaw Pact invasion of Czechoslovakia in August 1968, this orientation deepened into a demand for absolute autonomy and independence. By the early 1970s, the PCE leadership—especially Carrillo—recognized the broad political and ideological implications of organizational independence: because the prospects for socialism in Spain as in other countries were inextricably linked to the general fate of the European Communist movement, a regional approach by the Left to the problems of socialism and democracy was not only inevitable but vitally necessary.

The Soviet Union surely understood the threat posed by the ideas the Spanish Communist leadership advanced, and this perhaps explains why they went to such seemingly disproportionate lengths in the years after 1968 to bring to heel a small, clandestine party like the PCE. Certainly, Moscow hoped to make the PCE an example to other independent-minded Communist parties, and, given its tradition of reflexive support for the Soviet Union, the PCE offered an appealing target. When in February 1974, the Soviet journal *Partiinaia Zhizn* launched a bitter and apparently unprovoked attack on the principal Spanish Communist theoretician, Manuel Azcárate, the Soviets attacked more than just a critic of the Czech invasion or a party that had tenaciously fended off attacks by pro-Soviet dissidents. Rather, they were going after the most active exponent of the formation of a rival center for the international Communist movement focused in Western Europe. The Soviet blast was, in short, a conscious attack on a party that advocated the creation on a European level of that same "socialism with a human face" symbolized by the Prague Spring. Then as today, Soviet policy-makers considered this approach a challenge not only to their system of imperial control over Eastern Europe but to the political and social hegemony of the CPSU within the Soviet Union itself.

I

Only a very reckless gambler would have bet in 1948 that twenty-five years later the Spanish Communist party would be one of the most acerbic critics of the Soviet Union in the international Communist movement. At that time, the PCE was one of the most orthodox parties in the world, loyally following the twists and turns of the Stalin line, denouncing the Marshall Plan, NATO, and the pro-Western orientation of other opposition groups and sparing little in its adulation of the Soviet dictator. If all this was more or less standard operating procedure in the Communist movement, the Spanish Communists refined their slavishness more than most. Once the bright star in the Comintern galaxy, the PCE was not even invited to the founding session of the Cominform and rated no advance warning at all of the impending Soviet-Yugoslav break. Yet, when it came, the Spanish Communists conveniently forgot that Tito and the League of Yugoslav Communists had only recently figured prominently in the PCE pantheon or that party-to-party relations had been rather close. Typically, they denounced Tito as a spy, a traitor, a fascist, and an assassin[1] and then used the opportunity afforded by that split to dispose of troublemakers within the party.

The PCE spent the 1940s and 1950s under the stultifying influence of the French Communists, adhering to Moscow with a similar stolidness. The Spanish Communists wholeheartedly approved the invasion of Hungary and warned sharply of the dangers posed by "counterevolutionaries" in Poland. With respect to the Yugoslavs, they faithfully followed the Soviet lead. Party-to-party relations were resumed in 1956, ending without so much as an apology or a self-criticism what *Mundo Obrero* called "the disagreeable situation" that had devloped after 1948.[2] When Moscow again attacked the Titoists for their refusal to sign the declaration issued by the November 1957 meeting of ruling parties, the Spanish reversed once more and joined the chorus of criticism directed at Belgrade.[3]

A change in the orientation of the Spanish Communists began to develop in the wake of Khrushchev's speech denouncing Stalinism and the cult of personality at the Twentieth CPSU Congress. Earlier, we discussed how Carrillo and those close to him used de-Stalinization to gain the upper hand in an intraparty battle. Their accession to dominance marked a first phase in the agonizing reappraisal of PCE domestic and foreign policies. The Spanish Communists began in the early 1960s to tilt away from Moscow, Prague, and Paris and toward Rome, though the party was, of course, careful not to stray too far from the fold. It still relied heavily on financial assistance from the Soviets and, perhaps more important, party leaders believed that under Khrushchev "proletarian internationalism" would assume a new vitality. Nevertheless, the PCE now injected a note of independence into its relationship with the Soviet Union.

While Spanish Communist relations with the PCI warmed up, the PCE developed new ties with the upstart Eastern European maverick, Rumania. In April 1966, the two parties signed a joint communiqué incorporating the most important elements of the

now-famous Rumanian April 1964 statement on the need for absolute independence and noninterference in other parties' internal
affairs.[4] The Spanish Communist posture on the Sino-Soviet split
was relatively moderate, even if at times Ibárruri lent herself more
completely to the Soviet campaign by accusing the Chinese of
"pseudo-revolutionary adventurism" and of making "hysterical
cries, clumsy maneuvers, low slanders, and Philistine policy."[5] A
November 1963 Central Committee resolution, though condemning the positions articulated by the Chinese and upholding Soviet
calls for an international conference, also noted the party would
not support efforts "to place this or that party [an obvious allusion
to the Chinese and the Albanians] among the accused and condemning it."[6] The PCE abandoned its efforts to work out those
differences only in early April 1964, when the first pro-Chinese
groups sought actively to split the Spanish Communist organization.

Khrushchev's ouster in October 1964 spurred the Spanish drive
toward greater, if still limited, independence. He had become a
symbol for de-Stalinization; the manner of his departure was not
overly reassuring to those hoping for greater liberalization in the
Soviet Union. His successors had none of Khrushchev's spark, and
foreign Communist leaders like Carrillo could be forgiven if they
thought those men did not have his commitment to the fight
against Stalinism. Friction with the CPSU now manifested itself
more clearly. In early 1966, the PCE Secretary General himself
criticized Soviet violations of what he termed the "norms of
socialist legality" in the cases of two dissidents, Yuli Daniel and
Andrei Siniavski. The Spanish leader also took steps in two books,
Después de Franco, Qué? (1965) and *Nuevos Enfoques a Problemas de Hoy* (1967), to dissociate the PCE from what was "purely
Russian in the Soviet revolution": the repression of political
liberties and the implantation of a single-party state.[7]

Perhaps the clearest indication that the PCE was moving toward
independence from Moscow came in late 1967, when the Spanish
Communists publicly rebutted an article in the Russian daily *Izvestia* suggesting that Franco might be willing to restore the
monarchy in Spain, step aside, and allow the democratization of
Spanish political structures.[8] The PCE responded with such unexpected sharpness that *Izvestia* promptly published a retraction.
Evidently, the Spanish Communists chose to view the episode as
felicitously resolved. Still, the unavoidable conclusion was that, in

publishing the article, the Soviet government had intended to lay the groundwork for eventually developing diplomatic relations with the Franco regime. Such a move ought to have alerted the PCE that the Soviet Union was not above putting state interests ahead of those of revolution or change.

Nevertheless, the Spanish Communist leadership had probably not yet fully appreciated that the Soviets would not easily permit individual Communist parties to elaborate and pursue national roads to socialism, that Soviet interests might diverge fundamentally from those of other parties, or that Moscow could not be convinced to reform and liberalize the Soviet system. After all, not so long ago Krushchev undertook well-publicized efforts to restore the so-called Leninist norms to Soviet Communist party life and make it more responsive to the demands of the general population. The invasion of Czechoslovakia finally disabused Carrillo of these notions.

The Spanish Communists had been unrestrained in their support for the Czech reforms,[9] believing that the renovating dynamism of the post-January 1968 Dubcek leadership offered the international movement an opportunity to recover the "ideological offensive" it had lost as a result of the excesses of Stalinism. Shortly after the new Prague regime's "Action Program" appeared in April 1968, Santiago Alvarez, a member of the PCE Executive Committee, expressed hearty approval for the new course, going so far as to identify Dubcek's Czechoslovakia as "the type of socialist society which, given our concrete conditions and experiences, we think we must have in Spain."[10] The spring and early summer of 1968 were a time of exhilaration for the PCE. The speeches of party leaders and the articles in the party press during this period strikingly reveal the naiveté of these seasoned Communists in their belief that if Moscow could be made to understand what was really going on in Prague, they would actually support Dubcek's efforts.

The PCE leadership followed with growing concern Soviet efforts to restrict the scope of the Czech reforms during the summer of 1968, and it publicly supported French Communist attempts to defuse the crisis after five members of the Warsaw Pact sent a letter to the Czechoslovak Central Committee in mid-July that implicitly threatened military intervention if events were not brought under control.[11]

The invasion found Santiago Carrillo and Dolores Ibárruri on vacation near Moscow. The next morning, these two along with Luigi Longo, Secretary General of the PCI, and Gian Carlo Pajetta, the Italian Communist leader responsible for relations with foreign parties, met with Mikhail Suslov. Suslov reportedly turned to Carrillo during the conversation and remarked with ill-disguised curtness that the latter's objections to the invasion carried little weight: "After all, you represent only a small party."[12] On August 23, *Radio España Independiente* broadcast the PCE's official condemnation of the invasion, although a majority of the Executive Committee was not to gather and approve a formal declaration until September.

It was not until mid-September 1968 that the Central Committee of the PCE met in southern France, to ratify the Executive Committee's earlier condemnation of the invasion. The vote, sixty-five to five, was overwhelming. However, it is doubtful that at this juncture anti-Soviet sentiment in the Central Committee was so strong or that it reflected the feelings of the rank and file. Moreover, an editorial in the party paper, *Mundo Obrero,* broadcast into Spain over the PCE radio transmitter, confessed that the party was having difficulty convincing both "old and some young" members of the correctness of its policy with regard to the Soviet intervention.[13] This was hardly surprising in view of the long history of unconditional support for the USSR among party members: their prolonged clandestine status and isolation from other political forces had preserved the tendency to identify the actions of the Soviet Union with the best interests of the international movement and of the Spanish revolution itself.

After the invasion, Carrillo moved to distance the PCE from the Soviet Union, though an irremediable breach had not as yet developed between the two parties. The ambivalence of the PCE is attested to by the fact that, despite his support for the Soviet invasion of Czechoslovakia, Eduardo García was allowed to retain the post of organizational secretary until April 1969, when he was compelled to resign from the Central Committee. A month later, Agustín Gómez was ousted in turn. These developments were not announced by *Radio España Independiente* until the end of July, and they were not reported in *Mundo Obrero* until October.[14] By mid-December 1969, however, whatever chances existed for a compromise had evaporated, and García had moved to a position of open factionalism, drafting an open letter and circulating it among Spanish Communist emigrés in the USSR. To the Carrillo forces, this was the last straw. They responded by convening a Central Committee meeting in late December which voted to expel García and Gómez from the party.

Their expulsion opened a new front in the internecine war being waged within the Spanish Communist party: it was led on the pro-Soviet side by old-guard elements rallying around Enrique Líster, Executive Committee member and Civil War veteran. Líster had watched developments within the party after August 1968 with alarm, and although he apparently had not voted against the resolution condemning the invasion of Czechoslovakia, it is not surprising that he felt uncomfortable with the new line. Initially, and probably with Soviet acquiescence,[15] Líster had hoped to play a mediating role in the conflict. But Carrillo's later decision to deal forcefully with García, and his refusal to tone down PCE criticism of the "normalization" in Czechoslovakia, dashed whatever expectations Líster may have had of smoothing over the situation. In January 1970, he circulated a document to other Central Committee members denouncing Carrillo's management of party affairs as a "caricature of democratic centralism." He was thereafter excluded from most Executive Committee activities, until his expulsion from the party in September 1970, at which time he could rally only token support for his position. Líster then joined forces with García and Gómez. The first issue of their newspaper, which appeared a few weeks later (under the name *Mundo Obrero,* but printed in red rather than black), accused Carrillo of "opportunist deviations of the right and of the left" as well as of "systematic violations of democratic centralism."

Líster could not have realistically expected a majority to side with him, but he may well have had some reason to believe that he could garner a sufficiently large minority to force Carrilloist elements to temper their independent outlook. Unfortunately, from his perspective, two developments foiled his plans: first, Carrillo coopted twenty-nine new Central Committee members for the special plenum convoked to deal with Líster's challenge; next, Dolores Ibárruri elected to throw the considerable weight of her prestige behind Carrillo. It was Ibárruri's decision in particular which settled the issue for Líster. She had never really gotten along with Carrillo, and considered this man who replaced her as secretary general of the PCE in 1960, and kicked her upstairs to the post of president, to be little more than an opportunist and a usurper. She was very close to the Russians for political and

sentimental reasons and undoubtedly viewed his criticisms of the
Soviet Union with a most jaundiced eye. An old Stalinist at heart,
she had lived in the Soviet Union for nearly forty years, or her
entire exile. Moreover, her son's death in the battle of Stalingrad
tied her even more to the Soviet view of the world. Despite all this,
if Ibárruri did not side with Líster, it was perhaps because the CPSU
International Department considered Líster something of an un-
guided missile, an eccentric though loyal fool who could be used to
pressure Carrillo but not to lead a Communist party. Ibárruri, in any
case, was conscious of her position as the foremost living link with
the PCE's historic past; she may not have been willing to cast her
support to a "splittist" and potentially disastrous effort that could
only render the PCE a marginal force in the opposition to Franco.
Ibárruri may also have been moved by a sentiment difficult for
those outside "cultist" organizations to understand: "Without the
Party, none of us would be what we are; and, against the Party we
would return to the nothingness from which we came."[16]

Ibárruri's refusal to join forces with Líster in some ways sealed
his fate with the Soviets as well. They were willing to give him
money and organizational facilities, particularly in the bloc countries, but he never received the open and unabashed support he
demanded and which the CPSU had given other pro-Soviet factions, notably in the Greek and Australian Communist parties.
Moreover, Líster had little genuine support among Communists in
Spain. His support was primarily among emigré Spanish Community groups in the USSR, Eastern and Western Europe, and
Latin America.

Also important in explaining Soviet reluctance to come out flatly
in Líster's favor were the links the PCE forged with other parties in
the international movement after 1968. In 1969–70, party representatives met with delegations from no less than nine countries,
including Cuba, Japan, North Vietnam, and Yugoslavia. To varying
degrees, all these parties shared one characteristic: they were interested in reducing their dependence on Moscow, even if it is
unclear how far most of these parties would have been willing to
go had the CPSU taken a public and irreconcilable stance against
Carrillo. Indeed, only the Italian and Rumanian parties truly stood
by the PCE during this period.

Relations with the PCE's Italian counterparts gathered momentum after 1968. When open dissident activity broke out in the PCE,
the Italian Communists left no doubt as to where their sympathies

lay. A few days after the first expulsion, the two parties issued a lengthy communiqué underlining agreement between the two parties on all major questions. Shortly thereafter, *Rinascita,* the Italian Communist political weekly, published an article by Central Committee member Renato Sandri, endorsing Carrillo's handling of the split:

> [The schism] is a sad undertaking by dogmatists who have not hesitated to trample underfoot the "principles" of which they are so fond. But the undertaking is bound to fail. It must fail precisely because it is contrary to the processes and demands of the reality in which the Spanish comrades sink the roots of their thought and action.[17]

In October 1970, a few weeks after Lister's expulsion, the PCI rendered a similar show of support, calling the Spanish Communists "a most important part of the international Communist movement" and publishing the text of the September Central Committee plenum resolution on Lister.[18]

Not surprisingly, the PCE's other staunch ally proved to be the Rumanian party.[19] The earlier noted communiqué, signed in April 1966 in Bucharest, gave the first clear indication that the Spanish Communists were making efforts to shift from their traditionally unconditional pro-Soviet stance. It marked the opening of an era of extremely close ties between the two parties and particularly, between Carrillo and Nicolae Ceausescu. Since then, at least one Spanish Communist delegation a year has visited Bucharest.

The closeness of Spanish Communist relations with the Italians and Rumanians during this stage (and in subsequent years) stands in marked contrast to their cooler, more formal relations with the French Communist Party (PCF). No mention was made in the French Communist press of the García expulsion, and it was only several weeks after Lister was expelled from the PCE before *l'Humanité* published a report on those events, citing *Le Monde* as its source. The article alluded to the principle of noninterference as codified in the June 1969 Conference document in explaining why the PCF had "deliberately abstained from publishing the least commentary."[20] Formal recognition of the Carrillo/Ibárruri leadership came only at the end of November 1970—not until it had become abundantly clear that the Soviets themselves did not intend to "recognize" the Lister group. The coolness in PCE/PCF relations dated from the May 1968 riots, when Carrillo had implicitly criticized the conservative French Communist stance.

Then, in the spring of 1969, Carrillo opened the pages of the Spanish Communist theoretical journal, *Nuestra Bandera*, to Roger Garaudy for a study on the "problems of revolution in evolved capitalist countries," and rubbed salt in the wounds.[21]

Meanwhile, the struggle between the regular party organization and the dissident group moved into high gear. Striving to overcome their well-publicized (though perhaps not altogether well-deserved) image as nothing more than a Soviet pressure group, the dissidents embarked on an effort to gain international recognition. First, they needed to "authenticate" themselves, and the best means was to convene an "official" party congress. This rump congress, held in April 1971, formally ousted Carrillo and his supporters and elected a new Central Committee. The congress was, in fact, no more than a preliminary step in the dissidents' strategy: it was scheduled to coincide with a World Peace Council (WPC) meeting in Budapest that same month. Enrique Líster attempted to use his position as an incumbent member of the Presidency of the WPC to gain entry for the dissidents at the gathering. The organizers of the affair acted in concert with Líster, offering the regular PCE delegation led by Spanish poet Rafael Alberti, a Lenin Peace Prize laureate, joint representation on the World Peace Council with delegates from the dissident group. Alberti refused the offer and withdrew his delegation from the assembly. This bold move met with partial success. Although Líster was not removed from the WPC presidency, the new World Council posts allocated to Spain were not filled by members of either delegation.[22]

The dissidents courted emigré Spanish Communist groups in the USSR, Eastern and Western Europe, and Latin America. Although the pro-Soviet faction obtained backing from Spanish exiles in the Soviet Union and France, the great majority remained loyal to the regular party organization. The Líster-García organization found the greatest sympathy among the exiles and came closest to wresting control from the regular party among the Spanish Communist groups in Cuba and Mexico, where Líster visited for three months in late 1971. His efforts bore some fruit. For example, when the emigré organization in Mexico held its Ninth Conference in May 1972, it approved a political resolution accusing Carrillo of "opportunism."[23] Despite encouragement from supporters of the dissident faction, however, the Conference did not decide to sever all ties with the regular party. The dissidents' inability to persuade the emigrés in Mexico to join their ranks was symptomatic of a serious defect in their strategy. Even those persons predisposed to agree with the substance of the dissidents' criticisms of Carrillo saw their challenge as too great a threat to the unity of Spanish Communism and feared that a bitter, prolonged, intramural struggle would only result in the PCE's self-elimination from the Spanish political process.

At the same time, the regular PCE organization responded to the efforts of the dissidents and their Soviet backers on other fronts. In May 1971, the party's Executive Committee declined an invitation to attend the Fourteenth Congress of the Communist Party of Czechoslovakia.[24] This decision coincided with the publication of an article entitled "On the Use of Marxist Method" by PCE ideologist and international affairs expert Manuel Azcárate. Formally a critique of a document adopted at the Czechoslovak party's December 1970 Central Committee meeting, the article represented a direct challenge to all Soviet justifications for the August 1968 invasion. "Was socialism in danger?" Azcárate asked rhetorically. "To say yes," he declared, "is not only to laugh at truth but also to insult socialism."[25] In June 1971, the PCE followed up these verbal thrusts with a demonstration of the party's mass following: it organized an enormous rally at Paris' Montreuil Park which drew some fifty thousand people, mostly Spanish immigrants.

Yet these undertakings could not negate one aspect of the dissident critique of Carrillo and his leadership: no party congress had been held since 1965. To remedy this situation, the official Spanish Communist party finally held its own Eighth Congress in September 1972. Thirty-seven parties, including the Soviet one, sent fraternal messages to the Congress. Only Czechoslovakia, Albania, and China were conspicuous by their absence. This is not to say that all problems had been resolved. Rather a temporary accommodation had been reached. In fact, no fewer than eighteen of the messages combined their greetings with Soviet-style allusions to the need for loyalty to "Marxism-Leninism and proletarian internationalism." The Soviet message specifically wished the Spanish Communists "success in the consolidation of [their] ranks in the organizational and ideological plane." Nevertheless, although these messages may not have been particularly congenial, they represented an important victory for Carrillo and showed the Soviet bloc was at least willing to deal with him and his party.[26]

III

That the Soviets had their reasons for exercising restraint when dealing with Carrillo could not obscure their growing concern with Spanish Communist efforts to devise a theoretical framework justifying their position of autonomy and independence. For example, in his article in the theoretical journal *Nuestra Bandera*, Carrillo sought to explain the military intervention in Czechoslovakia and the Sino-Soviet conflict in terms of Marxist theory. He noted the existence of something akin to a "cold war" among the socialist countries, blaming this and other problems dividing Communists on ruling Communist parties. These, he declared, were influenced, as often as not, by "reasons of state rather than proletarian internationalism." While admitting the duty of every Communist was to defend the accomplishments of the "socialist community," he insisted that under no circumstances should non-ruling Communist parties become "satellites of one or another socialist state." Blind allegiances would not cure the international Communist movement's present troubles. What was required was not a "directing center or a common discipline" but recognition of the need for each Communist party to elaborate its strategy independently, that is, "to reaffirm its national personality."[27]

With greater moderation and restraint, Carrillo made similar points in his speech to the June 1969 Moscow Conference. Speaking for the Spanish Communist delegation, he called upon Communists everywhere to overcome their "incomprehension and resistance" to youth, to assume an open stance toward the myriad changes taking place in all societies and in the international system. His own position was perhaps not yet strong enough to make these points in polemical fashion, as Ibárruri had not yet committed herself against García, and Líster—although isolated—remained within the Executive Committee. Carrillo announced that the Spanish Communists approved the Basic Document, but would have preferred a reference to "evident realities" such as the existence of contradictions between socialist states. He reemphasized the internationalist dimension of PCE policy, but now insisted (soon to become the refrain of the Spanish party in the 1970s) that proletarian internationalism could only be measured by "the capacity of a party to elaborate a national and international policy which impelled revolution in its own country and at the same time drove forward the world revolutionary process."[28]

Carrillo's speech to the June 1969 Moscow Conference, like his article in *Nuestra Bandera*, was relatively mild and only suggested the origins of the "present difficulties." He left to others the task of making that fundamental point explicit. With that purpose apparently in mind, *Nuestra Bandera* in 1970 published two essays, one by Juan Diz (Manuel Azcárate) of the Executive Committee, the other by Ernest Martí (Joaquim Sempere) of its Central Committee.[29] Both authors attributed the stagnation and crisis of the international Communist movement to the "monolithic and authoritarian tradition" inherited from Stalin. His "despotic authoritarianism," they argued, had affected not solely the Soviet party but all other Communist parties, which in the post Lenin period had become little more than "executive organs" repeating and assenting to the dogma propagated from above. While other parties had arrived at similar conclusions after 1956, they had seldom been as blunt as the PCE in declaring it, much less in acting upon it.

Events in the years after 1968 further eroded any lingering sense of loyalty Carrillo and his closest associates retained toward the Soviet Union. Nonetheless, the PCE was loathe to abandon the notion that a spiritual, internationalist bond joined the international working-class movement and all Communist parties in the struggle against capitalism. The Spanish party held to that ideal even while insisting that fidelity to and defense of the Soviet Union were no longer, in the Marxist-Leninist jargon, the touchstone of proletarian internationalism. Such an interpretation, the Spanish argued, had been acceptable—indeed, praiseworthy—when the USSR had been the only "socialist" country. But with more than a dozen such regimes established in various parts of the world, no single party could claim to be the fountainhead of the international Communist movement. Pretensions along these lines had led to the Czech invasion, and the PCE believed that, while nonruling parties should maintain a basic solidarity with all those countries, they should never give any one ruling party uncritical support. Individual Communist parties, particularly those in Western Eruope, had to be extremely careful in this regard, since their model of socialism was radically different from Eastern bloc practice.

The most provocative argument the Spanish Communists offered to justify loosening their ties with the Soviet Union was their position that the vanguard role in the worldwide process of social change now belonged to the national liberation movements and so-called progressive forces in the capitalist countries. This scheme relegated the Soviet Union and its bloc allies to a back seat in the revolutionary movement and implied that it would be the forces of the Left in the advanced capitalist countries that would lead the international revolutionary movement.[30]

Moscow could tolerate the Spanish insistence that all Communist parties have the right to be independent and could even perhaps tolerate some aspects of PCE criticism of its foreign policy. Nonetheless, they could not permit the PCE to argue for autonomy or to claim that the mantle of revolutionary leadership should now pass to Europe. Unlike the Chinese, the Spanish Communists had no pretensions of becoming a rival, national pole in the Communist movement, but they did aspire to a catalytic role in forging a regional Western European alliance joining Latin European Communist parties of Spain, Italy, and France with all other forces interested in socialism. This coalition would build a new Europe, independent of both superpowers, and with its own specific weight in the international arena.

Particularly demonstrative of the independent role the PCE had come to play in the world Communist movement was the visit to China in November 1971 of a Spanish Communist delegation headed by Secretary General Carrillo. The PCE had been trying since early 1970 to arrange such a visit, and it marked the first time a nonruling Communist party had resumed relations with Peking after severing them in the heat of the Sino-Soviet polemics in the early 1960s. Although the Spanish delegation did not manage to meet with any figure more important than Keng Piao, Central Committee member charged with overseeing relations with foreign Communist parties, Carrillo was more than willing to accept the partial snub. After all, the trip could not but underscore that the "new" unity which the Spanish hoped to build in the international movement would in no case be based on proletarian internationalism *qua* unconditional loyalty to the Soviet Union. A *Mundo Obrero* article in early December 1971 reiterated the party's position and signaled the beginning of a new stage in the Spanish Communist revolution:

> There must be no guiding party or ruling center. No party has the right to impose its views on another or to interfere. Each party has its own forms and methods of action which are different from someone else's. These are general principles we regard as essential to arrive at a new unity—a unity of diversity of the Communist movement and of anti-imperialist forces.[31]

I V

The visit to Peking marked the end of one chapter in the PCE's post-1968 development, during which Carrillo and those supporting him successfully defended their independence from Moscow. Meanwhile, the PCE had been elaborating its own—ambiguous and ambivalent—vision of a Spanish road to socialism. This had been done primarily in the books and articles written by Carrillo and a few other key personalities in the party like Manuel Azcárate; for the party had been unwilling, perhaps out of caution, perhaps because the ideas were still inchoate to express publicly its conviction that the Western European Communist parties had to elaborate a regional strategy and a democratic model of socialism for the entire Continent. The PCE now turned its attention to this task.

This strategy and model have been called Eurocommunism. The term has drawbacks, not the least of which is that it suggests something completed, whereas the process it describes is incomplete, uneven, and contradictory. But, whatever the felicity of the term, the enormously important role Carrillo and the PCE have played in the development of this process cannot be denied.[32] It is perhaps a manifestation both of his personal projection and its organizational weakness that Carrillo cast a shadow beyond that of his party. He and Marshal Tito have been the outstanding figures of European Communism. Carrillo probably began to develop his ideas on autonomy and independence as much out of pique with the treatment he and his party received from Soviet leaders as anything else. His was a small, clandestine party with a glorious history in the international Communist movement; he resented the raw and unrefined attitude of Soviet leaders who, like Suslov in August 1968, felt no compunction about belittling the PCE and its prospects. Carrillo was a man with a powerful sense of history, the only Western European Communist leader in the 1970s who could claim a revolutionary lineage going back not only to the Popular Front but, through his father, to the Socialist movement of turn-of-century Spain. The PCE became in some ways the vehicle for Carrillo to rise to a broader Continential role. A stubborn streak of Spanish nationalism was transfigured into a commitment for Europe. Once he became convinced that the Europeanization of Communism was vitally important (though the exact moment is difficult to pinpoint), Carrillo seized on the idea. Having little to lose, he saw the heretic of today enshrined as the saint of tomorrow.

Following the Peking visit, Spanish Communist efforts shifted from primarily defensive measures aimed at blunting Soviet interference and establishing independence from Moscow to attempts to marshall support for a regional coalition of the Left. The Spanish Communists now moved openly to relate their domestic strategy to a regional Western European perspective and to lend that perspective primary importance in their foreign policy analysis. In the 1950s and early 1960s, the PCE, like other Communist parties on the Continent, looked with distrust and disdain on the idea of Europe as proposed by people like Schumann. Denouncing the European Economic Community (EEC) as an instrument of domination by North American and European monopolies, it thus rationalized total opposition to any Spanish association with the Common Market.[33] This assessment was premised on the notion that the world was irrevocably split into two antagonistic and competing blocs, led by the Soviet Union and the United States. The Czech invasion in 1968, the worsening of Sino-Soviet relations, Soviet overtures to the Franco regime for diplomatic relations, and Soviet acquiescence to the Spanish government's inclusion in the European Security Conference encouraged the PCE to reexamine carefully the motives behind Soviet foreign policy. By 1972, the party leadership had concluded that Soviet support for detente and peaceful coexistence concealed a determination to accept a divided Europe, a Europe in which the Kremlin would for a long time permit United States dominance in the West, while retaining its own in the East. Soviet acquiescence in the status quo in Europe only reaffirmed to the Spanish Communists the determining role of *raison d'état* rather than proletarian internationalism in Soviet policy. At the same time, new perspectives for the transformation of European societies had developed.

In his report to the Eighth Congress in 1972, Manuel Azcárate had analyzed this process and suggested several factors which signaled a decisive shift in the European balance of forces: (1) a crisis in social-democratic parties and their affiliated trade unions; (2) the eclipse of the Cold War and anti-Communism in general, both of which contributed to the "unity of the Left"; (3) the growing student movement and the influence of technocrats—the so-called forces of culture—in advanced industrial societies; (4) a growing antagonism between the peasantry and vast sectors of the middle class, on the one hand, and monopoly interests, on the other; (5) the growth of "progressive" tendencies in Catholicism; and, (6) a general crisis of bourgeois ideology that had deeply affected the youth in Europe. Those factors created, in Azcárate's opinion, a favorable climate for the "joint elaboration of strategic choices" among Western European Communists, all of whom would invariably come to share a view of socialism as "the development and broadening of democracy, creating a real workers' power, recognizing the value of political, cultural, and scientific liberties and as a society that does not give the state an official ideology and which accepts a plurality of parties and the autonomy of the labor movement from any political movement." The "growth of those ideas," he concluded, "on an international, European level will permit huge numbers of workers and citizens to have a new, concrete, and mobilizing image of what socialism can be and what it must be in this part of the world." A Europe where "Communists, Socialists and other forces" worked together, he added, could be called on to play an important, independent role, forcing a political space between the competing global superpowers.[34]

Against the backdrop of PCE efforts to forge a united front of the European Left, a highly polemical, anonymous article attacking the Spanish Communists appeared in the CPSU Central Committee journal *Partiinaia Zhizn* in February 1974.[35] This article singled out for harsh criticism four aspects of a report by Azcárate to a September 1973 PCE Central Committee plenum: (1) what it called "his incorrect and absurd thesis that there [were] contradictions between the state interests of the revolutionary movement"; (2) his invectives against the Soviet Socialist system, which, according to the piece, amounted to "spreading all manner of lies about the absence of democracy in the USSR"; (3) his outlook on the "problem of autonomy and equality of rights of the fraternal parties," which, the article declared, "includes not one ounce of proletarian internationalism"; and, (4) his call—"which reeks with nationalism"—for a democratic and socialist Europe. What seemed particularly offensive about this last point was that such a Europe would evidently have "no ties whatever to the present socialist community."

The *Partiinaia Zhizn* synopsis presented a distorted picture of the Azcárate report in question, as the Spanish were quick to point out, but it by no means misrepresented the position of the PCE on a number of issues. Most specifically, it accurately gauged the intent behind the PCE call for a European model of socialism: the creation of a European Socialist Community under the influence of neither superpower in which socialism and democracy would be complementary. Of all the sins Azcárate could have commited, clearly the implicit call for an autonomous, socialist Europe disturbed the Soviets the most. The other criticisms, while certainly not insignificant, acquired a special, provocative importance only when coupled with the regionalist perspective. In choosing Azcárate as their target, the Soviets were attacking the Spanish Communist who, after Carrillo, was the principal exponent of Spanish Communist revisionism. Yet the vituperations directed at Azcárate may well have been intended for another target: the PCE's Program Manifesto presented at the September 1973 Central Committee plenum, discussed in the previous chapter. After 1968 the PCE had on more than one occasion criticized what it saw as the fusion of party and state in Eastern Europe, the authoritarianism and bureaucratization exhibited by those societies, and the absence of fundamental democratic freedoms there. With the publication of the Program Manifesto, however, the PCE leadership not only codified those criticisms but pointedly contrasted the PCE's proposed solutions for Western Europe with the practice of the East.

Just what Moscow's motives were in approving the publication of the article in *Partiinaia Zhizn* is, in any case, difficult to determine. Assessment becomes even more complicated when one examines the joint communiqué issued in Moscow in October 1974 at the end of top-level talks between the two parties. As the communiqué makes amply clear, the PCE representatives' journey to the Soviet Union was no pilgrimage to Canossa.[36] While the Russians took a major step in publicly disowning the splinter Spanish group and "promis[ed] by every means an improvement in relations and mutual trust, even when differences exist on certain questions," the PCE made no significant concessions. Only with respect to the Soviet policy of detente did the Spanish Communists shift their stance and agree that the policy of peaceful coexistence as practiced by the Soviet Union "not only did not restrain the class struggle and the activities of Communist parties in the capitalist countries, but on the contrary created more favorable conditions for their development." And yet, too much should not be made of even this concession; for, the shift may have come in response to Soviet assurances that Kremlin policy toward Europe would soon change.

The chain of events poses a major question. If *Partiinaia Zhizn* in February 1974 had accused Manuel Azcárate (and by implication the Spanish Communist leadership) of "siding with the declared enemies of the Soviet socialist system," why in October did a Soviet delegation sign a joint communiqué with the same leadership group in a "spirit of sincerity and mutual understanding"? What happened in the months after the *Partiinaia Zhizn* article that could have induced the Soviets to institute such a sharp reversal in its policy toward the PCE?

There were in all probability two basic reasons for the turnabout. One relates to developments in the Iberian peninsula. The rapidity with which the Portuguese military overthrew the ultraconservative Caetano regime in April 1974 and the evident deterioration of the Franco government after the December 1973 assassination of Admiral Carrero Blanco confirmed to the Soviets that the Iberian peninsula was potentially the most revolutionary region of Europe. The overthrow of the Spanish and Portuguese regimes would create very favorable conditions for the "democratic and progressive" forces of other European countries. The other reason for the reversal in Soviet policy had to do with the pan-European Communist conference. The PCE and CPSU published their communiqué two days before the opening in Warsaw of a meeting of European Communist parties, the first in a series aimed at establishing the terms of a forthcoming meeting. With the support of the Italian Communists (who served with the Poles as cohosts to the meeting), the PCE probably made a formal communiqué with the Soviets the price for its attendance.

Those preparatory meetings lasted well over a year and a half and were marked by a tug of war between the Soviets and their bloc allies, primarily the Bulgarians and East Germans, who insisted the eventual conference issue a programmatic document with ideological overtones, and the Yugoslavs, Rumanians, Italians and Spanish, who tried to make sure whatever document emerged from the meeting would be as vague as possible. After extended debates, the Soviets capitulated on nearly all their demands and agreed to such a document. The pan-European conference held in East Berlin in June 1976 saw the public victory of the Eurocommunist bloc. As might be expected, it was Carrillo who was the most quotable exponent of national Communism:

For years, Moscow was our Rome. We spoke of the great October Socialist revolution as if it were our Christmas. That was the period of our infancy. Today we have grown up. We Communists do not have a leading center, no international discipline which can be imposed upon us: what unites us are ties of affinity based on the theories of scientific socialism. We will not return to the past structures and conceptions of internationalism.[37]

Spanish Communist differences with the Soviet leadership deepened as a result of the April 1974 Portuguese revolution. The PCE welcomed the Portuguese revolution at the outset, seeing in it a prelude to an offensive by the Left in Spain and throughout Mediterranean Europe.[38] Thus, *Mundo Obrero* described the downfall of Portuguese dictator Marcello Caetano as coming about through a process which closely resembled Spanish Communist proposals for a *Pacto para la Libertad*,[39] and Executive Committee member Santiago Alvarez, speaking upon his return from a trip to Portugal, remarked that "seeing what the PCP is today, one cannot help but think of what will be very quickly, with liberty, the PCE."[40] The euphoria quickly dissipated. The Portuguese Communist party, making little effort to conceal its disdain for "bourgeois" political institutions, was quick to attach its fortunes to the radicals in the *Movimento das Forças Armadas*. The Portuguese party thus emphasized how its tactics for exploiting the changed balance of forces on the European Continent differed from those of the PCE.

This is not the place to consider whether or not the radical politics of the PCP were out of synch with the domestic situation in the country. I have argued elsewhere they were not.[41] Regarding PCE-PCP-CPSU triangular relationship, it is important to note that the Portuguese Communist vision of socialist society did not have much in common with the *via española al socialismo*. Moreover, the Spanish leadership also became convinced that the Soviet Union's acquiescence in the PCP's quest for power was at least in part, an attempt to place an obstacle in the way of the PCE and like-minded parties. Carrillo implied as much in a November 1975 interview when he warned that no one should nourish

excessive illusions . . . about the way the USSR will react to the formation of socialist countries—or ones in the process of becoming such—not dependent on the USSR itself, and which will have a political structure different from those in the peoples' democracies. There is no doubt that the latter will look more and more toward European

models of socialism, if we reach that point. . . . Whether one likes it or
not, the socialism in Western Europe will become a pole of reference
for the whole working class movement and . . . [we] cannot ignore the
fact that this will be viewed with concern in Moscow.[42]

The PCE's policy toward NATO, the Atlantic Alliance, and the
presence of United States bases on Spanish territory acknowledged that in order to succeed, the parties of the European Left
must avoid being destabilizing forces in their own countries as
well as on a regional scale. On the subject of the bases, the party
abandoned its position of the 1950s and 1960s, in which it called
for the abrogation of the agreement.[43] Although as late as 1974, the
Spanish Communist newspaper *Mundo Obrero* called the American bases a "mortal danger for our motherland," the PCE repeatedly declared in public that it would accept their presence in
Spain for the foreseeable future or at least until Soviet forces
withdrew from Eastern Europe.[44] Negotiations for the dismantling
and withdrawal of the American military presence from the country should take place in the context of pan-European talks on force
reduction.

While the PCE accepted the presence of American bases in
Spain, the party generally opposed Spanish involvement in NATO.
In fact, at a private colloquium organized in Cologne late in 1975,
Manuel Azcárate made every effort to convince his audience that
Spain's inclusion would lead directly to Soviet moves aimed at
Rumania and Yugoslavia to reinvigorate the Warsaw Pact. Despite
this, the PCE went on record as saying that, while it would campaign against entry into NATO, it would accept whatever decision a
new and democratic *Cortes* rendered on the issue. Further indi-
cations of a greater Spanish Communist flexibility on this matter
came in the summer of 1976. Hoping to encourage the United
States to raise its veto against Communist participation in a provisional coalition government which would oversee the transition to
the post-Franco era, Carrillo offered not to oppose formal Spanish
entry into the Alliance.[45]

Nonetheless, it is important to remember that, despite their perceptions of the Soviet Union and the Warsaw Pact as threats to the
PCE's domestic and regional ambitions, the Spanish Communists
had not become converts to the idea of NATO. The Alliance could
be sure the Spanish Communists would oppose the use of Spanish
bases for delivery of arms or supplies to Israel in the event of a

new Middle East confrontation or to support increased allocations for defense in the event of Spanish entry into NATO. The PCE, advocate of gradual and balanced dissolution of both blocs, wanted the European Left to contribute to the development of Europe as an independent actor in the international system.

Spain stood outside the EEC in the mid-1970s; as a consequence, the Spanish Communists did not have to take a specific stand on issues affecting the Community, such as the direct election to the European Parliament. Similarly, they did not have to define their position toward existing institutional arrangements. However, the general thrust of Spanish Communist policy continued to be that the European Left must work within existing institutions to change their character and effect social and economic change. Entry into the Community and a corresponding Europeanist perspective thus were an integral part of the argument Carrillo developed.

With participation in Community institutions out of the question, how did the PCE seek to implement its European strategy? One level of activity was the establishment of contacts with social-democratic and socialist parties. Mario Soares's Portuguese Socialist Party (PSP) was a case in point: during the most turbulent moments of the Portuguese revolution one would have thought the PSP and not Cunhal's PCP to be the Spanish Communist homologue. Carrillo was an honored guest at the PSP Congress in October 1974; neither Cunhal nor the Communist newspaper *Avante!* found time or space for him. When Soares proposed a Latin European Socialist-Communist summit meeting to discuss the deteriorating situation in Portugal in mid-1975, the PCE was one of the few enthusiastic supporters of the idea. There were also Spanish Communist efforts to enter into formal contract with Mitterrand's PS and with the West German SPD, but these floundered at the time, particularly in the latter case, due to the intransigent opposition of the Spanish Socialist party, the PSOE.

One reason for the lengthy interval between the first calls for a European Communist summit and its realization in East Berlin in June 1976 was the demand voiced by the PCE and others that any resulting document be acceptable to socialists and other "progressive" parties. Indeed, it appears that Carrillo became convinced that over the course of the next decade or two the chasm separating Communists and Socialists would greatly narrow, and perhaps one day even the reunification of the two principal sectors of the European Left could occur.

The PCE also pursued its European strategy at the international syndical level with the *Comisiones Obreras* as the instrument for this policy. Seeking to overcome its image as a narrowly Communist trade union, *Comisiones* had become an associate member of the World Federation of Trade Unions (WFTU) and applied to join the nascent European Trade Union Confederation (CES). As noted in chapter 2, Communists active in the labor movement were forced by circumstances beyond their control to abandon the hope that the *Comisiones* would be the axis upon which the united labor confederation would be built in Spain. They considered the CC.OO., with its amorphous structures based on factory assemblies, as the prototype of the *sindicato de nuevo tipo* "new type of trade union" an original Spanish contribution to the reunification at the national and international levels of the labor movement. At the European level, *Comisiones'* efforts suffered from the veto of the Socialist UGT, its principal domestic rival. Although the CC.OO. had good relations with both the *Confédération Générale du Travail* (CGT) and *Confederazione Generale Italiana del Lavoro* (CGIL), its ties with the latter were particularly close. Nicolás Sartorius, one of the principal theoreticians of the Spanish labor movement, was close to his Italian counterpart Bruno Trentin, and in his writings sought to adapt the lessons of the Italian experiments with factory councils to Spanish conditions.

The third and perhaps most visible level of Spanish Communist strategy consisted of efforts to catalyze a "joint elaboration of strategic choices" with other Communist parties in the region. The PCE encouraged holding multilateral meetings to deal with important European problems, such as that in West Berlin in December 1973 on the monetary crisis, another in Brussels in January 1974 on the problems of the EEC, and one held May 1978 in Sweden on the European labor movement. But because these meetings were dealing with broad, Continental problems, they may have suffered from excessive diversity. More important were the links the PCE forged with its Italian and French counterparts. As noted earlier, it was the PCI that gave the Spanish Communists crucial moral and organizational assistance when Carrillo was under heaviest fire from the Soviets and the dissident groups they spawned.

Spanish Communist relations with the PCF, as we have seen, were less cordial. Carrillo and Marchais never really got along and, although the two leaders lived within a very short distance of each other in the Parisian suburbs, they rarely met. This was in marked contrast to the relations Ibárruri and others in the Spanish Communist leadership had in the 1940s and 1950s with Maurice Thorez. Earlier in this chapter, we alluded to the noncommittal stance the PCF adopted toward the Líster faction, at least until it became evident that the Soviet Union was not going to abandon Carrillo and the PCE entirely. The pro-Soviet orthodoxy of the French Communists offended many Spanish leaders after 1968, as did the chauvinism betrayed by the PCF on numerous occasions. The PCE, for example, had been allowed to maintain a separate organization in France since the end of World War II (a concession not accorded everyone: the Italian party has never been allowed to create a section in France, all its members in that country had to join the PCF), but in the mid-1970s, as the Franco era was coming to an end, the French began to insist that the Spanish, too, dismantle their organization and instruct its members in France to join the French party.

Perhaps the most obnoxious act of the PCF toward the Spanish Communists came in January 1974 at the Brussels Conference of the Western European Communist parties, shortly before *Partiinaia Zhizn* published its polemical attack on Azcárate. At that conference, Carrillo had proposed that migrant workers be accorded the status of national minorities within the countries where they worked. The proposal elicited a harsh and vituperative reaction from PCF Secretary General Georges Marchais, who called it a "false and dangerous thesis, one without objective foundation and sure to contribute to xenophobia and racism in France."[46] He may have been correct, and there certainly was a polemical thrust to the idea advanced by Carrillo; yet the French reaction was so disproportionate to the importance of the issue that it baffled many observers, and the Spanish as well. The latter did not think it simply coincidental that Marchais spoke shortly before the Soviets attacked Azcárate. What French connection did exist for the Spanish Communists was primarily at the trade-union level, where the good offices of the CGT served as a conduit for funds from the WFTU and Eastern European countries for the *Comisiones Obreras*.

Only in late 1975, when the PCF began to move away from pro-Soviet orthodoxy and made explicit its criticisms of the status-quo orientation of CPSU and USSR foreign policies did relations between the PCE and PCF begin to thaw. Even so, the process of convergence between the French, Italian, and Spanish parties was not without its ambiguities. In general, Spanish Communist criticism of Soviet domestic policies and of the status-quo orientation of Soviet European policy was more strident than those of the PCI, let alone the PCF. The results of the 1977 summit in Madrid reinforced the impression that the French and Italians preferred to be more vague in their criticisms and hoped to limit the joint declaration to general statements in favor of pluralism and the like. The PCE, by contrast, wished to include a public, critical analysis of the Soviet and Eastern European regime and the handling of dissidents in the East. One specific passage the Spanish proposed was rejected by the French and Italians, but found its way into introductory remarks Carrillo made at a press conference:

> But liberty and democracy are today a common patrimony of all peoples, of all advanced [*sic*] humanity. There where democracy and liberty are wounded, there where national independence is trampled upon, there where human rights are profaned, all the men and women of this world suffer [an assault] against their dignity and interests even though we be far away geographically. For this reason, we Communists do not hesitate energetically to condemn the violations perpetrated against this common patrimony, whatever the place they happen, regardless of social or political regime that causes them, even when those individuals responsible belong to parties which affirm socialist ideals.[47]

Statements such as this may have troubled the Soviet Union, but their impact was rather marginal when compared to the theses Carrillo defended in *"Eurocomunismo" y Estado* which appeared a few weeks after the tripartite conference. Completed in late 1976, the book may be viewed along several dimensions. At the most tactical, it (like the Madrid summit) was a public-relations effort, one of whose immediate political objectives was to boost the party in the forthcoming parliamentary elections. The book had a more substantive side, however. It represented an effort, admittedly a preliminary and rather hastily sketched one, to provide a theoretical framework which could serve as "the revolutionary model for developed capitalist countries." Drawing on such disparate sources as Gramsci and Althusser, and insisting on the social functions now performed by the state in advanced capitalist countries, Carrillo argued it was now possible to combine socialism and democracy in the countries of Western Europe.

The other substantive, theoretical dimension of the book concerned Carrillo's argument as to the nature of the Soviet system, how it differed from socialism, and the prospects for change there.[48] Briefly, Carrillo argued that the October 1917 revolution had laid the structural foundation for socialism in the USSR, but in the ensuing years a bureaucratic stratum had emerged—not a class, since it did not own the means of production—which prevented the democratization of political life in the country and blocked its passage to a *socialismo evolucionado*. Failure to consider the Soviet Union a socialist country was a major heresy, but Carrillo did not stop there. He went on to discuss the prospects for transformation in the USSR and explicitly linked change in Western Europe with the transformation of the Soviet State "into a democratic workers' State." Carrillo referred to "Eurocommunism" as a "tendency" (it did not have either an organization or an elaborated, common program, he said), but there was no mistaking the thrust of his remarks: he envisioned the eventual creation of a rival center that would show the Soviets the way to socialism.

Not surprisingly, the book earned Carrillo a vituperative personal attack from the Soviet journal *New Times* in June 1977.[49] Beginning with a recapitulation of the usual Soviet views of the international scene, the article emphasized how in the present period a triad led by the Socialist countries and including the international working class and the national liberation movements participated in the world-wide battle for socialism. Borrowing the old Stalinist saw that things inevitably get worse as they get better, the anonymous polemicist noted that "the more the political positions of monopoly capital totter, the more refined and perfidious become the actions of the enemies of communism": a situation demanding even greater unity in the Communist movement than before. Members of the Communist movement were not immune from such corruption, and some of them, the author went on, "unfortunately act from positions opposed" to its principles. In *"Eurocomunismo" y Estado*, Carrillo had revealed himself as one of those unfortunate souls. The Soviet writer then went on to distinguish between two "Eurocommunisms." One "belonged to the Left and to the Communist parties" (an obvious allusion to the Italians) and argued that the struggle for "socialism and democracy" in advanced capitalist countries had certain characteristics. The writer found this argument too narrow and simplistic; it omitted consideration of parties operating in Japan, Australia, or the United States and assumed a commonality of conditions in Europe. But one could at least carry on discussions with those who held to this position. Not so with the advocates—like Santiago Carrillo—of the other interpretation of "Eurocommunism." Carrillo, the article went on, might appear at first glance simply to be talking about differences in the strategy and tactics of Communist parties, but his real views were "exactly [those] of the imperialist adversaries of communism."

The article did not mention Manuel Azcárate, but evidently what turned the Soviets so bitterly against Carrillo was that he, like Azcárate, had proposed an independent Western Europe. Such a proposal was, at least formally, the Soviet line as well. But when Moscow talked about an independent Western Europe, it meant a Western Europe independent of the United States and with preferential ties to the East. From the Soviet point of view, to speak of a Europe with no ties to the socialist community was tantamount to adopting a pro-American position. For these reasons, the Soviet polemicist said that the interpretation of "Eurocommunism" advanced by Carrillo "responded exclusively to the interests of imperialism, to the forces of aggression and of reaction." The Soviet author admitted the temporary gains "concessions to opportunism" might bring, but warned that in the longer run, "they hurt the party."

The timing of the blast was not coincidental: it came on the eve of a meeting of the PCE Central Committee in late June 1977 that was to assess the Spanish Communist performance in the first elections of the Franco era. These had been disappointing, and one interpretation has it that the Soviets hoped through the *New Times* article to galvanize latent discontent within the party and maneuver Carrillo into a corner. If this was their strategy, it did not immediately produce the intended results. The Central Committee rallied around Carrillo, declaring that an attack on him and his views amounted to an attack on PCE policies as well. It then issued a statement pointedly drafted by eight Central Committee members, all of whom had close personal ties to the Soviet Union.

A different interpretation of the reasons for the *New Times* article asserts that the Soviets knew perfectly well that Carrillo, although vulnerable because of the electoral setback, would be able to survive any effort at defenestration. Still, attacking him with vigor could serve a purpose: it would let those who might be unhappy with the anti-Soviet thrust of Carrillo's writings and

speeches know that their concern was not an idle one. Symptomatically, during the Central Committee debate on what sort of
a reply to make to the *New Times* article, the motion to criticize
the absence of democratic liberties in the Soviet Union did not
prosper, receiving the vote of only about one-third of those
present, and with some prominent party leaders like Ibárruri abstaining.[50]

According to this interpretation, the blast on Carrillo had an international objective as well in trying to force the French and Italian Communists to mark their distances from Carrillo and PCE.
The Soviets had a partial success in this effort—the PCI immediately sent a high level delegation to the Soviet Union; the
Italians then explained how they objected to the tone of the *New
Times* article because it implied a desire to reassert control over
the international Communist movement. But the PCI also understood why the Russians were upset, since they too disagreed with
some of the opinions voiced by Carrillo.[51] The PCI did not specifically support the thesis that the Soviet Union and its allies in
Eastern Europe were not yet socialist countries, but its extensive
media coverage was largely favorable to the PCE position on the
New Times controversy. The PCF, however, adopted a hands-off
stance. It briefly reported the Spanish Communist reaction to the
articl⌐ and did not for some time make any public statements on
the issues. This posture changed only after a second *New Times*
article appeared claiming that the original essayist had only meant
to criticize Carrillo. This argument apparently hit a sensitive spot
in Marchais, and *l'Humanité* replied that "trying to detach a secretary general from his party . . . [was] an inadmissible procedure."[52]

The reaction of the French and Italian Communists—not to
mention that of the more pro-Soviet parties like those in Finland
or Austria—put Carrillo on notice that any move in the direction
of a definitive rupture with the CPSU would be very costly. It
would isolate the PCE internationally and probably bring little
tangible domestic benefit.

V

The changes in the foreign-policy orientation of the Spanish
Communists were profound. Beginning in the 1960s, Carrillo was
able, through charisma and adroit use of the organizational instruments at his disposal, to impel the PCE away from Moscow.

Earlier in this chapter, we considered some of the reasons why Carrillo opted to push the evolution of the Communist party in this sphere. Nationalist pique, personal conviction, and a desire to overcome a Stalinist past all played a role in that process. But perhaps the most important element encouraging the Spanish Communists was the realization of how difficult it would otherwise be for the party to overcome its own past and the propaganda of the Franco regime. Even so, the changes the PCE made with respect to its international ties and perspectives were insufficient; they would not bring the party the sort of broad support and legitimacy for which it had hoped.

Chapter Six

The PCE and the Politics of the Transition

WE HAVE DISCUSSED the sources, substance, and limits of the PCE's evolution since 1956, focusing on the changes in Communist policies toward the Catholic Church and its subculture and toward the labor movement. We have explored as well the transformation of Communist ideological, organizational, and international perspectives. The shift toward more adaptive, flexible, and moderate policies coincided with Santiago Carrillo's assumption of a dominant role in PCE affairs. Convinced that his party could only break out of the ghetto to which it had been relegated after the Civil War by establishing a Communist presence among the growing middle and professional classes, he injected an activist note into the policies of the PCE. Although many aspects of the Spanish Communist evolution away from Leninism were ambiguous and the results of specific initiatives uneven, over two decades the party laid a relatively solid groundwork from which to expand its audience. Indeed, in the twilight of the Franco era, the PCE's influence was acknowledged by the regime and by others in the opposition.

Communist organizational/political strength in the early 1970s was far superior to that of other political groups advocating change. Earlier, we noted what Juan Linz said about the effects an authoritarian regime has on moderate and liberal oppositionists. Such groups were either easily coopted into the Francoist system or, if they managed to develop as a party of the semilegal opposition, were little more than groups for discussion. This was true, for example, of the Christian Democratic movement in Spain. The various national and regional organizations in this *familia política* had a potentially important audience, but, except for the pre-Civil War *Partido Nacionalista Vasco* (PNV) in the Basque country, none of them was really more than a "testimonial group," coalescing around individuals of evident personal prestige but with little effective political organization.

The Communists had also developed an important edge over their competitors on the extreme Left and in the Socialist camp. These had proliferated in Spain during the 1960s, largely in reaction to the perceived abandonment of revolutionary principles by the PCE.[1] Some of the groups were avowedly Maoist and had split off from the Communist party in the wake of the Sino-Soviet dispute. Others eventually assumed rigidly dogmatic Marxist-Leninist positions but owed their early development to the radicalization of apostolic labor organizations in the 1960s. These groups developed some influence in the universities and among the working class, but, for the most part, their predictions about the necessity for armed revolution to put Spain quickly and irreversibly on the road to socialism had an air of unreality about them and alarmed most Spaniards. Although some of them eventually moderated their views, these groups remained small and posed little real challenge to the PCE.

The Communist party was in a strong position with respect to the Socialist movement as well.[2] Once the premier party on the Spanish Left, the PSOE had had difficulty adapting to underground conditions. By the late 1960s, its organization had atrophied considerably, and the party remained active primarily in Asturias and the Basque country. Repression was only partially responsible for the withering away of the PSOE however. The almost obsessive anti-Communism that became the hallmark of its exile leadership also worked against the party. Socialist sympathizers during the 1960s were hardly ready to leap into the arms of the Communists. In fact, there was a good deal of resentment among younger people in the country of the perceived Communist tendency to claim credit for initiatives undertaken by the entire opposition; likewise, there was considerable distrust following the Communist attempt to infiltrate the *Agrupación Socialista Universitaria.*[3] But the Communists were one of the most resolute opponents of the regime, and joint initiatives with them could only with difficulty be avoided.

The new generations of workers and students reaching political maturity in the Franco era and sympathetic to the opposition could not understand an anti-Communism as visceral and unflinching as that preached by the exiled PSOE leaders. Such anti-Communism too closely resembled Francoist rhetoric and seemed to be used by the exiles more than anything else to keep control over the organization. Disenchantment with the PSOE spawned quite a few national and regional Socialist groups, each seeking to claim the political space of democratic socialism. Yet most of these groups had an ephemeral existence and were little more than a name and a group of friends. It was largely in response to the loss of PSOE influence that discontented party members in Spain finally ousted the exiled leadership under Rodolfo Llopis in 1972 and started to rebuild the party. The effort would be ultimately successful, but in 1973–74 the PSOE was still quite weak vis à vis the Communists.

The advantage the Communists had developed over other opposition groups convinced PCE leaders that their party was well on its way to dominating the Left. It was felt that the regime would not long outlast its aged leader, and that the PCE could aspire to a leading role in national politics during and after the transition to the post-Franco era. Communist leaders generally refrained from making specific predictions about such matters, talking mostly in terms of the influence "progressive" forces would exert in the politics of a democratic Spain. But there were times when party leaders shed their caution and publicly expressed confidence.[4]

More recently, and as a result of the relatively poor Communist showing in the June 1977 and March 1979 parliamentary elections, many observers of the Spanish political scene have emphasized the virtual inevitability of that performance. Similarly, Communist leaders have downplayed the expectations they had in the early 1970s. And yet, although the Communists certainly had their work cut out for them at the time, their hopes for influence were by no means outlandish. But to force a change in the regime and insure for themselves an important role in that enterprise, the Communists needed both to frustrate the efforts of those who wanted to reform the regime and to block the emergence of a new Socialist party, be it the PSOE or any other.

Obviously, Communist objectives might have been attained through a dramatic change in government such as had occurred in Portugal in April 1974, when the military took power. But the PCE did not favor such a development, since any military adventure in Spain would probably come from the Right. Moreover, most

Spaniards wanted nothing to do with a situation that might lead to a new civil war. Accordingly, the PCE called for the peaceful transformation of the regime. The Communists felt that as long as the break with the past were clearcut, swift, and were presided over by a provisional government independent of Franco, they could gain advantages similar to those of their Portuguese counterparts without becoming a clear target for the Right.

For its realization, the scenario depended on the Communist ability to seize the political initiative. It was to this battle that the PCE turned in the early 1970s. This chapter will analyze Communist efforts to use the leverage they had developed since 1956 and will suggest some reasons why the PCE did not become a major electoral force.

I

The battle to determine the post-Franco future entered its decisive phase nearly two years before the death of the *caudillo*, with the assassination of Admiral Luis Carrero Blanco in December 1973. That brutally effective act of political violence, attributed to a branch of the Basque terrorist organization *Euzkadi ta Askatasuna* (ETA), sounded the death knell of the regime.

While opposition organizations like the Communist party had long been active in the struggle against the dictatorship, their predictions of its imminent downfall had been marked by an air of unreality. The regime had defeated the opposition-sponsored guerrilla movement in the 1940s and had weathered the international isolation accompanying the defeat of the Axis powers. More recently, it had withstood the resurgence of powerful strike movements. In late 1973, only the most diehard anti-Francoists were willing to hazard a guess as to how quickly democracy might come to Spain.

This reticence changed abruptly after the death of Carrero Blanco. He was not only the titular head of state and the *eminencia gris* of the regime but also the man Franco counted on to insure the continuation of his system. Whether he could have held the system together is open to question: what is clear, however, is that after Carrero's death the Franco regime entered a phase of slow but noticeable decomposition. Meanwhile, political maneuvering within the regime and among the opposition groups picked up markedly.

Spurred by the evident deterioration in Franco's own physical condition, the jockeying for position among the various factions of the regime began in earnest. Some held that the democratization of Spanish society within the inherited structures was not only possible but necessary, and the only way of avoiding disastrous political and social conflict. Their opponents, known as the *ultras*, represented the most conservative trend in Spanish politics. They saw the slightest deviation from pristine Falangism as a betrayal of the ideals Franco fought for during the Civil War. Carrero Blanco's successor, Carlos Arias Navarro, tried to steer a middle course between these factions, presenting a very modest reform program that called for the establishment of "national political associations" within the existing state party, the *Movimiento Nacional*. The 1974 overthrow of the Cactano regime in neighboring Portugal gave his most vociferous critics an opportunity to point to Portuguese events as confirmation of what would happen in Spain if Franco did not snuff out all attempts at liberalization.[5]

We have seen how the Communist leadership seized on the growth of student and worker dissent in the late 1950s and early 1960s to predict the overthrow of the Franco regime in the not-too-distant future. The failure of those predictions to materialize forced the PCE to reassess its analysis of the regime and to broaden its search for potential allies. The first steps in this direction came in *Nuevos Enfoques a Problemas de Hoy* (1967), in which Carrillo called attention to the emergence of an *evolucionista* current within the regime opposed to the more conservative sectors. The *evolucionistas*, as he defined them, were the political representatives of the most advanced and dynamic sectors of Spanish neocapitalism.[6] Though Carrillo did not argue for an outright alliance with this group in 1967, he did suggest that the neocapitalists, whose own economic interests were being damaged by the regime, would be willing to sacrifice the existing authoritarian political structures in return for "social" peace. The PCE would not explicitly admit a need to cooperate with these elements for several years, but it did promise that, in exchange for neocapitalist support of a *Pacto para la Libertad*, the change in the political system would take place with a minimum of social disruption.[7]

By the spring and early summer of 1973, the PCE had already entered into unofficial contacts with individuals it considered representative of that sector. However, it was not until August of the same year, when a government reshuffle made conditions more favorable, that the PCE Central Committee gave permission for party representatives to enter into formal negotiations.[8] The talks gathered momentum after Carrero Blanco's assassination, receiving further impetus from the Portuguese revolution.

The PCE had by now broadened its contacts to include Don Juan, son of the last reigning Spanish monarch Alfonso XIII and father of Prince Juan Carlos, whom Franco in 1969 had invested with the rights to the throne. The party suggested a role as arbiter of the post-Franco transition for Don Juan, if he were to make an explicit condemnation of the regime and claim the succession rights for himself. To minimize the chance that a possible conflict with Juan Carlos might give Don Juan second thoughts, and without consulting others in the opposition, the PCE generously declared that the dauphin could have a role in setting up "a provisional government of national reconciliation."[9]

Contacts and negotiations with various Socialist and Christian Democratic groups had also been underway when news about Franco's illness broke in June 1974. The Communists, convinced that Franco would not live through the summer and that the regime would disintegrate rapidly after his death, insisted on the immediate creation of a unitary opposition front. Don Juan declined the Communist offer, adopting a wait-and-see attitude, as did most of the other groups with whom the Communists had been in contact, including the PSOE. The Socialists insisted that only political parties and trade unions be permitted to join the proposed alliance. They rejected the Communist insistence on the participation of "representative" individuals and of neighborhood and housewife associations which were often little more than Communist-front organizations. More important, the Socialists detected an undue haste in the matter and felt, not unreasonably, that they were being asked to join in a project that would only help establish Communist preponderance over the rest of the opposition.[10]

Convinced that the other groups were making a major error, the Communists went ahead with their plans and announced, just as Franco left the hospital, the creation of a *Junta Democrática*. The *Junta* was an unlikely coalition. In addition to the Communists and the *Comisiones Obreras*, it included groups like the PSP, the *Partido Carlista*, the *Alianza Socialista Andaluza*, and independents like Rafael Calvo Serer, Antonio García Trevijano, and José Vidal Beneyto. The coalition rallied around a twelve-point program (to last only until the convocation of elections to a Constituent Assembly) calling for the establishment of a provisional government, total amnesty, the legalization of all political parties, syndical liberties, separation of church and state, and eventual Spanish entry into the European Economic Community (EEC).[11]

The *Junta* was decidedly heterogeneous and, in large measure, a union of convenience. For the Communists, it represented a shattering of their post-Civil War isolation and confirmed their emergence as a pivotal force on the Left. For a group like the PSP, in competition with the PSOE for international recognition, entry into the *Junta* established its credentials as more than simply a university group united around the figure of Enrique Tierno Galván. Similar considerations must have entered the mind of Alejandro Rojas Marcos, who thought his ASA might become the principal Socialist group in Andalucía. Calvo Serer saw the *Junta* as the ideal vehicle for demonstrating the depth of his conversion from regime luminary to opposition stalwart. After all, what group could be considered more diametrically opposed to Franco and all he stood for than the PCE?

Strictly speaking, the *Junta* did not represent much other than the PCE and *Comisiones*. With the possible exception of the PSP, the other organizations and individuals joining the *Junta* had little real or potential strength. As a consequence, there was something theatrical in the Communist insistence over the next year and a half that the *Junta* was the embodiment of the "democratic alternative" to the regime and as such would provide the nucleus for the provisional government to replace Franco. Creation of the *Junta* was, nevertheless, a significant political victory for the moderate policies of the PCE and an outstanding public-relations success. Impressive confirmation of this latter fact came with the revelation that, in August 1974, Nicolás Franco, nephew of the *Generalísimo*, traveled to Paris for a meeting with Carrillo and other *Junta* representatives. The *Junta* also served as the ideal vehicle for the Spanish Communists to establish a formal dialogue with others in the opposition, thus insuring they would be full participants in the political process of the post-Franco era.

Moreover, as the first national opposition-coalition to emerge in the twilight of the Franco era, the *Junta* and the groups composing it received an inordinate amount of recognition and favorable publicity. Its representatives traveled extensively, visiting the United States, Mexico, and various European capitals, where they successfully presented the organization as the principal opponent of the regime. This was particularly galling to other groups in the opposition; but their efforts to form a rival organization failed, largely because elements of the PSOE leadership did not want their party to be directly identified with what was essentially an anti-PCE bloc.[12] It was not until June 1975 that many of the groups outside the *Junta*—like the PSOE, and Social as well as Christian Democratic groups—joined together to form the *Plataforma de Convergencia*.

The *Junta* appeared on the Spanish political scene at a particularly fortuitous moment, when the country's political underpinnings were coming apart. There was a growing awareness among Spaniards of all classes that the status quo could not long endure.

Symptomatically, the changes taking place in Spanish society had begun to undermine two fundamental pillars of the Franco regime: the Catholic Church and, to a lesser degree, the armed forces. Government efforts in February-March 1974 to exile the bishop of Bilbao had brought relations with the Vatican and the Spanish Catholic hierarchy to the brink of total rupture. Although the regime ultimately backed down, relations were irreparably damaged. Subsequently, in March 1975, the government prohibited an assembly in the working class district of Vallecas sponsored by an auxiliary bishop of Madrid. Then, one month later, the episcopate joined those wanting change by issuing a proclamation urging national reconciliation. In doing this, the hierarchy tacitly admitted the seriousness of that discontent which was visible among the lower clergy and among Catholic Action militants, many of whom had moved toward outright anti-regime positions.

Nor were the armed forces immune to change, although their greater discipline had kept things under firmer control. It had become manifest after Carrero Blanco's assassination that a generational cleavage existed in the military. On one side stood many officers who had fought in the Civil War and wanted the army to function as a partisan political instrument, maintaining the state's fidelity to the Francoist heritage. On the other, younger officers who were uncomfortable with such an orientation and wanted to professionalize and depoliticize the military. Some of these founded a clandestine *Unión Militar Democrática* (UMD), which supported democratization of the political system. Unlike the situation in Portugal, most of the officers involved in the UMD believed that change should occur without the military playing a major role. The government arrested eight officers affiliated with the UMD in June 1975, but exact figures on the organization's strength were never revealed and the extent of its influence can only be surmised.[13] Luckily for the regime and the Spanish people, the army was not involved in a disastrous colonial adventure which might have, as in Portugal, provoked a military coup.[14]

Hardly an issue of the PCE newspaper *Mundo Obrero* went by in 1974 and 1975 without citing some new evidence of discontent within the regime or claiming the end of Francoism was in sight. In retrospect, Communist assertions that a national strike would take place under the direction of the *Junta*, that it alone could unleash a strike movement powerful enough to neutralize the army and the fifty-thousand-man paramilitary *Guardia Civil* were far off the mark. In fact, a trial-run *acción nacional democrática* called by the *Junta* in June 1975 had little success. The Communists, as on other occasions, not only overestimated their strength and that of the opposition, but decisively undervalued that of the regime.

With the wisdom of hindsight, we can see that the *Junta* did not muster a sufficiently broad spectrum of the opposition to force a radicalization of the prerevolutionary situation in Spain after December 1973. Whether responsibility for this fact should be apportioned to the Communists for their obstinacy in insisting that Calvo Serer (to whom they obviously owed a political favor) be included in the *Junta* and the other organizations—to which the PSOE objected—or to the Socialists for objecting depends largely on ideological perspectives and personal preference. Both sides bear responsibility: the Communists for being eager to ride roughshod over groups that they deemed had become politically irrelevant, the Socialists for being unwilling to accept the PCE as a key actor in the democratization process.

In this context, we should also mention the revitalization of the PSOE. The ouster of General Secretary Rodolfo Llopis in 1972 had been followed by an internecine battle, with both sides claiming to speak in the name of the PSOE. Not until early 1974 did a commission of the Socialist International vote to grant official recognition to the group which had defeated Llopis. That decision was appropriate since the overwhelming majority of the members in Spain and a large proportion of those in exile opposed Llopis, but it also reflected the International's belief that the fate of Spanish socialism depended on what was done inside Spain and that the PSOE had to move quickly with the task of overcoming the Com-

munist advantage. This had become a priority in the wake of the
Portuguese revolution and reflected the concern of European Social Democrats that the PSOE build up its presence before the
change in regime took place. The Socialists were strengthened by
the shift in the party leadership from exile to interior forces, and
by the recognition accorded that party by the International. The
latter should not be underestimated, for it insured West German
and Swedish organizational, financial, and moral support and
guaranteed that, all other things being equal, the PSOE would
stand well above other groups calling themselves Socialists. Both
factors were important in rejuvenating the PSOE and in bringing
about a unified Socialist movement capable of competing with the
Communists.

The disunity of the opposition was not the sole reason for the
failure of the efforts to bring down Franco and his regime at this
time. The other side of the coin was that few in the political and
economic elite were willing completely to break with the regime.
Discontent was one thing; active opposition quite another. Many
incipient oppositionists still entertained hope that after assuming
the throne Juan Carlos would force a genuine liberalization of the
regime, thus paving the way for economic and political integration
into Western Europe. Many had been deeply affected by the
radicalization of the Portuguese revolution and feared the consequences if the situation were to get out of hand in Spain. Most
Spaniards, in any case, remained allergic to politics and, even if by
the mid-1970s few felt any enthusiasm for Franco, neither did they
wish to jeopardize increasingly widespread economic benefits and
security.

The PCE, in any case, was not as finely honed a political weapon
as its leaders might have desired. Communist organizational
strength was impressive when measured relative to that of other
groups, but the party was not exempt from problems. This was
particularly true in Madrid, where the party had suffered a heavy
blow in early 1974 with the arrest of Executive Committee
member Francisco Romero Marín, who had spent seventeen years
directing the party in the capital. His arrest resulted in the
confiscation of an important part of the propaganda apparatus and
forced the restructuring of the organization, difficult enough to
achieve without having to prepare simultaneously an assault on
the citadels of power. His immediate successors did not distinguish themselves, and the party organization was roundly crit-

icized at a clandestine meeting with Carrillo and other members of the Executive in the summer of 1974. There were, moreover, important sectors of the party (not just *leftist* intellectuals but working class activists) who were skeptical of the *Pacto para la Libertad* insofar as it meant alliance, however temporary, with the representatives of "monopoly capital." Leftist dissidents in Madrid and Valencia had sought to draw these discontented elements from the party by forming a separate organization in 1973.[15]

The party had its share of problems in the labor sphere as well. Through its influence in the Comisiones *Obreras*, the PCE had developed into the leading force in the Spanish labor movement. Originally, the *Comisiones* had benefitted from an ambiguous judicial status, but by the late 1960s and early 1970s, the regime had begun to crack down harshly on labor dissidence. One particularly successful raid in June 1972 netted most of the top leaders of the movement. This blow and others like it effectively decapitated the *Comisiones* in Madrid and elsewhere, thus eliminating many leaders who might have helped force the *ruptura*.

I I

In November 1975 Francisco Franco died, after a prolonged agony lasting well over a month and involving no fewer than half a dozen major operations. Many had feared and others anticipated the event would open the floodgates; paradoxically, the length of the deathwatch made the moment of his passing anticlimactic and contributed to a smooth transmission of power. In the end and despite the aggressive bravado of the *Junta*, Juan Carlos ascended to the throne, forty-six years after the abdication of his grandfather.[16]

The first government of the monarchy took office in December 1975. Those expecting a rather clearcut break with the past were disappointed. Unsure of where real power lay within the regime and unwilling to test the extent of the powers he had inherited from Franco, Juan Carlos retained Arias Navarro as premier. The Cabinet, on the other hand, included several reformers, the most important of whom were Manuel Fraga Iribarne and José María Areilza. Arias appointed them to the Interior and Foreign Affairs ministries respectively. Areilza, a former ambassador to the United States and France, had joined the moderate opposition by the late 1960s. As Foreign Minister, he would show Europe the regime's more liberal side. The other reformist figure in the Cabinet was Fraga Iribarne. A former Minister of Information, Fraga had gone into voluntary political "exile" as ambassador to Great Britain in 1974, after refusing to participate in the "political associations" charade Arias had authorized at the time. He, like Areilza, must have received some assurances either from the King or Arias prior to entering the new government. Fraga proved to have too authoritarian a personality to preside over the transition to democracy in Spain, but in late 1975 and early 1976, his gesture of having dinner with PSP leader Tierno Galván was still quite out of character for a government leader.

Although Fraga and Areilza held strategically and symbolically important ministries, the government as a whole was only marginally more liberal than traditional Francoist governments. The period from November 1975 to July 1976 was characterized by a struggle between the *reformistas* and their opponents within and outside the Cabinet. The latter successfully weakened reform measures, drawing support from *ultras* entrenched in the largely nonelected *Cortes*, in the state bureaucracy, and in the highest ranks of the military. As before, Arias sought to convey the impression that he stood above the fray but, those in the *bunker*—as Carrillo and others in the opposition pointedly called them—[17] knew very well that he was their ally.

Although the Communists remained convinced that all efforts to reform the political system would fail, the entry of the reformist wing into the government in December 1975 visibly complicated the situation. The PCE now had to worry that other groups in the opposition, particularly the PSOE, might accept preferential treatment and perhaps even legalization in an effort to weaken the Communists. From the PCE point of view, these circumstances made a quick showdown with the regime imperative.

The PCE had originally hoped for a united opposition front able to go on the offensive immediately after the death of Franco. In June 1975, the *Junta* had engaged in talks in an effort to bring about the rapid unification of the two organizations. Though spurred by an August decree suspending *habeas corpus* for two years and by the subsequent execution of several terrorists in September, the talks had not progressed as the PCE had wished, and the opposition faced the first government of the monarchy still divided. The most important issues dividing the *Junta* and the *Plataforma* were the former's call for a provisional government and the Communist rejection of Juan Carlos as "a slightly dis-guised continuity."[18] The PCE, moreover, had been instrumental in having the *Junta* say in its March 1975 *Manifiesto de Reconcilia-ción Nacional*, that "the democratic evolution of the State by way of legal reforms [was] objectively and subjectively impossible."[19] The groups in the *Plataforma* opposing such a stance were not sure the King would push for change, but they at least held open such a possibility, arguing that, in any case, a frontal assault on the monarchy was impolitic and might precipitate a military *putsch*.

   With a united opposition front impossible for the short term, the PCE shifted its emphasis to mass mobilization. Such an approach would not only channel growing popular discontent with the de-teriorating economic situation (over 20 percent inflation and rising unemployment) against the regime but, by aggravating the politi-cal situation, might prevent any rapprochement between the gov-ernment and the moderate opposition.

   Demonstrations and strikes began in December 1975, with the party instructing its militants and sympathizers in the *Comisiones Obreras* and in neighborhood and housewife associations to organ-ize protests against the suspension of collective bargaining and government-imposed wage freezes. The movement began where the party was strongest—among transport, metallurgical and con-struction workers, and in the industrial belt around Madrid and Barcelona—but soon spread. At its apogee in January and Febru-ary, the strike movement involved over three hundred thousand workers in the Spanish capital, virtually paralyzing Madrid and Barcelona.[20] In the former, the government had to order the militarization of the Metro and mail services, and the same mea-sures were required with the municipal employees in Barcelona.

   The success of those strike movements and the tragic deaths of five demonstrators during a march calling for a general amnesty impelled the opposition toward a general agreement. By early April 1976, the PCE could at last see the fruit of its unremitting efforts: representatives of the *Junta* and the *Plataforma* held a press conference at a prominent Madrid hotel at which they an-nounced the constitution of *Coordinación Democrática*.

   It was a pyrrhic victory. Although *Coordinación* brought to-gether a multiplicity of opposition groups, ranging from Maoists to the liberal *Partido Democrático Popular* headed by Ignacio Camuñas, the very extension of the coalition impeded concerted and decisive action. The PCE justly congratulated itself about outbidding the government for the temporary allegiance of the moderate groups, but for *Coordinación* to become a reality, the Communists had had to abandon some of their most cherished notions. The new coalition's declaration of principles issued no call for a provisional government, talking instead of the need for a "constituent process," and made no reference to Juan Carlos or the monarchy.[21] Despite the relative success of the earlier mobilizations, few groups in the opposition saw these as the vehicle for changing the political system. Although they might be useful as a way of showing the opposition's determination, they could not take the place of negotiations under the present circumstances. It was not enough to be able to call more or less effective strikes; the opposition needed to present a credible alternative.

The formation of *Coordinación* and its acceptance of the need for a *ruptura pactada* ensured the defeat of the mass-mobilization tactics supported by the Communists and various extreme Left groups and the victory of those who argued that the opposition should eschew confrontation. Ruíz Giménez's *Izquierda Democrática* (ID) had defended the latter option with particular vehemence, and the Communists badly needed this Christian Democratic group in *Coordinación*. Not only would ID compensate for the absence of most Liberal and Social-Democratic groups, but the presence of the universally respected Ruíz Giménez in the coalition would serve as a counter to those who saw *Coordinación* as a vehicle for revolution and disorder.

The governmental policy of selective toleration was evident in the authorization of the Christian Democratic *Equipo* meetings in January 1976 and of congresses like those of the PSP, the PSOE-affiliated UGT, or the *Federación de Partidos Socialistas* in May and June; whereas prohibiting of provincial and regional *Comisiones Obreras* assemblies and other organizations linked to the PCE increased the friction between the Communists and the moderate opposition groups. By late June, the PCE even had to swallow remarks like those of *Izquierda Democrática* Secretary General Jaime Cortezo that there was no contradiction between having some parties in *Coordinación* legalized while others, although tolerated, remained illegal.[22]

Communist leaders complained bitterly in 1975 and 1976 about the government's tolerance—indeed, some said favor—toward the PSOE. Whether the government preferred the PSOE or as is more likely, was in some way pressured by that party's powerful international friends is not altogether clear. Some in the government wanted to encourage a relatively strong Socialist party as a way of isolating the Communists, but others doubted that the PSOE with its radical rhetoric and Jacobin tradition could ever assume the role.

Yet, the government headed by Arias Navarro proved incapable of taking advantage of the obvious divisions in the opposition. Indeed, it was unable or unwilling to discipline the surprisingly defiant *Cortes,* which threatened to emasculate what were little more than cosmetic revisions of the Penal Code and political associations law. One prominent Christian Democrat, José María Gil Robles, the former leader of the *Confederación Española de Derechas Autónomas* and a man who could hardly be accused of being radical, warned the King that failure to press vigorously for democracy would imperil the future viability of the monarchy.[23] Juan Carlos had voiced his keen disappointment with the premier's performance, calling Arias an "unmitigated disaster" in one interview.[24] Finally, perhaps in part due to assurances of support received during a visit to the United States in mid-1976, Juan Carlos broke the stalemate. He asked for and received Arias Navarro's resignation.

III

If Juan Carlos had resisted replacing Arias Navarro, it was primarily because he was unsure of who might replace him. The appointment of a new Premier was no simple matter. Among the procedural obstacles Franco had laid for his successor, the most important was the power granted to the Council of the Realm to select three candidates from which the King could choose the new premier. The monarch could refuse to pick one of those chosen and instruct the Council to give him a new selection; however, this process could create a constitutional crisis.

In July 1977, the Council of the Realm presented Juan Carlos with the names of former Foreign Minister Gregorio López Bravo, former Public Works Minister Federico Silva Muñoz, and Adolfo Suárez. In choosing the latter, the King appointed as Premier a relatively young man of forty-three years who had been Secretary General of the *Movimiento Nacional* and a Cabinet minister under Arias Navarro. There has been some speculation that Suárez and the King had been consulting with each other for some months and had reached an understanding as to what measures were necessary and tolerable in order to democratize the political system. If this is true, and it is entirely plausible, then there was little of the accidental in the rise of Suárez. Nevertheless, few people in Spain thought the decision to appoint Suárez a sound one at the time. The then-Communist economist, Ramón Tamames, called the designation "a historic error," and *Mundo Obrero* referred to his first nationwide telecast as "purely verbal reformism."[25] They were not alone. Only the more conservative elements applauded the choice and, then, primarily because Suárez had made his career as an *apparatchik* in the Falange and seemed a fairly traditional sort.

That Suárez would last out the summer, much less preside over an almost historically unique peaceful transition from authoritarianism to democracy, was a thought that entered few minds. And yet, the young Premier, not lacking in opportunism and with a political future still before him, did just that. Suárez understood that decisive government action was necessary to break the superficial unity of the opposition and impose the reformist solution. In retrospect, there appears to have been little that separated the Suárez reform plan from that of someone like Fraga, except that the new Premier, besides not having immediate responsibility for a thankless ministry like that of Interior, was very much at home on television and understood the political importance of style. He also had a more pragmatic cast of mind than Fraga. Whereas Fraga opposed the legalization of the Communist party as a matter of principle, Suárez was more flexible. When it became apparent that to resist on this score might lead the PSOE to boycott the reform process, he legalized the PCE.

The Suárez Cabinet was largely homogeneous. It contained no important political figures who might tower over the Premier (people like Fraga and Areilza had been asked in a lukewarm fashion to join the new government, but had declined), consisting instead of what 'have been referred to as technicians of power. Suárez presented his *reforma política* to the nation in September 1976. The program anticipated approval by the *Cortes* that fall, by the electorate a few weeks later and called, finally, for parliamentary elections by mid-1977. The *reforma* had critics on both the Right and the Left. Suárez dealt with the former by threatening to have the King dissolve the *Cortes* if it rejected his program. He dealt with the latter more circumspectly, showing a willingness to listen absent in his predecessors. As some wags explained the differences between Arias and his successor: Arias did not bother to listen; Suárez listened but then went his own way.

Suárez faced an opposition which at first glance appeared more united and impressive than ever. Indeed, in October 1976 a new opposition coalition named the *Plataforma de Organizaciones Democráticas* (POD) had appeared on the political scene. It included all of the groups in *Coordinación* as well as *asambleas regionales* of Cataluña, Valencia, and Galicia, with only some Catalan and Basque nationalist groups conspicuously absent. Beneath the surface unanimity, however, the opposition was deeply split. The more moderate groups like the Christian Democrats, the PSP, and the Liberals considered the Suárez political reform program insufficient in many aspects, but thought it offered a solid basis for negotiation, particularly with respect to certain aspects of the electoral law.[26] The openness with which these groups received the government's proposals could not have surprised many people. Already at the time of the constitution of *Coordinación,* Ruíz Giménez and his *Izquierda Democrática* had made clear they would consider the holding of free elections to be the political or moral equivalent of a *ruptura.* The ID and others in the Christian Democratic *Equipo* entered into contacts with the Suárez government within weeks of its formation, as did the PSOE. Indeed, the latter now acted more and more as the fulcrum of the opposition.

By contrast, the Communists and others to their Left bluntly rejected the *reforma.* At a public Central Committee session in Rome in July, PCE Secretary General Santiago Carrillo laid down the core of Communist demands: a general amnesty, overturning of the political associations law submitted to the *Cortes* by Suárez, formation of a provisional national government, the creation of autonomous governments for Cataluña, the Basque country, and Galicia, and elections to a Constituent Assembly.[27] A September 1976 statement by the PCE Executive Committee called the *reforma* a "fraud" and "undemocratic."[28] Before any discussion of the electoral process, the Communists demanded the legalization of all political parties and the neutralization of the state apparatus. The PCE was also instrumental in drafting the so-called Valencia document, which took a hard-line approach and called for the creation of a broad-based provisional government, the adoption of emergency economic measures, and the consummation of the *ruptura.*[29] The document drew instant criticism from the moderate opposition groups, and *Coordinación* shelved it.

Publicly, then, the PCE remained committed to a *ruptura*, but we can wonder how much of the intransigence was simply posturing with a view to strengthening the party's hand in eventual negotiations or to insuring its legalization at roughly the same time as other opposition groups. In any case, the PCE could hardly keep repeating that things had not changed. They had, and substantially so. There was a de facto toleration of the party, which could not have been imagined a year before. The unofficial headquarters of the PCE had been installed in downtown Madrid, less than a half-mile from the *Dirección General de Seguridad*, where Central Committee member Julián Grimau had died in April 1963. The entire Madrid provincial committee had been presented at a public conference in October. Furthermore, police had been ordered not to arrest members of the Executive Committee at its meeting to decide the party's position with respect to an important strike called in mid-November 1976.

It should not surprise us that the rather rapid changes Spanish society had experienced in the year after Franco's death had an impact on the PCE. After all, those changes were taking place along lines quite different from past predictions by Spanish Communist leaders, particularly Carrillo. A close reading of Communist documents from that period suggests a perplexity in the party with occasional strong debates on how to adjust to the situation. Although the materials are not available for an exhaustive analysis of trends within the party, to unravel the political and personal elements which contributed to the debates, we can focus on the different perceptions manifesting themselves with respect to the nationalities question and the labor movement.

The PCE had traditionally presented itself as the most vigorous proponent of regional autonomy and self-determination, declaring its advocacy of federalism, but calling for referenda in Cataluña, Galicia, and the Basque country to determine whether the population wanted outright independence or some form of association with the Spanish state, the latter a position Communists favored.[30] There was little disagreement with these general theoretical propositions. The difficulties arose when one sector of the party, including various Basques and representatives of the Valencian branch of the PCE, among others, insisted on a call for self-government in *all* regions, not simply those mentioned above, as part of the program for the *ruptura*. Regional provisional governments should be set up the moment the Left consummated the *ruptura* at the national level.[31]

Though in many ways consistent with traditional party demands and expectations, this policy seemed dangerously utopian to a rival faction represented by then Executive Committee member Pilar Brabo. In several articles published in mid-1976, Brabo argued against the notion of *rupturas parciales*.[32] The call for regional provisional governments in the short-term, she declared, would only dissipate and obstruct the drive for a national *ruptura,* lending a certain credence to those who charged the Communists with advocating the dismemberment of the nation. The PCE already had its hands full dealing with those who, like Josep Pallach and Josep Tarradellas, advocated separate Catalan negotiations with Suárez; it did not need a similar problem in every region. While Brabo never explicitly said that the *ruptura nacional* was impossible, she did emphasize the difficulties the party would face in attempting its realization. In effect, she sided with Manuel Azcárate, also of the Executive Committee, who warned against too prolonged an insistence on a *ruptura* lest "[we] lose the train of reality."[33]

Similar differences of opinion between maximalist and possibilist postures developed in the labor movement. Here, the point at issue was whether to transform the *Comisiones Obreras* into a trade union. *Comisiones,* as we have seen, had emerged in the mid-1960s as an organization whose militants took advantage of syndical elections to infiltrate the regime-controlled *sindicato vertical.* Relying on this mixture of legal and illegal work, CC.OO. had emerged by the latter part of the decade as the principal labor organization in the country. Many Communist labor activists believed the *Comisiones* would one day simply take over the OS. So long as other groups in the labor movement were weak, *Comisiones* could eschew traditional labor structures with their bureaucracies and membership rolls, maintaining the fiction it was a *movimiento sociopolítico,* independent of all political parties. Thus, in the autumn of 1975 Marcelino Camacho called for a *congreso obrero constituyente* and offered *Comisiones* as a framework within which other trade unions like the UGT and USO could participate.[34] In a similar vein, in early 1976 the PCE theoretical journal *Nuestra Bandera* published an article stressing the continuing validity of *Comisiones* as a "trade union of a new type."[35] Publication of the article just preceded the January–February 1976 strike movement, when it was still believed the *ruptura* could be realized. By summer, the rapid growth of other labor organizations led to a reassessment of this strategy on the part of Communist leaders and to the decision to instruct militants active in the labor movement to push for the organizational transformation of *Comisiones*. Proposals along these lines were submitted and approved at a July 1976 *Asamblea General* of the CC.OO.; but, despite its inevitability, the move caused consternation among those who insisted a *ruptura* at both the political and syndical levels was possible and necessary.[36]

By early fall 1976 it had become generally apparent that the PCE could not impose its version of the *ruptura*. The party had lost two battles. It had failed to wrest the political initiative from King Juan Carlos and the reformist faction of the regime rallying around Premier Adolfo Suárez; it had also lost out in its struggle with the PSOE for the mantle of leadership on the Left. The Socialists had used well the opportunity provided by the emergence of Suárez to develop and strengthen their structures. If the Communists had viewed the decomposition of the PSOE under Llopis in the early and mid-1960s with a good deal of self-satisfaction, the shoe was now on the other foot. Their call for a negative vote on the referendum organized by Suárez to approve his political reform program was more or less pro forma. Several Executive Committee statements already indicated that the party had dropped its long list of demands and would participate "in a positive way" in the political process if there were democratic liberties.

IV

The focus of Spanish Communist efforts shifted in late 1976 and early 1977 to achieving the legal recognition of their presence in the country. In an effort to force the government's hand, Santiago Carrillo held a public news conference in the center of Madrid several days before the referendum. The uproar from the extreme Right was so great that the government had to respond: within two weeks, Carrillo and seven members of the Central Committee Secretariat had been arrested. The arrests triggered demonstrations in many major Spanish cities, and overnight Madrid and Barcelona were painted and papered with signs demanding his freedom. Though the government offered to drop charges if he left Spanish territory, Carrillo refused. In a few days, he was granted provisional liberty, given free rein to carry on his political activities, and had met secretly with Suárez. Less than a month and a

half later, Carrillo would host a "Eurocommunist" summit meeting with French and Italian Communist leaders in a not too subtle
effort to prod the government to legalize the PCE.

At this point, the illegal but no longer clandestine PCE became
an explicit target of the extreme Right. Isolated acts of violence
against party militants had already taken place, and the unofficial
party bookstore in the university section of Madrid had been
bombed, but none of those events compared to the cold-blooded
murder of four Communist lawyers at their offices in late January
1977. The assassinations came the evening of the same day an extreme leftist group kidnapped the head of the Supreme Military
Tribunal, thus demonstrating the degree to which the extremes in
Spanish politics coincided. Fortunately, no potentially disastrous
military adventure materialized, and the crisis drew opposition
and government closer together in the effort to forestall such an
outcome. The Communists responded to the provocation by organizing a peaceful, mass funeral demonstration for their dead,
with the participation of all major opposition figures, and called
again for national reconciliation and amnesty, even for the mur-
derers. This first overt PCE demonstration was an impressively
disciplined outpouring of grief with a clear political dimension.[37]

The restraint exercised on that occasion put the issue of PCE
legalization squarely on the political agenda. In mid-February, the
Council of Ministers issued a decree law adopting a simple de-
claratory procedure with notarized presentation of statutes for the
legalization of political parties. Most groups, including the Communists, filed their papers. The government legalized a number of
groups (including the PSOE) immediately, but declined to do so in
the case of the Communists and the parties to their left. Suárez
opted to send the matter to the Supreme Court for a judgment as to
whether those parties fell afoul of prohibitions in the penal code
of groups obeying an "international discipline" and whose goals
were the establishment of a "totalitarian" system. At first, overcoming these procedural obstacles appeared to be a mere formali-
ty, particularly in the Communist case, with a favorable decision
expected within thirty days. The normally docile Supreme Court
did not just go through the motions on this occasion however. At
one point, some feared it would rule against the party. The Court
ultimately declared itself incompetent after an emergency session
with the Minister of Justice, and handed the case back to the government. Suárez could not temporize much longer. Were he not to

decide in the Communists' fabor, many opposition groups were likely to refuse to participate in the elections, jeopardizing as a consequence the political reform program. Finally, during an Easter holiday weekend when the largest Spanish cities were virtually empty—eight days before the thirty-eighth anniversary of Franco's victory in the Civil War and shortly after a decision to dismantle the moribund *Movimiento Nacional*—the government announced the legalization of the Communist party.

News reports of the event and its aftermath focused on military discontent with the move, some even speculating of a potential coup attempt. There was dissatisfaction with the decision, but there was little chance of a successful takeover. What really disturbed the high brass was the way the government reached its decision. The issue of legalization of the Communist Party had been under discussion within the Cabinet since January, but the final decision was apparently made in the absence of the three service-branch ministers. As for the public at large, a poll published in the weekly newsmagazine *Cambio16* showed 55 percent of those surveyed approved the legalization, with only 12 percent opposed. However, another poll later released by the newspaper *El País* suggested at least one reason why the PCE would not do well in the forthcoming June 1977 elections: Carrillo had the second highest negative rating of any major Spanish politician, outdone only by Fraga Iribarne.[38]

While the delay in the legalization of the PCE may have been due in part to government fears of an adverse military reaction, this was not the whole story. By keeping the Communists in judicial limbo for several weeks, Suárez hoped to give extra advantage to himself and the various groups which might occupy the political Center. This was not an irrelevant consideration; for, although since the June 1977 elections we have become accustomed to speaking of the inevitable Suárez triumph, it was by no means clear in February or March that Suárez would capitalize so well on his pivotal political role during the transition.

Less than a week after the party's legalization, the PCE Central Committee in the Spanish capital met for the first time in thirty-nine years. With only party president Dolores Ibárruri absent (still in Moscow but to return a short while later), the ranking leaders of Spanish Communism met to prepare the strategy for the upcoming parliamentary elections.[39] Carrillo's report to the session emphasized the need for the party to follow a moderate course so as to avoid political destabilization. Calling for the establishment of a *pacto constitucional* among all the parties of the Center and Left, he repeated the party's oft-stated position that the new *Cortes* should draft a new constitution to replace the Francoist Fundamental Laws and should then be dissolved. He indicated the Communist leadership was open to the notion of forming a *frente democrático electoral* with the PSOE and other forces of the Left, but insinuated that such an alliance was unlikely, given "the weight of Atlantic politics."[40] This last proposal, it should be noted, was a demagogic straw-man: for quite some time the PCE had rejected anything smacking of a revived Popular Front.

The same Central Committee session approved the party's electoral program. It called for the constitution to make specific reference to the legalization of all political parties, to establish the supremacy of Parliament over other branches of government, to set the vote at eighteen, to grant autonomy for nationalities and regions and to separate church and state. In its economic aspects, the document called for fiscal amnesty and reform, the extension of unemployment insurance to those without jobs in the agricultural sector (a particularly serious problem in Extremadura and Andalucía), greater state participation in the social security system, and the creation of an "economic and social council" to function as the national planning board. The party did not advocate any major nationalizations and, on the whole, its short-term economic program was remarkably similar to that of the *Unión de Centro Democrático*.

Perhaps the most polemical aspects of the plenum were its decisions to shift the party's historical allegiance from the tricolor Republican flag to the traditional bicolor one associated with the monarchy, then reimposed by Franco after 1931, and to drop its insistence on a republican form of government. The decisions caused a commotion among some Communist militants, with eleven Central Committee members showing their opposition to the move by abstaining on the vote. In fact, the shift on the monarchy issue had been under discussion in the Executive Committee for several months and had been prefigured by a Carrillo statement to a Paris press conference in April 1976 that his party would not act as an obstacle if "through some miracle" the Crown brought democracy.[41]

V

The campaign for the June 1977 elections officially began three weeks before election day, but for the Communists, keenly aware of the rather low percentage given the party in most polls, it started immediately after the Central Committee meeting. In the months and weeks preceding the election, the Spanish Communists ran a campaign aimed at overcoming the bitter memories many Spaniards had of the PCE and its conduct during the Civil War and the virulent anti-Communist propaganda the Franco regime had directed at the country during the ensuing four decades. They tried to convey the image of a moderate, profoundly democratic party that had abandoned all reliance on Leninist methods of seizing power as well as any subservience to the Soviet Union. Basking in the limelight of "Eurocommunism," Communist leaders ceaselessly reminded their audiences of their commitment to political and civil rights and to the rules of parliamentary democracy. In keeping with the general spirit of the campaign was one election rally in the province of Teruel where the Communist candidates for Congress spent two hours addressing the crowd, never once mentioning the word "communism."[42]

Chapter Seven

The Search
for Political Space

THE JUNE 1977 parliamentary elections concluded forty years of authoritarian rule and ushered in an era of democratic politics for Spain and its citizens. No group participated in those elections with a greater sense of purpose and accomplishment than the PCE. But, if the occasion was a joyous one for the Communists because it marked their formal entry into the political arena, the moment brought disappointment as well. Despite their many years of activity as the best-organized and most effective opposition force, and despite the adaptive domestic policies and independent foreign policy the party had pursued, the Spanish Communists failed to secure either a dominant position on the Left or a decisive role in national politics.

This chapter will explore the reasons for the Spanish Communist failure in June 1977 and analyze subsequent PCE efforts to broaden its popular base of support. First, we shall assess the Communist performance in those elections. Our attention will then shift to the post-June 1977 period and PCE efforts to neutralize the effects of its initial electoral failure. We shall focus on Communist initiatives generally, assessing as well developments in the labor movement and in Communist ideology and foreign policy. A final section will assess the effectiveness of those efforts as reflected in the March 1979 electoral returns.

I

The Spanish Communists captured 9.2 percent of the national vote in June 1977 and received nearly 1.7 million votes. This made them the third largest electoral force in the country, but still they trailed well behind the *Union de Centro Democrático* led by incumbent Prime Minister Adolfo Suárez, and a resurgent *Partido Socialista Obero Español,* which took 34 and 29 percent respectively. As it was, despite the claims PCE leaders had made in the early 1970s about the future role and influence of their party, the Spanish Communists' performance in June 1977 did not compare favorably either with that of the French and Italian Communists in the post-World War II period or with the 15 percent the Portuguese Party polled in April 1976. The PCE did well only in the four Catalan provinces (eight deputies and over 550,000 votes, representing 18 percent of the regional total) and in parts of Andalucía (five deputies and nearly 250,000 votes in Cádiz, Córdoba, Málaga, and Seville). In the conflict-ridden Basque country and in Galicia, the party did not capture a single Chamber seat, and even in Madrid and Asturias, where the Communists had been thought to have a lot of influence, it barely topped 10 percent of the vote. Leaders of the PCE could take solace only from the fact that the various extreme Left groups—still illegal in June 1977 and forced to run in electoral fronts under assumed names—did considerably worse. Nevertheless, even if these groups received less than 3 percent of the national vote, this figure represented more than a third of the PCE vote (without counting Left nationalist groups) in 1977.

The political and economic program the PCE had presented to the nation placed particular emphasis on the need for measures to ensure the consolidation of the democratic system.[1] Unable to push through its plan for a provisional government to oversee the elections and rule the country during the transition to the post-Franco era,[2] the Communists called in early 1977 for the creation of an "arc of constitutional parties" ranging from the UCD to the Socialists and the Communists, to agree on a new national charter.[3]

The economic component of the Spanish Communist program had been similarly unprovocative.[4] It gave no hint of socialist transformations, and, although the PCE rejected any suggestion that it might agree to anything resembling a "social pact," the party showed a willingness to enter negotiations with other groups with a view to setting up a four- or five-year plan for economic recuperation. Their only condition, PCE leader Santiago Carrillo declared, was that "the sacrifices and advantages be adequately distributed."[5] Specifically, the PCE called for extensive fiscal reform, an end to urban speculation, and an attempt to restore confidence among small and medium entrepreneurs. All in all, the Communists' economic program could be judged less radical than that of the Socialists. Whereas the PCE generally avoided the subject of nationalization (declaring that expropriation with compensation would be indispensable in the longer run but that the issue should not be raised until democracy had been consolidated), the PSOE talked as if the nationalization of banking and credit institutions and energy-related industries was realizable in the not-too-distant future.

The Communists ran one of the best-organized campaigns. The size and orderliness of their rallies were impressive. One rally at Torrelodones outside Madrid and another at Gavá on the outskirts of Barcelona attracted over 500,000 people. (Such displays, on the other hand, helped mislead Communist leaders: after the June elections, it was evident that in places like Vizcaya, Seville, and Santander, to name only a few, Communists rallies had attracted more people than had voted for the party.) The PCE also organized work sessions where lawyers instructed militants and sympathizers on how to function as pollwatchers (interventores). In Barcelona, Madrid, and other large cities, the party mobilized thousands of these pollwatchers in an effort to minimize vote fraud. The strategy was particularly effective in Madrid, where the Communists were able to challenge successfully a sufficient number of votes to retrieve an apparently lost seat in the Chamber. Because the pollwatchers also participated in the vote-counting procedure, the PCE was able to tabulate the results coming in from urban centers long before the government itself could. Indeed, in some localities officials verified their numbers against those of the Communists in the hours after the polls closed.

The PCE directed most of its campaign fire at the Popular Alliance (AP) and its leader Manuel Fraga Iribarne. "Fraga, el pueblo no te traga" (Fraga, the people won't swallow you) became a favorite slogan at rallies, and Carrillo declared on more than one occasion that the former minister of the interior belonged in an insane asylum. Suárez, on the other hand, received little or no criticism. The strategy had its logic, but, as we shall see when we discuss the Communist performance in specific regions, it may well have hurt the PCE. Rarely did Carrillo lash out at the prime minister. For the most part, attacks on Suárez were left to second-ranking figures in the party like Simón Sánchez Montero or Ramón Tamames. This may have been because of a secret meeting between the two leaders in early January 1977. Although in the course of the meeting, Carrillo rejected a Suárez proposal that the PCE run in the elections under a different name and wait for legalization until after June 15, the two nevertheless came away with a respect for each other's political abilities.

Next to AP, the favorite Communist targets were Felipe González and the PSOE. True, Communist leaders could be heard to insist that the PSOE was a natural ally in the struggle for socialism, with much in common with the PCE; but they also strongly attacked the PSOE for its "social-democratic" orientation. The PCE held several things against González and his party. In the first place there was the fact that for the senate races the PSOE had allied itself with Joaquín Ruíz Giménez and José María Gil Robles's Christian Democratic Federation rather than with the Communists. Second, and perhaps more important, the PSOE, through a combination of skill and luck, seemed first in line to reap the fruits of what the PCE considered were its unique contributions to the anti-Franco struggle and the democratization process. Since Carrillo and other PCE leaders had been important members of the PSOE left wing before the Civil War and had abandoned it after becoming convinced that only the Communist party could lead the Spanish working class to socialism, it was difficult for many Communists to accept that the PSOE was far ahead of their party in the opinion polls.[6]

I I

The PCE's performance was not altogether unexpected, but it disappointed the Communists deeply. For one thing, garnering only 9.2 percent of the total vote constituted a political defeat of the first order for a party which a year before had been telling its militants that reform of the Francoist system was bound to fail and exhorting them to press forward and lay claim to "the hegemonic role in the process of change."[7] By late 1976, of course, the PCE had changed its public stance on this score and indicated a willingness to accept the legitimacy of Adolfo Suárez's reforms once the party had been legalized.

During the early stages of the campaign, PCE leaders had tried not to raise the expectations of their militants unduly. Instead of dwelling on the party's prospects, they emphasized the importance of minimizing the AP vote and bringing about a working Center-Left majority in the new *Cortes*. As election day approached, however, some Communist leaders, buoyed by the impressive turnout at rallies, began to talk of a surprising showing by "the party which had struggled most vigorously against the dictatorship and for democracy."[8]

After June 15, those militants had to be reassured. Carrillo did his best to comfort them, describing the Communist vote as "honorable" and emphasizing that the "most dynamic sectors of the population" had supported the party.[9] The Communist vote, he said, had "an enormous expansive capacity," and the vote certainly did not match the "outpouring of heroism and sacrifice" the PCE had made during the Franco years.[10]

The PCE Central Committee met in late June to analyze the Communist performance. In rationalizing their defeat, Communist leaders underscored the fact that their party, illegal until less than two months before the elections, could not in the space of a few weeks overcome the effects of forty years of anti-Communist propaganda. This had had to be done while radio and television remained under the influence and control of the government. Moreover, they said, there was the electoral system under which the balloting took place. The Suárez government had fashioned a law which quite clearly discriminated against the Left. Although it purported to set up a system of proportional representation, its provisions worked against the smaller parties and overrepresented the more conservative, agricultural parts of the country. The electoral law discriminated in other ways as well. It set the voting age at twenty-one, keeping out some 2 million young people among whom the Left generally and the PCE in particular had gained an audience; and it placed numerous obstacles in the way of the more than a half million Spaniards working abroad.

The extent of the Communist defeat in 1977 was magnified by the PSOE's remarkable performance. The *Partido Socialista Obero Español* received three times as many votes as the PCE and captured 118 seats in the Chamber, 47 in the Senate. Calling the

Socialist vote "disposable," "transitory," and "nonmilitant," Carrillo explained to the Central Committee in late June that the PSOE
had done so well because it had been legalized earlier than the
Communists and had been shown more toleration by the regime.[11]
He threw down the gauntlet with the charge that the Socialists
had found support among the "bourgeoisie," who believed the
PSOE more able to attract foreign investment, and among workers,
who thought it "in a better position to enter the government." The
PCE, he went on, had been victimized by fear: it had been unable
to overcome the atmosphere created at the time of the party's
legalization by statements like that of the army officers who expressed "revulsion" at the government's decision.

As we can see, the PCE leadership spared little in their efforts to
explain away the Communist showing in the June 1977 elections.
Many of the arguments made good sense, but they were not a
sufficient explanation. Indeed, after June 15, Communist leaders
worked hard at blaming extrinsic factors instead of taking a careful
look at their own analyses or strategy.

The Spanish Communists had assumed that the influence they
exerted as the best-organized opposition force in the country could
easily be translated into electoral strength. They were wrong, as
they were wrong in thinking that the virulence of their public disagreements with Moscow after the Czech invasion would overcome the visceral distrust many Spaniards felt for the PCE. Communist leaders not only misjudged and overestimated the efficacy
of their efforts within Spain but also failed to go far enough in
shedding the undemocratic attitudes and habits that had been so
much a part of the PCE for so long. These failures might not have
mattered quite so much had the Communists managed to wrest
the political initiative from King Juan Carlos and Prime Minister
Suárez in the year after Franco's death. But the fact is they did not.
Unable to galvanize the forces necessary to impose a clean break
between the Francoist past and the democratic future, the PCE
could not capitalize on its organizational superiority.

Communist discussions of the June 1977 election invariably
emphasized the negative impact forty years of anti-Communist
propaganda had had on the Spanish electorate. They were right, of
course, but there was more to it than that. Did not the propaganda
have some factual basis, and did not the PCE's analysis of the
changes needed in Spanish society bear the imprint of the Civil
War and of the hatred Communist leaders and militants had devel-

oped toward the regime? Certainly, the success the PCE had had with a Popular Front strategy during the Civil War encouraged the party leadership to pursue its broad alliance strategies and its remarkably prescient call for "National Reconciliation" in 1956. But the PCE did not emerge from the war with particularly clean hands, and there was no self-criticism, no public apology for the Spanish Communists' role in the assassination of Andreu Nín by the Soviet secret police and of Leon Trotsky by a Catalan Communist in Mexico or for the slavish adherence to Stalinist directives and the deaths of Anarchists at the hands of party members in Cataluña in 1937 and 1938. The enmities engendered by the Civil War isolated the Communists on both Right and Left and filtered down to the general population. The Communist insistence that the Franco regime could not be reformed but had to be brought down (a view the PCE did not abandon formally until 1976) led many people to wonder about the Communist commitment to moderation. Other groups in the opposition (including the PSOE) subscribed to the thesis that there had to be a clear break with Francoism, but it is likely that Spaniards took the Communist position a bit more seriously, saw the PCE as more radical and more likely to carry through on its intentions than the other parties. Indeed, one survey showed 40 percent of the Spanish electorate believed the PCE had no skill in avoiding confrontation between Spaniards.[12] To an electorate whose dominant desire was to forget the Civil War and the quarrels that had engendered it and to move quickly toward psychopolitical integration with Europe, the Communists resurrected unwelcome memories. Their still-fresh statements about the unviability of the Suárez reform program suggested a desire to reverse, not simply to forget, the verdict of the Civil War. Indeed, all who watched Santiago Carrillo on his one nationally televised campaign appearance in June 1977 saw a man whose repeated references to the war indicated he had failed to lay down the burdens of the past.

The moderation of the Communist campaign may well have been a two-edged sword. Had the PCE acted less "responsibly" during the transition, Suárez could easily have delayed its legalization until after the elections. Indeed, Communist leaders justified the moderate policies they pursued by alluding to that possibility and to the danger of an involution toward authoritarian government. This approach may have convinced some restive rank-and-filers of the virtues of restraint—but posing the alternatives as democracy or dictatorship and raising the specter of *pinochetismo* probably scared away some voters.

The PSOE undoubtedly benefited from this state of affairs. Led by a vigorous and photogenic thirty-four-year-old First-Secretary, Felipe González, the PSOE was successful in its effort to project a reformist image alongside a commitment to deep and thorough-going change. The PSOE retained its allegiance to Marxism, but the social-democratic Marxism of the early twentieth century, not that of Lenin and Stalin. Unlike the Communist party, it had never been subservient to Moscow. The PSOE had always been un-abashedly pro-European. Continental Socialists like Willy Brandt, François Mitterrand, Pietro Nenni, and Olaf Palme lent their prestige to a campaign promoting the PSOE as the best vehicle for European integration. This was important at a time when Spaniards badly wanted their country accepted at last as a full and equal partner in Europe. The PSOE was also helped by the phe-nomenon of historical memory—the return to the Socialist family of many Spaniards who might never have been members of the party or its trade union affiliate, the UGT, but who invariably had some relative who had once been.

The Socialists' success in preempting what might have been the political space of Eurocommunism in Spain was partly due to the ambiguities of the Communists' evolution and campaign. There was, for example, the openly pro-Soviet attitude of the eighty-three-year-old president of the PCE, Dolores Ibárruri, on her re-turn from exile in Moscow in early May 1977. The Spanish Com-munists had gone to great lengths in the years after 1968 to dem-onstrate their independence from the Soviet Union. As we have seen, relations had deteriorated sharply, and in early 1977 in his book *"Eurocomunismo" y Estado,* Carrillo had questioned the de-gree to which the Soviet system was socialist (an unprecedented step for the secretary general of a Communist party in Western Europe), implying that deep structural changes would be neces-sary before it could claim that status.[13] The presence of Ibárruri on the Communist list in Asturias and her statements during the campaign did little to back up what credibility Carrillo had devel-oped on this score. Though her appearances were short (Ibárruri suffered from a heart ailment and was growing senile), she wasted no opportunity to tell her audiences about the accomplishments of the Soviet bloc.[14] Indeed, her defense of the Soviet Union was so strong that on more than one occasion Carrillo felt compelled to explain away her remarks, reminding people that she had, after all, lived nearly forty years in Moscow and that her only son had died fighting in the Russian army at Stalingrad in World War II. Ibárruri was, of course, essentially a symbolic figure within the PCE. She wielded little effective power, but her statements lauding "those countries where socialism is being built," when coupled with the unwillingness of others in the leadership to address the issues forthrightly, undoubtedly raised questions about how deep Eurocommunist doctrines ran in the PCE.

Communist organizational practice raised similar doubts. The leadership openly admitted that during the Franco era their party (like all the others) had emphasized centralism over democracy. That was the only way, they argued, the PCE could have survived the rigors of clandestinity. They promised that once democracy were restored and the party legalized, they would put the combat-party model aside and begin the full democratization of PCE internal structures.[15] There was progress in this regard in the year and a half after Franco's death, but the Communist record up to and during the campaign did not help the party recast its image. The candidates were selected behind closed doors, with the decision as to which individuals would run and in what slot left largely in the hands of the party's Central Electoral Commission, especially those of its members who also sat on the Secretariat. The Central Committee, ostensibly the highest policy-making body in the party between congresses, was there to rubber-stamp the results. That would not have been so bad had the party leadership permitted at least a semblance of debate on these matters at the various provincial conferences that met during the spring. Instead, when individual members of the party or units like the lawyer's group in Madrid sought to spark a debate on organizational questions or specific party policies, they were quickly silenced.[16] The most glaring confirmation that old methods still had quite an influence in the PCE came in mid-April 1977 when the Central Committee dropped the traditional Communist opposition to the monarchy and its flag. The members of the Central Committee took what was for the PCE a decision fraught with symbolism after a largely pro forma debate, prior to which there had been no discussion within the party. As if this were not enough, the Communist leadership apparently ordered its security forces to remove all who shouted slogans during rallies in favor of the Republic or raised its flag.

III

There was keen disappointment in Spanish Communist ranks after the June 1977 election. Although most polls had indicated the PCE would garner no more than 10 percent of the national vote, many in the party had held on to the hope that the predictions would be proven wrong. In the end, of course, they were not; and, despite the preeminent role the PCE had played in the opposition to Franco, the Communists found themselves outstripped by a resurgent PSOE by better than three-to-one. Most galling to the Communists was their inability to translate their trade-union influence into votes. Not only did the overwhelming majority of people who eventually supported the UGT in the 1978 syndical elections vote for the PSOE in 1977 (72 percent versus a mere 2 percent for the Communists), but even among those who later voted for the *Comisiones Obreras*, the PCE did poorly. Thus, while 44 percent of the eventual *Comisiones* voters supported the PSOE in 1977, only 39 percent voted for the PCE.[17]

The Spanish Communists emerged from the June 1977 election keenly aware that they had to narrow the Socialist advantage before much more time passed. Were they to fail in that enterprise, the party risked finding the political/electoral boundaries frozen and itself in danger of becoming an essentially marginal spectator to the struggle for political power in post-Franco Spain.

The sparring between Socialists and Communists did not take long to begin. The latter had defined their objectives clearly: consolidate the nascent democratic institutions *and* stop the PSOE from consolidating its position as the Left's alternative to the Suárez government. In pursuit of those objectives, PCE leaders proposed the creation of a "government of national concentration" with the participation of the UCD, the PSOE, Catalan and Basque minority groups, and the Communists. The Communists insisted repeatedly during the summer and fall of 1977 that only such a government could rally the popular support necessary to stymie those who wished to destabilize Spanish democracy,[18] but behind their warning about the dangers of polarization, the PCE was also laying the rationale for collaboration with the UCD against the PSOE.

The Communists had several points in their favor as they tried to reverse the balance of forces on the Left and in the country.[19]

One was the presence they had developed in the labor movement. The Communists had begun to work within the official Francoist vertical unions as early as 1948. Although this policy did not bring them immediate results, by the late 1950s the structural conditions for worker unrest and dissent had developed and spontaneous workers commissions began to appear. When they did, the Communists were in place, ready to seize the opportunity. Communist labor activists created provincial and national structures to coordinate plant-level commissions. Eventually they developed a dominant presence in the organization which came to be known as the *Comisiones Obreras*. Leaders of the PCE had ceaselessly predicted that, after the break with Francoism, the CC.OO. would emerge as the core of the industrial-relations system in Spain. Their hopes had been dashed by the political dexterity of King Juan Carlos and Prime Minister Adolfo Suárez, but even so the PCE entered the post-Franco era with a decided advantage in organization and trained cadres over their closest rival, the Socialist *Unión General de Trabajadores* (UGT). The Socialists made a determined effort in the months after June 1977 to overcome the Communist advantage among organized labor, but without much success. With their presence in labor and the power to call strikes and demonstrations that went along with it, the Communists had an ace in the hole.

Another circumstance that worked in favor of the PCE was its organizational discipline and the influence it could exert through the network of organizations, such as housewife and neighborhood associations, it had developed since the 1960s. Surveys made in 1976 and 1977 indicate that the average Communist militant inclined more to the Left in his personal preferences than did official party policy; even so, there could be no doubt about the party's ability to deliver support for the "responsible" policies advocated by Carrillo and his closest associates. This discipline increased the PCE's political weight—and contrasted with the PSOE's apparent lack of cohesion.

A final element which worked in favor of the Communists was the electoral weakness of the UCD. That party had been able to parlay 34 percent of the vote into a nearly absolute majority in the Chamber (165 seats out of 350) thanks to the d'Hondt system of representation used to distribute the seats, but this was an artificial abundance. If push came to shove, Suárez could probably count on the support of the *Alianza Popular* (AP) and its sixteen deputies, but he did not relish this option. Suárez and Fraga

Iribarne, the secretary general of AP, disliked each other intensely, and the prime minister desperately wanted to avoid being tarred with the brush of Francoism. The presence of an aggressive Socialist party complicated matters for Suárez. The PSOE called for elections immediately upon completion of the constitution, denounced Suárez as the heir of an illegitimate regime, and saw itself as likely to succeed him.

The proposal for a "government of national concentration" did not elicit overly enthusiastic responses from the Socialists. Flush from their electoral triumph, Socialist leaders were staking out for their party a claim as immediate Left alternative to the government and had begun to envision the development of a two-party system in Spain: PSOE-UCD or PSOE and whatever the Center-Right might come up with. The PSOE expected to form a government on its own terms after new general elections and saw in the Communist call for a broad coalition government a rather transparent effort to weaken the Socialists.

As might be expected, the idea of a Socialist government did not sit well with either the Communists or the UCD. Relations between the PCE and PSOE had been poor before the June 1977 election and deteriorated in its aftermath.[20] Nor were Socialist relations with the UCD much better. Although the virulence of Socialist attacks on Suárez diminished after the elections and the UCD and the PSOE sometimes voted together in the first session of the *Cortes*, the honeymoon was brief.

The UCD and PCE shared a common interest in impeding a possible accession to power by the PSOE. Suárez, of course, wanted above all to remain Premier, but the Communists—who did not object to this ambition for the present—also wanted to prevent the UCD and PSOE from consolidating their electoral positions and cementing a bipolar political system in Spain. But the PCE had to be careful about how it went about achieving these objectives. Pursuing a strategy whose consequence would be the weakening of the UCD would probably result at once in a strengthening of the PSOE and of the more conservative forces in the UCD and on the Right in general. The alternative, then, was to insist on a policy of consensus. Such a policy had the advantage of helping to consolidate democracy in the country and of encouraging the PSOE to come to terms with the UCD.

By late summer 1977, the UCD and PCE were ready to cooperate in an attempt to trim the Socialists' sails. The *Pactos de la*

Moncloa, economic and political agreements signed in late October, was the most explicit manifestation of this confluence of Centrist-Communist interests. While the PSOE signed the agreement only reluctantly, warning it would be up to the government to make the *Pacto* work, the PCE hailed the agreement as a vindication of its policies and as the first move toward shifting the axis of Spanish politics from the parliamentary sphere (where the party was very weak) to another where the Communists' ability to maneuver was greater and their influence in the labor movement could be more effectively employed.[21]

Although the signing of the *Pactos* was a victory for the PCE, the party was not fully able to exploit the triumph.[22] The Socialists rejected the Communist suggestion of a supraparliamentary commission to oversee implementation of the accords, and the PCE just did not have the leverage necessary to compel the Suárez government to fulfill its ends of the bargain.

Outmaneuvered by the Center and the PCE, the PSOE responded to these developments by vigorously attacking the government, demanding that municipal and general elections be quickly convoked, and working to unify the various Socialist groups under the PSOE banner. That strategy was successful in many parts of the country—fusing groups from Cataluña, Aragon, Valencia, and to some degree, Andalucía, with the national party—and culminated in May 1978 with the entry of the PSP into the PSOE and the elevation of Tierno Galván to the post of honorary president. A similar effort was evident in the labor sphere, with the integration of an important part of the third largest union in the country, the *Unión Sindical Obrera,* into the UGT in late 1977.

IV

Indeed, labor was one of the principal battlegrounds for the PSOE and PCE. The Communists, as noted earlier, had developed an important presence in the Spanish labor movement in the 1960s and 1970s through their influence in the *Comisiones Obreras.* Party leaders had confidently expected to exploit their longstanding penetration of the official *Organización Sindical* by simply taking control of the national labor structure one day. The success of the Suárez *reforma política* foiled those plans. In the months after Franco's death, as it became evident that the *Comisiones Obreras* were firmly under PCE influence,[23] the CC.OO. also began to lose their suprapartisan image.

The impressive PSOE performance in June 1977 provided a shot in the arm to the UGT. Anxious to give their party an advantage in dealing with the Communists that no other Latin European Socialist party had had since the end of World War II, Socialist labor activists looked for the UGT to develop a hegemony in the labor movement analogous to that the PSOE was building in the political sphere. The Communists, for their part, were keenly aware of the need to hold the line in the working class: a UGT triumph in the upcoming syndical elections would be a serious blow to any hopes the PCE had of reversing the correlation of forces on the Left.

The animosity between Communists and Socialists, already evident in the *Cortes* and exacerbated by the Moncloa agreements, grew even more acute as a result of competition in the syndical elections. Many issues separated the two unions. There was sharp division over the *Pactos*, with the UGT criticizing the agreements (more than the PSOE, in fact, but inevitably coming around), while the CC.OO. early expressed its wholehearted approval. Other issues related to UGT claims about the properties and other goods confiscated by the Franco regime in 1939[24] and to the system used for the syndical elections.

The UGT favored closed lists, arguing that such a procedure encouraged the identification of the worker with a union rather than an individual, rendering an accurate reading as to the implantation of individual unions, as well as fostering the creation of a stable industrial-relations system in the country. Behind this argument, of course, lay the conviction that trade unions were the best instrument for the defense of the rights of the working class. Closed lists would also help the UGT attract the workers' vote, which had gone to the PSOE in June 1977. *Comisiones* and Communist labor activists had a different perspective. Drawing on a lengthy tradition of workplace *asambleas* and a disdain (although tempered over time by the need to consolidate control of the union) for trade union structures, the CC.OO. called instead for a system of open lists.

The dispute intensified as the UGT accused the government of favoring *Comisiones* by seeking to adopt the open list system. That the government did not want a UGT victory in the syndical elections is quite clear; that it favored a CC.OO. victory, much less. Some individuals in the government, notably the Minister of Labor, may have preferred such an outcome, but those close to Suárez and with real influence in the government were less interested in promoting the Communist-led union than in weakening the UGT and confusing the labor situation to the point where the UCD could promote either its own trade union alternative or a third force independent of both the Communists and Socialists. The extent to which this was the underlying objective of government labor policy became clear when the Suárez government issued its decree regulating the syndical elections.[25] The law set up a system of closed lists in enterprises with more than 250 workers (some 30 percent of the syndical electorate) and open ones in smaller factories. In the latter, moreover, there was no requirement that the prospective delegate's syndical affiliation appear on the ballot, which permitted the government subsequently to claim that many of the delegates in those factories were independents.

After several months of delay, negotiation, and procedural squabbling, the syndical elections began in early 1978. The results showed the *Comisiones* in first place nationally with 34.5 percent of the delegates elected, compared to 21.6 percent for the UGT.[26] The CC.OO. won most clearly in Asturias, Cataluña (particularly in Barcelona), Madrid, and Valencia, doing especially well in factories with fewer than 50 workers. There, its margin of victory over the UGT was more than 15 percentage points. That margin diminished as the size of the factory increased, until in factories with over 1000 workers the difference was only 6 percent. For its part, the UGT placed above its national average in several regions, most notably the Basque country and Extremadura, but in the end the Socialists just did not have enough cadres. Its policy of nonparticipation in syndical elections under Franco hurt the union, and this effect was only partially offset by the lengthy transition to democracy and by the assistance some of its Western European counterparts provided in the form of training programs and funds. Although the UGT did not do badly, especially given its atrophy in the early 1970s when it was active only in Asturias and the Basque country, on balance the CC.OO. must be considered the victor in 1978. The Socialists had hoped—it is unclear whether they really believed it was possible—to duplicate their June 1977 showing in the trade-union sphere; for the Communists to hold their own was a setback for the PSOE.

V

Our consideration of Communist strategy and politics in the post-June 1977 period would not be complete without an analysis of what we might call the ideological and propagandistic offensive which the PCE undertook to improve its popular standing. In this context, we shall focus first on the events which shaped the visits Carrillo made to the Soviet Union and the United States in the fall of 1977, then turn to a discussion of the Ninth PCE Congress in April 1978 and its decision to drop the term Leninism from the party program.

We have already discussed the controversy sparked by the book *"Eurocomunismo" y Estado* and the vitriolic personal attack directed at its author, Santiago Carrillo, by the Soviet journal *New Times*. Indeed, it appeared by late summer 1977 that an irrevocable split might develop between the CPSU and the Spanish Communists. Then, in early September the PCE announced that V. Pertsov, attached to the International Affairs Department of the CPSU Central Committee (ostensibly in Spain to attend the San Sebastián film festival) had met with Carrillo and other Spanish Communist leaders in an effort to reduce tension between the two parties. One proposal discussed was that the PCE might attend the sixtieth anniversary celebrations of the October 1917 revolution in Moscow. Both sides, it would appear, had at least a temporary interest in resolving the dispute. For the Soviets, the presence of as heterodox a party as the PCE would reinforce Moscow's fading status as the mecca of the international Communist movement. The Spanish also had an interest in attending: Carrillo planned to visit the United States in late November, and a trip to Moscow would lend his foreign initiatives a sense of balance, perhaps helping to undercut criticism within the PCE and certain West European Communist parties that he liked to grandstand and was too extreme in his criticism of the CPSU.

Negotiations continued into the fall, with final agreement reached in October. Carrillo and the Spanish delegation arrived in the capital of the USSR a few weeks later; where, in a move which made the PCE leader an international *cause célèbre*, the Soviets did not permit him to speak.

Press accounts generally placed responsibility for the incident on the CPSU or on some faction in its leadership, but there is evidence which suggests that Carrillo was not an innocent victim. The entire affair may have been a public relations stunt devised in anticipation of the Carrillo visit to the United States, designed to reinforce the impression, both domestically and internationally, that the Spanish leader was the most anti-Soviet Communist personality in Western Europe. What is the nature of this evidence?

First, all accounts of the affair agree that during CPSU Central Committee member V. Afanas'yev's Madrid visit in mid-October, both sides came to terms on the general guidelines for the Carrillo speech and the date of his arrival in Moscow. Perhaps one week before his scheduled arrival, Carrillo notified Moscow that he would not arrive in time for Leonid Brezhnev's inaugural speech, as he had in the meantime promised to attend the closing session of the Fourth Congress of the Catalan Communist party. With nearly 20 percent of the regional vote in June 1977, eight deputies in the *Cortes,* and some forty thousand members, the *Partit Socialista Unificat de Catalunya* (PSUC), the Catalan filial body of the PCE, was the most important component of the Spanish Communist Party. Nevertheless, Carrillo could easily have chosen not to go to Barcelona, and he undoubtedly knew the Soviets would interpret his absence for the snub that it was.

Besides this provocation, there was the question of the Carrillo speech. According to the official PCE version, Carrillo turned it over for translation upon arrival.[27] However, no text of the speech has ever been published. Some have speculated as to whether there ever was a speech (or merely vague outline notes unacceptable to Soviet leaders) or whether the speech was so weak compared to that of the PCI's Enrico Berlinguer that Carrillo, as the *enfant terrible* of the Communist movement, chose not to deliver it. Quite probably, Carrillo intentionally provoked the Soviets, hoping to insure himself not only a good reception in the United States, but access to the Carter administration. Carrillo perceived the United States as perhaps the principal obstacle to Spanish Communist entry into the government (thus, indirectly, to the legitimization of the PCE) and believed that were he judged sufficiently anti-Soviet, the United States might not pressure Suárez to keep the Communists out, depriving Suárez of supposed American displeasure as an excuse for excluding the PCE from the Cabinet. The gambit failed: although during his visit to the United States Carrillo spoke at prestigious universities and institutions like the Council on Foreign Relations, he had no official contacts with the Carter administration and concluded his trip without the expected waiver of the American veto. It is difficult to ascertain the degree to which such expectations were ever realizable, but unless Carrillo had been willing to break with Moscow completely (which would have meant a fundamental critique of the Soviet system and would have led to a break with his Italian counterparts as

well), there was little the leader could have offered the United
States in return.

It was during this trip to the United States that Carrillo first
mentioned the possibility that during the Ninth Congress, scheduled for early 1978, the PCE would drop the appellation Leninist
and define itself simply as a "Marxist, democratic, and revolutionary" organization. The proposal, like the foreign policy initiative
undertaken by the PCE with the publication of *"Eurocomunismo"
y Estado* and the visits to the Soviet Union and the United States
by Carrillo, undoubtedly had a substantive and serious side, but
their foremost objective was a quest for votes and democratic
credibility.

In the weeks and months preceding the Congress—the first
legal one held since 1932, when the PCE had had some five
thousand members—party leaders sought to make sure that the
debate on dropping Leninism did not get out of hand and, particularly, that it did not catalyze too deep a discussion of Communist
policies since 1956, when Carrillo had assumed leadership of the
party. It was to this end that Carrillo—who one former member of
the Executive Committee said behaved within the PCE "like Juan
Carlos in the country"[28]—presented the fifteen theses of the new
party program to the Central Committee only the day before that
body met to convene the national congress. Approval of the theses
was virtually unanimous, and even those Central Committee
members who were later to voice their opposition to one or more
of the theses did not object, an indication of how difficult it was to
have a real debate of opinions in that body. Carrillo also asked the
Central Committee to adopt a one-third rule: a minority thesis had
to collect at least one-third of the delegate votes at any assembly
in order for it to be raised at the next higher meeting.

Provincial and regional organizations moved to channel and
limit debate as well. In as important a province as Madrid, party
leaders first demanded that half the delegates from the region be
appointed by the provincial committee. Although the leadership
yielded on this score, it successfully opposed counterproposals
that delegates to the Congress be elected directly by the party
base, deciding instead that the participation of any party member
in the provincial conference could be prevented if 20 percent of
those in his neighborhood *agrupación* voted against him. Often
enough, recourse to such methods was unnecessary. There were
black lists circulating with the names of the worst troublemakers,

and the *comisiones de candidaturas,* which picked the "official" slates presented to delegates at the various levels, set aside ample representation for incumbent leaders.

The efforts to confine debate had their intended effect with respect to the Congress, but they were less successful at the earlier provincial and regional conferences. One reason for this was that many of the new members who had joined the party in the last decade (the PCE claimed 45 percent of its two hundred thousand members had entered after 1970) took party leaders at their word when they promised the democratization of party structures. Party leaders might channel dissent, but they could not afford to suppress it altogether.

Yet Carrillo and others in the leadership underestimated the emotive power of the Leninism issue within the party. It was one thing to abandon Leninism in practice, as the party had increasingly done in the years after 1956; it was quite another to recognize that rejection formally and develop a substitute doctrine. Some of those opposing Thesis 15 (the proposal to drop Leninism) wanted the PCE to uphold as still valid such fundamental Leninist notions as the armed seizure of power and the dictatorship of the proletariat. Others were less nostalgic and, recognizing how much the world had changed since 1917, saw no necessary contradiction between "Eurocommunism" and Leninism properly understood. However, they wanted the party to be clear about its desire for eventual working-class hegemony and desired a full-fledged debate on Leninism and its implications to promote the development of a coherent "Eurocommunist" alternative distinct from Stalinism and Social Democracy. This group (its adherents could be found primarily in the PSUC and in Asturias, Andalucía, and Madrid) feared that electoral avarice would lead the party quietly to drop fundamental principles. Still others would have liked to abandon Leninism entirely but voted with those who opposed Thesis 15 (and Carrillo's leadership) because they felt that only a thorough airing of this issue would permit the PCE to rid itself of the lacre caused by forty years of Stalinism.

Ideological, personal, and generational cleavages—all of which combined to create a serious PCE identity crisis—made the pre-Congress discussion rich and lively. The situation became particularly volatile in three zones: Asturias, Madrid, and Cataluña.

In Asturias, a region where the PCE had expected to do well in June 1977 but did not, disaffection had been growing for quite some time. The heavy-handedness of the central party organization in imposing Dolores Ibárruri as the head of the Communist list in the general elections had generated a good deal of resentment. The opponents of Thesis 15 capitalized on this sentiment. Indeed, tension within the party in Asturias reached such a point by late March 1978 that on the opening day of the regional conference nearly one-third of the delegates, including José Ramón Herrero Merediz, a member of the Central Committee, walked out.[29]

In Madrid, the battle over the theses became embroiled in a dispute over control of the provincial organization.[30] While the conference approved only three of the Central Committee theses as proposed, supporters of the official theses did manage to channel delegate discontent by supporting partial amendments which would "clarify but not contradict" the official proposals. As in Asturias, none of the rival theses received the one-third of the votes necessary to place it before the Congress as a minority position.[31]

It was in Cataluña that the pre-Congress debates reached their zenith. The PSUC had convened its Fourth Congress in early November 1977, where the delegates had included in the program an allusion to the PSUC as heir to "Marxism, Leninism, and other contributions to revolutionary thought and practice."[32]

Those who argued for the retention of Leninism—and their base was above all in the labor movement—were able to wrap themselves in the mantle of Catalan nationalism and to exploit the concern of many militants about the loss of definition and identity suffered by the party.[33] A further complication arose for Carrillo and Thesis 15 because those who had sided with the Central Committee theses from the beginning came from a faction derisively known as *banderas blancas,* long the object of bitter recrimination within the PSUC for its alleged "social democratic" orientation.

By the time the PSUC national conference met in early April, the lines had been firmly drawn. Though eventually the victor, Carrillo did not emerge unscathed. Thesis 15 was approved by a narrow margin of 97 to 81, but in the wake of this favorable vote eight members of the PSUC Executive, who had up to that point been bound by the rule of democratic centralism, threatened to resign if they were obliged once again to vote with the Executive Committee majority. Amidst talk of a split in the party, the others in the Catalan leadership prudently relaxed the rules of internal discipline. As a result of that decision, a motion to have Leninism mentioned in the statutes won by the same margin as Thesis 15.

After all this commotion, the PCE Congress was almost anticlimactic. Only in Cataluña had the minority theses prospered, and by the opening of the Congress, everyone knew what the outcome of the voting would be. As expected, the delegates approved the report Carrillo presented in the name of the Central Committee by a lopsided margin (898 for, 37 against, and 51 abstentions, but with 361 votes unaccounted for), despite broad criticism of its excessively personalistic thrust and lack of clarity about Communist medium- and long-term strategy.[34] Since the official theses had been substantially modified in the various commissions, the plenum approved most by large margins. The only electric moments in an otherwise dull congress came late on the third day when, after an at times stirring debate between spokesmen for majority and minority positions, the delegates voted on Thesis 15. The verdict: 968 votes in favor of a slightly revised version of the leadership's original proposal, 240 votes against, and 40 abstentions.[35]

Despite its predictability, the Ninth PCE Congress was important because it signaled the beginning of a renovation of the Spanish party. Of the 160 members of the Central Committee, 56 were new to that body, as were 14 of the 46 on the Executive Committee. One development, whose implications were not clear at the time, was the rise in the influence of labor activists. Nearly a quarter of the new Central Committee had *Comisiones* backgrounds (the proportion of those of working-class origins on the CC was over 50 percent, and seven CC.OO. leaders sat on the Executive Committee). Their entry was in no small measure due to the fact that everywhere except in Cataluña, those active in the labor movement distinguished themselves as Carrillo's most dependable supporters outside the *apparat*. Many of them, to be sure, were less than enthusiastic about some "Eurocommunist" tenets, but they sided with Carrillo primarily because this was the best way to insure that the debate within the party did not get out of hand.

In sum, Carrillo came out of the Ninth Congress firmly, if not necessarily comfortably, in control of his party's affairs; however, his victory there, and particularly securing approval of the thesis abandoning Leninism, had not been easy. To achieve it, he and others in the Spanish Communist leadership had to endure a debate and criticism which was in many ways unique in the experience of Communist parties.

While the Congress did not turn out to be as open as some had hoped, neither was it as controlled as others might have wished. Indeed, the myth of party unanimity lay shattered in the wake of the Congress. Moreover, debate over the issue of Leninism set in motion a process which the party apparatus would have a difficult time containing. The debates leading up to the Congress were the first salvos in what promised to be a long, drawn-out battle over the identity and policies of the PCE.

V I

A straightforward assessment of Communist policies in the months after June 1977 is difficult, if not impossible. In the weeks after the signing of the Moncloa agreements the PCE came close to forcing the PSOE into a government of national unity, but it ultimately failed—not only because of the Socialists' opposition but also as a result of Suárez's reluctance. Suárez did not relish the idea of sharing power and preferred to use the Communists to keep the PSOE off balance. And yet, despite this failure, any objective analysis of the PCE's strategy and its relations with Suárez and the UCD would have to emphasize that the Communists received as much from that relationship as they gave. The PCE captured only 9.2 percent of the vote in June 1977, but in the months after that election, Carrillo and his party became key figures on the Spanish political scene, playing important roles in the drafting of the constitution and legislative proposals. Suárez had to take their views into account, and occasionally he had to backtrack from his original intentions when faced with Communist opposition.

One example was the municipal-elections law debated in the *Cortes* in February and March 1978. Putting their heads together in an effort to extract maximum partisan gain, the UCD and PSOE had drafted a proposal that after municipal elections the head of the list with the most votes would automatically become mayor. There can be little doubt as to the intention of the document: it aimed to freeze out the other parties and distribute the mayoralties among the UCD and PSOE. Well aware of the likely impact of such a law, the Communists attacked the proposal and mounted a vigorous campaign against it. Needing the PCE to support him on various controversial provisions of the constitution, Suárez backed down and agreed (as did the Socialists, but they had little choice in the matter) to a compromise. Only a candidate whose list had won an absolute majority automatically became mayor. Otherwise, the councilors elected the mayor. On the first round, an individual had to receive an absolute majority of the votes cast by his fellow municipal councilors. Only if no victor emerged at that point did the second round become necessary, at which time a plurality sufficed. The change was vitally important for a smaller party like the Communists, as was amply demonstrated in the municipal elections of April 1979. Unable to win an absolute majority in most cities, the Socialists had to turn to the PCE for support on the mayoralties. The PSOE/PCE municipal pact put Socialist mayors in over twelve hundred Spanish cities, but in return the PSOE had to decentralize authority and grant patronage to the Communist councilors.

Whatever advantages the PCE may have derived from its privileged relationship with Suárez, it was nonetheless clear that the political initiative remained in the hands of the prime minister. He was the dominant partner, and when in December 1978 he decided to call new elections there was not much the Communists could do about it, even though they did not want a return to the polls. Indeed, it was reported that shortly before dissolving the *Cortes* Suárez asked the PCE to join his party in creating a stable parliamentary majority.[36] We do not know how serious he was in this matter or what the exact terms of the offer were, but Carrillo declined the overture, insisting that for the Communists to enter the government or sign some sort of agreement with the UCD, the Socialists also had to take part. The reasons for this stance should be evident. The Communists might not want an election, but they could reasonably expect to hold their own in one. There was not all that much to be gained from entering into the relationship proposed by Suárez. It might keep the PSOE out of the government, but, by making the PCE appear too blatantly anti-Socialist, it would also stoke the Socialists' fire and perhaps indirectly help them do well in the upcoming municipal campaign. The Communists preferred to chance new national elections. They clearly did not want the Socialists to win and would do their best to take votes away from them. If a close election materialized, a UCD-PSOE or PSOE-UCD coalition government might ensue, and the Communists could then be asked to join the government or support it informally in some way. If the Socialists were to veto such an arrangement, however, the PCE could assume the role of principal (albeit moderate and responsible) opposition party and thus benefit from the disenchantment which would set in once the inevitable austerity measures were instituted. On the other hand, if, as Carrillo believed, Suárez were to win again, little would change for his party, but the Socialists would lose much of their momentum.

The arrangement between the UCD and PCE managed to block the PSOE for nearly a year and a half, lasting through the negotiations for the new constitution. As a result, such traditionally thorny issues as church-state relations, the monarchy, education and the devolution of power to the regions were for the most part satisfactorily resolved or papered over to be dealt with later. But, while consensus politics had some very obvious advantages, its limits were also apparent. A recrudescence of terrorist activity, a growth of discontent within the military, and citizen boredom with what appeared to be endless parliamentary debates abraded the image of nearly all the parties by late 1978. The disenchantment peaked with the constitutional referendum in December. Although those voting overwhelmingly approved the charter, abstention was high. Averaging 30 percent nationally, it attained dramatic proportions in the Basque country.

Ever more convinced that Suárez was growing weaker and the UCD itself susceptible to a split, the Socialists stepped up their drive for new elections. In what came as a surprise to some observers of the Spanish political scene, Suárez took up their challenge, dissolving the *Cortes* and calling parliamentary elections for March 1979 to be followed by municipal ones a month later. This sequence would prevent the Left from capitalizing on what everyone anticipated would be a good showing in the municipal elections: when this happened in April 1931, the result had been the abdication of Alfonso XIII and the onset of the Second Republic. Suárez need not have called elections under terms of the new constitution. Although the UCD did not have a majority of votes in the *Cortes*, he could have opted for investiture. The Constitution provided for two rounds in any such vote. A premier-designate had to gain an absolute majority of the votes cast to win the first, but on the second round a plurality would suffice. Given the improbability of agreement among the other parties and the likelihood of Communist abstention, Suárez had little to fear on this score.

The decision to call new elections, therefore, represented quite a gamble by Suárez. True, he alone had access to the polls performed by the *Centro de Investigaciones Sociológicas* which probably confirmed his suspicion that most undecided voters (some 40 percent of those queried by pollsters) would opt for his party in the end, particularly given the growing national concern over terrorism. The realization that without elections any minority government would be confronted by constant Socialist demands for a return to the polls and that in this atmosphere making headway against mounting social and economic problems would be virtually impossible probably influenced his decision. So did the desire to rule without having to rely on agreement with other forces, particularly the Communists.

Although most polls in early 1979 showed a PSOE lead among those Spaniards who had already made up their minds, the Socialist machine was not as well-oiled as people supposed or party leaders suggested. For one thing, although the Socialist-backed UGT had been second to the Communist *Comisiones Obreras* in the trade union elections celebrated in early 1978, the union had not done nearly as well as Socialist leaders had originally predicted and had slipped even more since that time. Perhaps overly confident of victory over Suárez, the party had also fallen behind in its organizational reinforcement and consolidation. Many in the PSOE realized this was a serious problem even after senatorial by-elections in Asturias and Alicante in May 1978 showed the Socialist vote hurt by abstentions. Moreover, the unification of the various Socialist currents under the PSOE banner was not smooth as hoped, with some of the regional Socialist electorate resenting the unification. There had also been a good bit of grumbling in the ranks about a González remark to the effect that at its forthcoming Twenty-eighth Congress the party would drop the reference to Marxism from its program. An even more profound political miscalculation was the Socialist decision to attack Suárez as being a slightly disguised continuation of Franco. Suárez, it could hardly be denied, had made his career under the *ancien régime,* but only the most short-sighted could deny the decisive role he had played (along with King Juan Carlos) in bringing democracy to the country. The Socialists, in effect, overestimated their ability to overcome in two years the effects of four decades' hostile anti-Left propaganda. A story appearing in the leading newsmagazine *Cambio16* captures the popular climate: campaigning in a town twenty-five miles from Madrid, a UCD candidate put a pin with her party emblem on the coat of a prospective voter; before consenting, the voter asked if one could be put in jail for wearing it.[37]

There was a good deal of talk in Spain before March 1 about possible coalition governments, with most speculation focusing on the so-called grand coalition between the UCD and PSOE. Suárez, of course, did not call the elections to share power; sources close to the UCD insisted throughout the campaign that were their party to win at least one-hundred-sixty seats in the new Cortes, it would form a minority government. A coalition government, it should be stressed, would have benefited neither Socialist/UCD partisan interests nor those of democracy in Spain. It would only have muddied the political waters at a time when clearcut alternatives, put aside in part because of the exigencies of the transition from Francoism, needed to be emphasized once more. The Communists would have welcomed the opportunity to assume the mantle of opposition to a UCD-PSOE government.

VII

The Communists' chief objectives in the March 1979 electoral campaign were to prevent a PSOE victory and to prepare for the municipal elections by extending their organizational network and influence. To this end, they mounted an aggressively anti-PSOE campaign. Although there appears to have been some debate within the PCE as to how much criticism should be directed at the Socialists, the general tenor of the campaign was harsh. Communist speakers roundly denounced the influence the West German Social Democratic party was having on the PSOE and ridiculed the Socialists for thinking that they could constitute a left-wing government in 1979 Spain. In a clear pitch to the left-wing PSOE voter, Communist candidates argued that a vote for the PCE was the only way to keep the PSOE on a "progressive" course. Communists attacks on the Socialists were also aimed at discouraging PCE voters from going over to the PSOE. This possibility posed a real threat. Surveys taken over the previous two years indicated that half the Communists voters would opt for the Socialists as their second choice, and polls commissioned in January and February 1979 indicated some 8 percent of Communist voters from 1977 now intended to vote for the PSOE.[38] Some may have felt that Carrillo overdid his attacks on the PSOE—one highly respected independent on the Left described him after the election as having an "anti-socialist phobia"[39]—but his sarcasm sprang from a resentment deeply felt by the PCE rank-and-file over the

PSOE's ability to outmaneuver the Communists and maintain a position of strength on the Left. The standing joke in many Communist groups was that the PSOE had a record of one hundred years of honesty and firmness (this was the official Socialist slogan in 1979, the party's centenary) but had spent forty of them on vacation, a not too flattering reference to the atrophy of the PSOE organization during the Franco years.

Aside from the jabs at the Socialists, there was little electricity to the Communist campaign this time around. Once again, the PCE had the most impressive and largest rallies and mounted the best-organized campaign. But, perhaps because the novelty had worn off and the previous two years had been so exhausting, not to mention the fact that another campaign was looming in just a few weeks, there was little visible excitement. The program the PCE presented to the nation was like that of 1977 but, if anything, more moderate. There was no mention of nationalization in the short or medium term, just calls for greater efficiency. Who could quarrel with demands that the administrative apparatus, the municipal structures, and the social security system be reformed, that the fight against terrorism be carried forward, and that autonomy measures for the various regions be enacted? Perhaps the only controversial measures put forward by the PCE related to the *Estatuto de los Trabajadores*, a sort of labor charter, and its proposal for breaking government control and censorship over radio and television.

As slogans like "Put your vote to work" and "Employ your vote against unemployment" suggested, the Communists directed their campaign propaganda at the working class. At one level, of course, this was not surprising. The PCE claimed to be the party of the working class, found its raison d'être in representing proletarian interests, and had preferential relations with the largest trade union, the *Comisiones Oberas*. But, in fact, the Communists had received fewer working class votes than the PSOE in 1977. Communist leaders were determined to reverse this trend. Already at the Ninth PCE Congress, a definite effort was made to promote working-class activists and those with working-class backgrounds into the highest policy-making bodies of the party: over one-quarter of the new Central Committee were from the CC.OO., as were seven of the thirty-four members of the new Executive Committee. Many CC.OO. leaders—notably Marcelino Camacho, Nicolás Sartorius, Julián Ariza, Tomás Tueros, and Fernando Soto, all members of the CC.OO. National Secretariat and of the PCE Executive Committee—made their way onto PCE lists in March 1979. Although a detailed statistical breakdown is not possible given the paucity of biographical information about the *Cortes* candidates, it is worth noting that, according to a report published in *Mundo Obrero*, out of thirty thousand national and municipal candidates put forward in 1979 by the Communists, some ten thousand were members of the CC.OO.[40]

VIII

In an interview published the day after the March 1979 elections, Santiago Carrillo described the PCE's results as "what we had hoped for and somewhat more."[41] Carrillo was trying to put the best face on an election about which he must have had mixed feelings. Suárez had won and the Socialists were not going to enter the government, and this was, of course, reason for rejoicing in the PCE camp. The UCD had lost some 50,000 votes, but it had once again outdistanced the PSOE by nearly five percentage points. This was a serious setback for the PSOE, whose leaders had virtually predicted that they would defeat Suárez, at least in the popular vote, and form the government. Thus, the PCE's assessment of the election was generally favorable, for even though it had incorporated various regional Socialist groups and Enrique Tierno Galván's *Partido Socialista Popular* (PSP) and had made efforts to strengthen the UGT, the PSOE only increased its total vote by 100,000. The mergers did not bring an automatic gain for that party, much less the "multiplier" effect predicted by Socialist leaders. Only in Cataluña, where the *Réagrupment* organization formerly headed by Josep Pallach fused with it, did the PSOE improve perceptibly. Elsewhere, and particularly in Andalucía, there was a hemorrhage of the PSOE vote, with losses of 56,000 in western Andalucía. In Madrid, where the PSP had garnered 212,000 votes, the PSOE advanced by only 38,000; the admittedly heterogeneous PSP vote appears to have split several ways, part going to the UCD, part to the PSOE, part to the Communists. The Basque country had always been an area of PSOE strength, but when the returns were in this time around PSOE candidates had lost 70,000 votes relative to 1977, and three deputies.

Besides drawing favorable conclusions from the Socialists' failures, the Communists pointed to positive aspects in their own showing. The PCE increased its vote in forty-one of the fifty-one districts where it presented candidates and was the only national organization to register both a relative and absolute increase in its vote over 1977. The PCE gained the bulk of those 300,000 votes in a few provinces. Nearly 65,000 came from Andalucía, more than half from the provinces of Córdoba, Granada, and Jaén. The party also picked up 63,000 votes in Madrid province (going from 10.16 to 13.5 percent of the vote there) and 12,000 in Oviedo. Perhaps the most spectacular rise in the Communist vote came in the province of Valencia, where the PCE total increased by nearly 45,000 votes from 9.2 to 13.3 percent.

There was a less positive side to the Communist performance, however. The party had gained some 300,000 votes—but the lowering of the voting age to eighteen had brought in 3.2 million new voters, as few as 10 percent of whom may have voted Communist. In addition, as Communist leaders were well aware, their party had quite a distance to go before it could pretend to have a nationwide base: approximately 65 percent of its vote had been concentrated in just eight provinces, and five-sixths of that total came from five. The party had gained votes in parts of Andalucía, but in some provinces where it had expected to do much better than in 1977—like Cádiz, Málaga, and Seville—its increases had not been very significant. There had also been a loss (admittedly small) in the four Catalan provinces, a region where the Communists had done very well in the previous elections, and this was a source of concern for PCE leaders. Even more alarming were the results in the Basque country and Galicia: in none of the eight provinces there did the PCE win a single chamber seat or attain more than 5.1 percent of the vote. The party gained marginally in La Coruña, Orense, and Pontevedra, but lost votes in all the Basque provinces.[42]

There were several general characteristics exhibited by the Communist vote. By a margin of 65 to 35 percent, more men than women voted for the PCE in 1979—this compared to a 51 to 49 ratio for the Socialists and 41 to 59 for the UCD.[43] Along with this failure, and despite an ostentatious effort to make itself attractive to Catholics, the PCE attracted only 18 percent of those described as practicing Catholics.[44] The educational profile of the Communist voter showed him to be slightly better educated than his Socialist or Centrist counterparts. Although the Communists trailed the UCD and PSOE among voters in all educational categories, the proportion of the PCE vote coming from those with high-school degrees or higher educations was greater than for the UCD or PSOE,[45] an outcome that may reflect the influence the PCE exerted over the university and student movements during the 1960s and into the 1970s. Most predictably, the Communists did relatively well among the working class, with skilled and un-skilled workers making up nearly 32 percent of the Communist vote.[46] But, even so, it was the Socialists who gained the support of a majority of the working class (48 percent compared to 19.5 for the PCE) and could more accurately claim to be the principal worker party in Spain.[47]

Much of what we have said earlier about the reasons for the PCE's failure in June 1977 applies to its performance in March 1979, but some additional factors may have intervened. One factor contributing to that failure was the polarization of the electorate around the UCD and the PSOE. Neither party came out of the 1979 election unscathed, but between them they managed to collect nearly three-quarters of the votes cast. The PSOE did not do as well as many Socialist leaders had expected, but it was still successful in convincing those who voted Left that the only truly useful vote, the only vote that could have a real impact on policy, was one for the Socialist party.

A second factor that probably affected the PCE's performance was the dimming of its Eurocommunist image. We noted earlier the ambiguities in the Spanish Communists' evolution away from Stalinism, but insisted on the strength of the ideological challenge posed to the Soviet Union by Carrillo in *"Eurocomunismo" y Estado.* In the aftermath of the incident in Moscow and of his failure to have the Carter administration waive its opposition to Communist entry into the Spanish government, Carrillo backed off from confrontation with the Soviet Union and consciously with-drew from the limelight of controversy in the international Communist movement. While the Spanish Communists by no means abandoned the positions they had developed, they began to sound more moderate. They were now more ready to incline toward the Soviet Union and its allies—to take an anti-Chinese stance, for example, during the Sino-Vietnamese conflict in late 1978 and early 1979.

A third factor which might explain the PCE's failure to expand its electoral base significantly has to do with the political and organ-izational choices the party made after June 1977. Although the

Communist vote in the first election of the post-Franco era had
been remarkably broad-based (in the sense that a significant proportion came from outside the working class), in the months
thereafter the party had opted to strengthen its ties with the labor
movement. This was logical enough given the PCE's base in the
Comisiones Oberas, but it meant that within the party itself preference was to be given to labor activists over younger professionals. This choice made it much more difficult for the PCE to broaden
its electoral appeal and led to strong polemics within some provincial and regional organizations. In the final analysis, the campaign the party directed at the working class was a failure: aside
from picking up support among agricultural laborers in parts of
Andalucía and from workers in the industrial belt in Madrid and in
Valencia, the PCE did not reap a more bountiful harvest of CC.OO.
votes this time. Indeed, one post-electoral analysis suggests there
was no significant correlation between areas where the PCE vote
increased and where the CC.OO. had done well in the 1978 syndical elections.[48]

IX

The first two elections of the post-Franco era did not leave the
Communists in a very favorable position. Some consolidation and
broadening of the PCE vote took place in March 1979, but that
expansion brought the party nowhere near the take-off point anticipated by most party members. Indeed, it was the eruption of
nationalist sentiment in various regions and some misjudgments
by the PSOE, not the successes of the Communists, that made the
situation in mid-1979 still somewhat fluid and unpredictable. Unable to increase their vote significantly, the Communists were
very much dependent on the vigor of the UCD. So long as the Centrists kept the Socialists at bay, the PCE could hope to modify its
imbalance with the PSOE.

Chapter Eight

Crisis and Retrenchment

THE APPROVAL OF the new Constitution and the parliamentary elections of March 1979 marked the end of the transition from the Franco era and signaled a move away from a consensus-seeking style of government. This new phase led to a changed role for the PCE. Heretofore the Communists had been a valuable counterweight to the Socialists, and as such the PCE had developed a special relationship with Suárez and the UCD. Buoyed by his victory in the parliamentary elections and confident his minority government could depend ultimately on the support of Fraga Iribarne's *Coalición Democrática* and/or the Basque and Catalan nationalist parties, Suárez now turned to a more overtly partisan style of government. With the Socialists temporarily stunned and on the defensive, the UCD government was less interested in cooperation with the Communists. As a result, the PCE had to stress even more its competition with the PSOE.

The aggressively anti-Socialist strategy of the PCE had contributed to the PSOE's defeat in the parliamentary elections, but there was no great shift of votes to the Communist standard. Indeed, the PCE had increased its share of the vote by only 1.5 percent over 1977, and most of the Communist vote was still concentrated in the metropolitan areas of Barcelona and Madrid. The PCE had done very poorly in the Basque country and Galicia. Even in Andalucía, where the party had performed creditably, the margin separating it from the PSOE was quite large. The Communists also faced formidable organizational and ideological problems. By dropping the Leninism label and substituting a description of the PCE as a "revolutionary and democratic" organization, the Ninth PCE Congress in April 1978 had purportedly resolved the issue of how deeply the Spanish Communists held their "Eurocommunist" identity. But this had been little more than a change in label and, in the wake of their poor electoral showing and of the breakup with the Centrists, latent and unresolved policy divisions opened up. Compounding and exacerbating these divisions was the organizational transformation the PCE was undergoing. The explosion in membership—the PCE went from approximately thirty thousand members in 1976 to an estimated two hundred thousand by the Ninth Congress—overwhelmed party organizations in many parts of Spain. The ensuing struggles for power in regional and local organizations, the unsuitability of many Communist veterans for routine political tasks, and the growing conflicts between intellectuals and professionals on the one hand and labor activists on the other hinted at further problems to come.

But the magnitude of these problems was not at first glance apparent. The Socialists' failure to defeat Suárez and the UCD in the legislative contest had caused much internal commotion within the PSOE, provoking a debate over party alliance policies. The municipal elections in April 1979 increased this tension; and, the PSOE, badly needing to show some gain from its efforts, was forced to settle for an agreement with the Communists. Although Socialist candidates led in most major cities (for example, in Barcelona, Madrid, Seville, and Valencia), they had not won the absolute majority needed to insure the election of mayors. With Communist support, however, Socialists mayors would be elected in most cities of more than fifty thousand people. Political realism thus impelled a Socialist-Communist municipal agreement, and in exchange, the PCE could reap the benefits of political patronage in the nearly twelve hundred cities where the Left had a majority. Because the Communists had been instrumental in organizing neighborhood and housewife associations under Franco and wielded a decisive influence in many of them, the PCE also anticipated having a much greater role in the city halls than their percentage of the vote suggested.

Broadening the opportunities for the Communists was the crisis loosed within the PSOE by the motion Felipe González presented at its May 1979 Congress to drop Marxism from the party program.

The original plan was for González, having just won the parliamentary elections and therefore leading his party into the government, to preside over a triumphant celebration at which delegates would readily approve anything he proposed. This plan was derailed by the March 1979 elections results and the face-saving agreement signed with the Communists in April. By the time the Congress met, the motion González presented in the name of the Federal Committee had become a defensive maneuver aimed at broadening the Socialists' electoral appeal. González believed that "the Socialist party's capacity to attract [voters] diminish[ed] in inverse proportion to links through stable agreements with other parties and, especially, with the PCE."[1] But this was not the posture of the more leftist *sector crítico*, which favored alliance with the Communists. As a result of the March 1979 elections and of the impact of the April municipal agreements, many of those elected as delegates to the PSOE Congress supported an opening to the Left. Under these circumstances, and with the PSOE still in the throes of its transformation from cadre- to mass-based party, the González proposal was defeated. As a result, González refused renomination to the post of First Secretary and pushed for a special Congress in September. Eventually, a compromise solution would be found and González would return to his post, but not before bitter intraparty polemics eroded the Socialists' public image.

I

The situation created by the Socialist-Communist municipal pact and the convulsions shaking the PSOE suggested to the Communists that their party was not hopelessly locked into a marginal position on the Left. Thus encouraged, the PCE moved to attack the PSOE where the Socialists were weakest and the Communists strongest: in the labor arena. In the previous chapter, we discussed the competition between the Socialist UGT and the *Comisiones Obreras*, noting the victory the latter had gained in the 1978 syndical elections. The Communists retained their strength in labor during the next year, profiting from their position as architects of the Moncloa agreements signed in late 1977. By early 1979, as the spirit of consensus that had animated the Moncloa agreements weakened and the economic situation worsened, the Communists sought to galvanize worker discontent. The moment was a propitious one: the sluggish economy rendered the govern-

ment especially vulnerable, and the UCD wanted a new version of
the Moncloa agreements—but not at the price of allowing the
PSOE into the government. The Communists had no objection to
another agreement, so long as they were treated as the Socialists'
equal. Indeed, the Communists were anxious for a new pact to
compensate for their poor electoral showing and to facilitate an
expansion of their influence in the working class. After all, the
system of industrial relations had not yet been fleshed out; and,
were the Communists to play a major role in a "social pact," they
could anticipate that future legislation would favor the factory
councils structure they and the *Comisiones* supported.

The *Comisiones'* strategy of riding the tide of strikes and work
stoppages had first become apparent in late 1978, and had accelerated following the parliamentary and municipal elections in
1979.[2] The economic downturn favored this strategy, as did the
internal problems the UGT faced. Partly due to the incorporation of
labor leaders from the *Unión Sindical Obrera*, but for other reasons as well, the closeness of UGT relations with the PSOE became
the subject of debate in the union. With the passage of time,
moreover, it had become evident that the UGT did not have
enough cadres to compete with the *Comisiones'* mobilization
strategy or to outmaneuver more radical elements during worker
assemblies. If the Socialist presence in the labor movement could
be undermined—and this was the Communists' ultimate
objective—it would be impossible for the Socialists to govern
alone. Needing to appear serious and responsible, and conscious
of the disadvantages the Portuguese Socialists faced because of
Communist hegemony in the trade-union movement there, the
PSOE also understood what was at stake in the battle over labor.

While the Communists and *Comisiones* sought to exploit what
they perceived to be a rightward drift in the PSOE and to use an
aggressive strategy not only to outflank the UGT but also to increase membership in the *Comisiones*, the Socialists and the UGT
adopted a different tack. Although joining in strikes and mobilizations, the UGT sought to reinforce its serious and moderate image
by pursuing either plant- or national-level agreements with management. This would furthermore increase its chances for tapping
into the large numbers of nonunionized workers whose politicization was not very great and whose primary concern in economically turbulent times was to stay on the job. It was to this part of
the labor force the UGT Secretary General Nicolás Redondo ad-

dressed himself at the Third Congress of the Federation of Agricultural Workers in September 1979: "We shall move toward all those mobilizations which are necessary, but always after an absolutely clear negotiation."[3] Reinforcing this thrust toward accommodation was the conviction that approval of legislation favoring a trade-union role in the factories could best be obtained if the UGT demonstrated to the government and the business community its willingness to make concessions during a recession. Thus, during the summer of 1979 the UGT entered into negotiations with the largest employer association, the Spanish Confederation of Employer Organizations (CEOE), signing an agreement in July that recognized trade-union sections in factories of more than 250 employees and allowed trade unions to sign collective-bargaining agreements in factories where they had elected more than 10 percent of the syndical delegates.[4] These agreements, moreover, were not limited to salary questions, but could include broader work-related issues as well. The UGT negotiations with the CEOE had been encouraged by the Suárez government, which promised that whatever agreements were reached on a labor-relations system would be included in a soon-to-be-elaborated Workers' Statute. By late 1979, when the Parliament debated this statute, the PSOE joined with the Centrists in approving legislation that incorporated the principal points of the UGT-CEOE agreement and weakened (particularly in Article 85) the role of the workers' councils.[5] The signing of an *Acuerdo Marco Interconfederal* (AMI) by the UGT and the CEOE in early January 1980 capped the process begun a half year before. Under the AMI, a set of guidelines for collective-bargaining agreements, salaries in most factories could be increased from 13 to 16 percent but would be dependent on increased productivity; furthermore, the trade-union section, not the factory council, would negotiate the contracts.[6]

The Communists and the *Comisiones* reacted with bitterness and some condescension to the UGT and PSOE initiatives. The PCE had already presented its version of the Workers' Statute in April 1979, and had called on the Socialists and the UGT to back that version in negotiations with the government. The Communists hoped to regain some of their lost prominence by compelling the UCD and the Socialists to include the *Comisiones* as well as the PCE in any discussions regarding an economic recuperation program. This they hoped to accomplish by mobilizing workers in the factories: in late June *Comisiones* leader and PCE Executive

Committee member Nicolás Sartorius warned of a general strike in October.[7] During the months of July, October, November, and December, the CC.OO. and the Communists organized demonstrations in various cities, with Madrid site of the largest, drawing nearly two hundred thousand people. As the pace of the demonstrations increased, so did tension between the PCE and PSOE, provoking a rhetorical duel between Carrillo and González over the Workers' Statute in the *Cortes*. The Socialist leader pointedly reminded his audience of how "a Communist syndical philosophy upholding the values of pluralist democracy has yet to be demonstrated to exist."[8]

The approval in December 1979 of the Workers' Statute (which the PCE described as "leaving the workers still without rights") and the signature of the *Acuerdo Marco* in January 1980 was the UGT and PSOE answer to the Communist offensive begun in the aftermath of the parliamentary elections. During those months, the Spanish economy had further deteriorated: unemployment had risen to nearly 10 percent (twice that in areas like Andalucía), and numerous firms were close to bankruptcy. The divergent postures now assumed by the Communists and Socialists reflected not only their differing strengths, but their contrasting evaluations of how to improve their respective positions in Spanish politics. As it was, the Communist gamble on an offensive strategy failed to pay off. By summer 1979, the PCE leadership was already losing control over the more radical elements in the *Comisiones Obreras*. At this point, most were members of small leftist *groupuscules* active in the CC.OO. By late 1979, however, the bacillus of radicalism had spread to Communist labor activists.[9] They responded to the confrontation with the Socialists by becoming increasingly sectarian in their attitudes, dismissing UGT policies as those of a "yellow" trade union. More moderate elements in the party had warned of "the danger should a gap develop between the most politicized sector of the working class and the bulk of the class itself,"[10] but such words were ignored by labor cadres whose political weight in the PCE increased even as the general prospects for the party dimmed.

The apogee of the *Comisiones'* mobilization strategy came in January 1980, several weeks after the signature of the *Acuerdo Marco*, with a general strike at the SEAT plants in Barcelona.[11] The strike took place in the context of negotiations for a new collective-bargaining agreement. *Comisiones* leaders pursued a hard line, organizing mass assemblies and shutting down the factories. In the end, not only did *Comisiones* lose control of the strike (when its activists called for a return to work, their suggestions were rejected in the assemblies), but it gave the impression of being much more extremist than the UGT. The latter had urged the use of secret ballots to gauge the true sentiments of workers, and had argued that, with demand for SEAT cars dropping by 40 percent compared to the previous year, the unions should show a greater willingness to compromise. In any case, by the end of January, the strike had been broken: workers had gone back to work, and *Comisiones* had egg on its face. The depth of worker discontent with the *Comisiones'* role was revealed in late April when syndical elections were held at the SEAT plants. With participation at an all-time high of 82 percent, the UGT won handily. Whereas in 1978 the *Comisiones* had elected 57 delegates and the UGT 54, this time the UGT elected 78 and the CC.OO. only 46. A number of factors lent a special character to the election in the SEAT plants—for example, a visit by Felipe González in support of the UGT; a bitter internecine struggle between hard-line and more moderate elements in the PSUC and in the *Comisiones;* a SEAT announcement in the middle of the campaign that its financial losses meant twenty-five thousand workers had to be put at 75 percent salary for a month. The elections also showed that the *Comisiones* and the PCE were out of step with the great majority of workers there and perhaps elsewhere in Spain.

The SEAT elections and others in the spring of 1980 (such as that involving sixteen thousand workers in the FASA-Renault plant, in which *Comisiones* suffered heavy losses) threw the political momentum on the side of the UGT and, indirectly, of the PSOE. Although many *Comisiones* leaders were astonished, the UGT and PSOE support for the Workers' Statute and the signature of the *Acuerdo Marco* evidently paid off. Within two months of the signature of the *Acuerdo Marco,* one hundred sixty collective-bargaining agreements involving approximately 2.5 million workers were signed, and the *Comisiones* could do little to block their implementation. Indeed, as Nicolás Sartorius admitted in an article aptly entitled "The Red Light Has Turned On," workers had reacted "above all other considerations to the fear of losing their jobs."[12] In an effort to avert a disaster in the national syndical elections scheduled for later that year, the PCE leadership called a meeting of the Central Committee and later one of Communist labor activists. The resolution approved by the Central Committee warned of the danger when "the vanguard radicalizes itself, separates itself from the broad masses and seeks, without taking into account the real relation of forces, a frontal and solitary confrontation, falling therefore [victim to] impatience and subjectivism."[13] The special cadre meeting held a few days later presented a tumultuous scene, with hard-line Communist *Comisiones* leaders like Francisco Frutos, Fidel Alonso, and others challenging the party leadership's call for moderation.

The defeat of the Communist labor offensive begun in mid-1979 coincided with the consolidation of the Socialists' position. The municipal pacts and the PSOE crisis during the summer of 1979 had at first encouraged the PCE to believe it would not long remain a minority party. But the satisfaction and confidence with which the Communists viewed their future faded by early 1980. Not only did González reimpose his authority at the Extraordinary Congress in September 1979, defeating decisively the *sector crítico* (whose rival list only garnered 14 percent of the delegates' votes), but the UGT successfully expanded its influence in the labor movement. The Communists' inability to make headway against the PSOE was also evident in the municipal sphere, where expectations of their being able to outmaneuver the PSOE fell in the face of Socialist political skill and general budgetary constraints. Given the highly centralized nature of government in Spain, left-wing city councils could hardly embark on ambitious community projects or significantly expand social services. Moreover, popular participation in civic associations was declining and so did the influence the Communists exerted through these associations.

By early 1980, then, the Communists had failed to significantly expand their audience or influence. Party activists realized increasingly—if reluctantly—that a long, drawn-out battle would be necessary before the PCE could reverse the balance of forces on the Left. This revised vision of the future coincided with important changes abroad, which did not augur well either. In France, the PCF had deliberately sabotaged a possible leftist majority in the March 1978 National Assembly elections, and the outlook for it was bleak indeed. In Italy, the assassination of Aldo Moro in mid-1978 and the resulting political cross-fire directed at the PCI by the Socialists and Christian Democrats, as well as by extraparliamentary and terrorist groups, rendered unlikely any "historic compromise." Enthusiasm for detente was waning, and a new

Cold War loomed; the Soviet invasion of Afghanistan undermined an already tenuous superpower condominium. These circumstances had affected the PCE. With the seemingly inevitable success of Spanish-style Eurocommunism no longer assured, debates within the party became acrimonious. It is to a discussion of the organizational and ideological crises these tensions provoked that we now turn.

I I

The PCE had entered the post-Franco era after four decades of repression and underground activity. Its task was to transform itself into an organization with a broad presence in Spanish society and with a capacity for electoral competition. Although its history, rituals, and organizational continuity made it an established political force in Spanish society, the PCE *qua* mass-based organization was still in its infancy. Until 1976, several groups operated under the PCE standard. One group was in exile, with its headquarters and the majority of its leaders in Paris. By the early 1970s, however, most PCE members were living in the major industrial centers in Spain. Although the exiled leadership had laid the broad policy guidelines for the party, on its return to Spain it nevertheless faced the task of molding units that had developed a good deal of autonomy into an effective organization.

The organizational transformation of the PCE was also conditioned by the depoliticization of Spanish society. This phenomenon, which became especially evident once the euphoria over the newly instituted democracy passed, coincided with a more general crisis many European political parties faced when they could neither perform traditional socialization and recruitment functions, nor address new issues that superseded or modified long-standing class, religious, or regional cleavages. This European-wide trend manifested itself in Spain, where it was reinforced by popular demobilization and lack of civic education— products of the preceding forty years of authoritarian rule.[14] Although the Communists initially saw themselves as immune to these pressures, the problems they faced after 1977, as well as their electoral weakness shattered that illusion.

Another organizational challenge the PCE faced was how to handle the centrifugal regionalist tendencies that emerged, more virulent than ever, in the 1970s. Earlier, we talked about the fragmented nature of the Communist organization—in part the result of physical isolation and the difficulties this created for coordination and communication. However, the PCE faced a second problem in this regard: the strains placed on party organization by peripheral nationalisms. In many ways, the belligerent chauvinism of the Right belied the unstable foundation of the Spanish nation. Four decades of Franco rule, with its treatment of areas like the Basque country and Cataluña as if they were occupied territories, exacerbated this tension. Eventually regional frustration exploded, and, because regional sentiment was almost by definition anti-Franco, most national opposition groups supported demands for regional self-government. It was easy enough to criticize the "centralist" character of the Franco regime and call for a devolution of tax and administrative powers. But after this much had been done, the appropriate vehicles had to be found for articulating those regional demands in the regions. As the various political groups tried to develop a presence throughout Spain, they were incorporating regional cleavages into the incipient party organizations. For the Spanish Communists, this center-periphery tension posed a challenge unique from those facing other West European parties.

During the Franco era, the PCE dealt with the issue of peripheral nationalism by upholding the right of historic nationalities to self-determination while emphasizing Communist support for a federal solution to the problem. In terms of organization, the PCE sought to integrate some "nationalist" sectors into its ranks, particularly in the Basque country and Cataluña. In the first region, the effort generally failed. Despite the entry of some dissident members of ETA into the PCE in 1970, most Basque radicals considered the party too tame and too Madrid-oriented for their tastes. Cataluña, on the other hand, provided a more favorable arena, and the PSUC a more effective instrument, for Communist efforts.

Conflict between different generations also had an impact on the national Communist party as it expanded and consolidated its organization. At the onset of the Franco era, several generations coexisted in the PCE. The oldest and least powerful were the septuagenarians and octogenarians who joined the party in its early years, achieving positions of importance prior to the Civil War and retaining these positions until the late 1950s and early 1960s. While these individuals have not been particularly active in setting the course of recent party policy, they (particularly Dolores Ibárruri, the matriarch of the PCE and its living link with the past) exercised a restraining function. In exchange for lending legitimacy to the changes Carrillo made in party policies, they imposed limits on the adaptation.

A second generation of party members joined the PCE just before and during the Civil War. Communist fortunes were on the rise at that time, and many of these people joined the party because it was the politically opportune thing to do. In the decades following the Civil War, however, few of the rank-and-file of this generation remained active in the PCE. The most resolute handful lapsed into the vague status of sympathizer or sometime-collaborator. But these people, like others who dropped out of party politics, were not irretrievably lost to the PCE. Many reentered the party in the post-Franco era and, by then eager to prove they had remained *real* Communists, they often supported those who tried to slow the "Eurocommunization" of the PCE. There was as well a tendency toward obedience (or *seguidismo*, which roughly translates as "followerism") among them, which those in positions of power within the PCE did not hesitate to draw on.

A third political generation had entered the PCE after the consolidation of the Franco regime, but in the context of the demonstrations and strikes that shook Spain beginning in the late 1950s and early 1960s. These people, generally workers, students, or professionals, joined the PCE in those years because it was the principal force in the anti-Franco movement. Those from the working class entered the party after participating in the semiclandestine *Comisiones*. The others, sometimes scions of the wealthy or the social elite and in any case privileged because of education, became active during their university years and retained party links as they entered professional life. Prior to the death of Franco, there was little sign of any conflict between the workers on the one hand and the students and professionals on the other. Student activists led strikes in support of working-class demands in the late 1960s, at a time when the labor movement was reeling under the harshest repression. Members of the various professions either signed public manifestos demanding political and syndical liberties or, if they were lawyers, openly defended labor activists who had been arrested. Although many who remained in the PCE after their university days did so less out of loyalty to the PCE per se than because the party was the most effective instrument for opposition to the regime, party leaders nevertheless gave these people special status, delegating important duties to them without requiring formal participation in cells.

Perhaps the high point in the influence of the professional sector (popularly known as the "forces of culture") occurred in late 1975 and early 1976. During that time, PCE members came out into the open, as the party committed all its forces to press for a peaceful break with the Francoist past. Intellectuals and professionals were in the forefront of the battle, which lasted until mid-1976: their status rendered them less vulnerable to the police and to the risk of losing their jobs. By mid-year, as we have seen, the PCE had failed to seize the initiative from the reformist faction led by the King and Suárez, and the influence of the professional sector within the party waned. The PCE now had to worry about insuring its existence as a national movement; and, to this end, it relied not on the "forces of culture," but on activists it had developed in the labor movement. As a result of this reorientation, many professionals lost positions of power. At the same time, members of the exiled Communist hierarchy were returning to Spain and reestablishing their control over party politics.

The problems and cleavages just described became more pronounced as the PCE moved to transform its structure and create a mass-based organization. This process, which the Communists described as the "homogenization" and the "territorialization" of the party, involved the elimination of separate organizations for professionals, the creation of local and neighborhood party committees, and the reorganization of the party along either plant-level or territorial *agrupaciones*.[15] Lawyers, teachers, doctors, and other professionals entered the latter, and their expertise was put to use primarily on municipal and local government concerns. Communist workers, for their part, participated through the plant-level *agrupaciones*: their principal task was the consolidation of the *Comisiones Obreras* in the plants. This distribution of responsibilities made sense; however, it also led to a growing division, first physical and then of orientation, between the factory *agrupaciones* and the party committees that were charged with overseeing Communist activities within specific geographical areas. The initial success of the *Comisiones* and the Communists' reliance on their influence in labor to balance their electoral weakness also encouraged increasingly open manifestations of *ouvriérisme*. The head of the PCE Madrid organization, Victor Díaz Cardiel, thus stressed the need for labor militants to be active in party affairs in order to "guarantee the [worker] character or nature of the Party."[16] Ironically, all this occurred as the labor cadres were gaining power within the PCE and achieving greater autonomy from party leaders in the elaboration of policies in the syndical arena.

The rise in the influence of labor activists within the PCE stemmed in part from the success the *Comisiones* had enjoyed in the 1978 syndical elections. At the Ninth PCE Congress, numerous labor activists were elected to the Central Committee, and seven of the thirty-four Executive Committee members were from the *Comisiones*. This pattern was also evident in Communist organizations in the Basque country, Galicia, Valencia, and Cataluña. In Cataluña especially, veteran labor activists such as Cipriano García, Francisco Frutos, José María Rodríguez Rovira, and José María López Bulla played major roles in party affairs. But the influence of labor activists was not solely a product of the social presence they gave the PCE. The labor activists represented a relatively solid and dependable bloc around which the party leadership could rally its initiatives. This was especially true in the case of the 1978 proposal to drop Leninism. As we discussed in chapter 7, that move represented an effort by Carrillo to further legitimize the PCE in Spanish society and to broaden its electoral audience. It unleashed a storm of controversy within the party, however, with many intellectuals and professionals calling for a much more thorough purging of "Stalinist" traditions. Anxious that the debate not extend too far, Carrillo relied on an alliance forged between delegates with links to the party apparatus and others tied to the *Comisiones* to carry the day at most regional conferences and in the Ninth Congress. Each side had its own reasons for not wanting the debate to get out of hand, the *Comisiones* activists being, for the most part, uncomfortable with too "liberal" an interpretation of Eurocommunism.

The political and organizational influence of the labor activists drew on and fostered the latent *ouvriériste* bias of the PCE. The PCE, it was true, had made great efforts during the 1960s and 1970s to attract non-working-class elements to the party, focusing on the "forces of culture." Communist initiatives in this respect had been presented as innovations comparable to what Lenin had done by incorporating the peasantry into the traditional Marxist scheme of alliances. And in a certain sense they were; but, as with so many of the ideological changes made by the Spanish Communists, the ambiguities were patent. People from outside the working class were accepted on condition that they would "[become] converted into proletarians."[17] This anti-intellectual strain had always been part of the PCE and had played a role in numerous conflicts, but the *ouvriérisme* became more prominent after 1977. During discussion of the Leninism proposal prior to the Ninth Congress, traditional elements within the PCE pointedly criticized the so-called gold peaks who demanded greater internal debate and democracy. Ibárruri herself rallied to the charge, blaming turmoil in the Asturias branch on the fact "there were more intellectuals than workers" in the party there.[18]

These attacks alienated many intellectuals and professionals. Although many of them had been in the party since before the death of Franco, they had never become as dependent on it as labor activists or members of the apparatus. Economically and socially independent, the intellectuals-professionals were less vulnerable to the innumerable psychological pressures the leadership could bring to bear when enforcing discipline. Beginning in 1978, a growing number either dropped out of or were expelled from the PCE. Francisco Alvarez Areces, a university professor who had been head of the Communist organization in Asturias, and who led a walkout of more than 110 delegates from a regional meeting in early April 1978, was kicked out. Party lawyer José María Mohedano resigned in early 1979, his departure preceded by those of Carlos Borasteros, a well-known physician, and Mario Trinidad, editor of the left-wing monthly, *Argumentos*. By early 1981, when the First PCE Assembly of Intellectuals, Professionals, and Artists met, group membership had dropped from three thousand in 1977 to four hundred in late 1980.[19] The hemorrhage showed no signs of stopping, and soon after the Assembly, two well-known professionals who were in the PCE Executive Committee, Eugenio Triana and Ramón Tamames (a member of Parliament and deputy mayor of Madrid), resigned from the party.

III

The organizational tasks confronting the party, the generational and regional cleavages, the growing tension between professionals and labor activists, the failure of *Comisiones'* mobilization tactics, and the more general Communist inability to cut into the Socialist advantage generated profound uncertainty and discontent in Communist organizations throughout Spain.[20]

Virtually no important regional organization escaped the turmoil provoked by these problems. The Madrid provincial party suffered through a bitter internecine struggle, pitting moderates against labor activists who wanted a return to more aggressive political and trade union tactics. In Asturias, regional Secretary General Gerardo Iglesias moved against dissidents with a fury not seen in other parts of the country, decimating the local PCE. In the Basque country, the poor electoral performance precipitated a debate over the alliance policies of the party. A razor-thin majority grouped around Secretary General Roberto Lertxundi—a former member of ETA and a man Carrillo had believed would breathe life into a moribund party—who called for greater sensitivity to Basque problems and eventual unification with the leftist, regionalist group, *Euzkadiko Ezkerra*. Ranged against Lertxundi were those with a more "national" vision, among them former Secretary General Ramón Ormazábal, and numerous leaders of the *Comisiones*, headed by Tomás Tueros.[21] Valencia was likewise the scene of bitter political struggles with hard-liner Antonio Palomares effecting an alliance with representatives of the central party apparatus against a younger group of "nationalist" leaders headed by Emerit Bono and Ernest García, who was forced to resign as Secretary General in September 1980. The Communist organization in Andalucía did not escape similar tumult. Generational conflicts (pitting, for example, the 43-year-old "historic" leader Fernando Soto and his allies, Eduardo Saborido and Francisco Acosta, against peasant leader Juan Antonio Romero and Juan Bosco),[22] policy differences over how "leftist" an orientation to give municipal policies in Anadulucía, and the problems of articulating an organizational relationship between the regional party and its provincial branches led to the resignation of Soto in January 1981.

It was in Cataluña, however, that the crisis facing the Communists became most public and pronounced. In the first post-Franco elections, the Catalan Communists received over 550,000 votes—18.2 percent of the total votes cast in the region and 19.9 percent of those in Barcelona province)—and elected eight deputies to the national parliament. This performance contrasted with the 9.4 percent share of the national vote garnered by the PCE. Indeed, the PSUC accounted for 47 percent of all Communist votes in the country. And, although this percentage dropped to 35 in March 1979, the results of both elections underscored the importance of the PSUC for the Spanish Communist cause.

If "Eurocommunism"—which was, at least in part, a strategy aimed at attracting more moderate voters to the Communist

standard—had failed generally in Spain, the same was not true in
Cataluña. Data from a 1978 survey show the profile of the PSUC
voter to be somewhat different from that of his PCE counterpart.[23]
Of PSUC voters asked to place themselves on a 10-point Left-Right
scale, only 17 percent chose the two leftmost positions, as opposed
to 43 percent of PCE voters. Only 46 percent of the PSUC voter-
sample accepted the label "Marxist," in contrast to 64 percent of
the PCE voters. On a third question—asking voters how close they
felt to the Socialist Party—over 20 percent of the sample from the
PSUC electorate said "Very," while only 8 percent of the PCE voters
gave that answer.

Another index of the importance the PSUC had for Spanish
Communism was its size. During the last years of the Franco regime, the Catalan Communists developed an impressive organization, and by early 1977 the Barcelona city federation boasted
some 5,500 members. By April 1978, the PSUC had 40,000 members, nearly one-fifth of the Communists in Spain—entitling the
Catalans to the largest delegation at the Ninth PCE Congress. What
was more, the results of the 1978 syndical elections showed that
the margin of victory scored by the *Comisiones* over the Socialist
Unión General de Trabajadores (UGT) in Cataluña was the largest
in Spain, with between 42 and 56 percent of the delegates elected
belonging to the CC.OO.[24]

As it sought to adapt to the political environment in post-Franco
Spain, the PSUC faced many of the same organizational and
ideological problems as the PCE. Not surprisingly, the changed
circumstances triggered a power struggle within the PSUC. As we
have seen in chapter 4, various factions or groups were already
visible by early 1977, and the competition between them grew
more acrimonious, especially as Carrillo and the PCE sought to
influence the outcome of their battles.

Some Catalan Communists had objected to the April 1977 decision by the PCE Central Committee to drop the traditional Communist support for a republic. The mild treatment Suárez and the
UCD received from the PCE during the campaign preceding the
1977 parliamentary elections provoked more grumbling. So, too,
did PCE efforts in the wake of June 1977 to work with Suárez
against the Socialists. The PSUC's electoral success sparked further
calls for greater autonomy vis-à-vis the national party.

The events surrounding the Ninth PCE Congress generated a
profound resentment among many Catalan Communists, not only

(or even mainly) over policy, but because of Carrillo's style of leadership and his efforts to control the PSUC. In the ensuing months, these feelings deepened, and supporters of the PCE secretary-general—for example, the so-called white flag group we discussed in chapter 4—came under fire, losing influence to factions with a more hard-line orientation. The principal beneficiaries of this trend were a "Leninist" group associated with a younger generation of activists from the *Comisiones Obreras*, and a smaller pro-Soviet contingent in the PSUC.

Up to mid-1979, the accomplishments and rising expectations of the Catalan Communists created what we might term "structural" conditions for conflict between the PCE and PSUC. By late 1979 a new element—diminished prospects for the PSUC—was added, and this heightened tensions among the Catalans. The PSUC had premised its strategy on the possibility, indeed the probability, of an alliance with the Socialists. While the PSUC did not seek an outright Popular Front, the party did believe that with a popular majority in tow, the Catalan Left could compel the moderate nationalists in *Convergencia* to form a regional coalition government. The results of the municipal elections suggested the conditions were being met for such a process.

It was against this background that the March 1980 elections to the Catalan parliament took place. The results were a clear-cut defeat for the Left. Although the PSUC more or less held its vote (its percentage increased relative to 1979, but its total number of votes declined), the Socialists lost over 200,000 votes, dropping into second place with 22.3 percent. Meanwhile, *Convergencia* became the leading vote-getter in the region, increasing its vote by nearly 250,000 over March 1979. With a 28 percent share, it was now in a position to elect its own candidate as president of the Catalan regional government, the *Generalitat*.[25]

As a result of the setback suffered in the regional elections, the internal struggle within the PSUC stepped up. Moderates blamed the vote loss on the strikes called by the *Comisiones* in late 1979 and early 1980 that were part of its mobilization strategy.

As the crisis within the PSUC intensified, so did the battle between the "Leninists" and the more moderate sectors of the PSUC for control over the *Comisiones Obreras*. In full swing since 1978, the battles ended in June 1980 with a victory for the "Leninists" at the Second Congress of the National Workers' Commission of Cataluña (*Commissió Obrera Nacional de Catalunya*—CONC).

The more moderate sectors had argued against a strategy of strikes and work stoppages, insisting that industrial workers were more interested in maintaining their jobs than in demanding (and not achieving) higher wage increases. At the CONC Congress, this view—more in tune with official PCE policy—was supported by only 20 percent of the delegates; its defenders gained only six of the fifty-five seats on the CONC's new Executive Committee. Moreover, the general program and statutes approved at the Congress contained strong criticisms of the *Pactos de la Moncloa* and the policy of consensus. The strength of the more hard-line elements was particularly visible on international questions, with 285 delegates calling for "preferential relations" with the Soviet-controlled World Federation of Trade Unions (WFTU). Although a motion to have the CONC affiliate only with the WFTU was rejected, this group managed to pass a resolution condemning the U.S. bases in Spain and supporting entry of French and Portuguese Communist unions into the European Syndical Confederation.[26]

Along with the reinforcement of hard-line groups in the labor movement came increasingly vocal Catalan criticism of PCE foreign policy positions. Disenchantment with the "Eurocommunism" Carrillo preached had been evident since early 1980, when the PSUC organization in Baix Llobregat approved a resolution supporting the Soviet invasion of Afghanistan. The official PSUC posture (like that of the PCE) was to condemn the Soviet action, but more moderate—relatively speaking—party leaders sought to derail the growing internal dissent by stepping up attacks on the United States and NATO.[27] At the same time, PSUC leaders called for greater Catalan input into PCE foreign policy decisions. What was more, in a direct slap at Carrillo and Azcárate, during a PSUC Central Committee meeting devoted to international issues, Secretary-General Gutiérrez quoted approvingly the remarks made by a prominent "Leninist," José Rodríguez Rovira:

> We are not neutral. . . . That is the first fundamental question. It is necessary that we leave quite clear the fact we are not neutral in relation to the Soviet Union, the Warsaw Pact and the Socialist countries. . . . [There are] interimperialist contradictions which we should know how to stimulate and take advantage of in favor of a policy of peace, disarmament, detente and the overcoming—in any case simultaneous—of the blocs. This policy is not only best for us but the socialist countries as well.[28]

That statement represented a step back from the foreign-policy positions articulated since 1968 by Carrillo, and it reinforced doubts as to the commitment to political democracy (as understood by the West) of Rodríguez Rovira and others in the PSUC. To make matters worse, numerous voices now called on the PSUC to pressure the PCE to adopt a less "critical" attitude toward the USSR, to diversify its links in the international Communist movement beyond the PCI, to temper its acerbic criticisms of the PCF, to attend events like the May 1980 Paris Conference sponsored by the French and Polish Communists, and to tone down its support for the European Economic Community.

The publication in June 1980 of the Draft Theses for the Fifth PSUC Congress represented for Carrillo and the PCE a further slap in the face. The document repeated well-known Catalan criticisms of Spanish Communist failures during the transition to the post-Franco era. It also attacked the "policy of concentration" followed by the PCE since June 1977, blaming that policy for "creating confusion among workers and the popular classes."[29] Moreover, the Draft Theses called for unity between Socialists and Communists in the context of a Catalan *bloque de progreso* and (in a further, not too veiled reference to internal affairs) for greater democratization of the party.

These events climaxed in the weeks preceding the Fifth PSUC Congress in January 1981. The temper of the debates in local organizations and the tone of letters sent to the party weekly, *Treball*, reinforced the impression the Congress would not be a routine affair. So did the discovery that the PSUC organization in the Vallès Occidental, which would send the largest single bloc of delegates to the Congress, was circulating amendments toughening the Draft Theses among other local organizations.[30] The document was in flagrant violation of the rules of democratic centralism, which prohibit horizontal communication between organizations. Several Central Committee members—among them, Alfred Clemente and José Valdivieso, the visible heads of the pro-Soviet group in the PSUC—were responsible for this effort. It is therefore also likely (given Soviet efforts since early 1978 to woo Spanish Communist labor leaders and potential dissidents, as well as a more general Soviet offensive against Eurocommunism in the previous year and a half) that Soviet diplomats in Madrid encouraged the effort.[31] And well they should have; the document defended the Soviet invasion of Afghanistan as having been requested by the government in Kabul, and called on the PSUC to oppose European integration.

By late December, the delegate selection-process was completed, and there was talk of eliminating the term "Eurocommunism" from the PSUC program at the Congress. Aware of this, Gutiérrez tried to defuse the situation by declaring a few days before the Congress that "the errors of the USSR [came] from its desire to help in the revolutionary transformation of society."[32] Moreover, in his own speech to the Congress, he criticized the term but argued against dropping it, on the grounds that doing so would be "to abandon (the concepts of) revolution of the majority and socialism in liberty." The report he presented in the name of the Central Committee, including the reference to "Eurocommunism," drew the support of only 53 percent of the delegates voting (with approximately 100 votes unaccounted for). The following day, however, an amendment to remove "Eurocommunism," from the party program was approved by a margin of 424 to 359, with 21 abstentions.[33]

The vote was unquestionably a victory for the critics who, galvanized by pro-Soviets like Clemente and Leopold Espuny, acted decisively. And yet many of the 424 delegates voting to exclude the term "Eurocommunism" could not be described as reflexively pro-Soviet. Most voted against the term because it was a symbol—a symbol of Carrillo and the PCE, a symbol of failure. The pro-Soviets simply took advantage of this sentiment.

The Fifth Congress threw the PSUC into the most severe crisis it had ever experienced. The previous secretary-general and president refused reelection, and the Central Committee elected in their place Frutos and Père Ardiaca respectively. Despite an effort to fashion an "integrated" leadership, in the end Frutos formed an Executive Committee whose overwhelming majority was "Leninist." Representatives of the "white flag" group declined to join, as did many pro-Soviets and supporters of the former leadership.

The Fifth PSUC Congress reflected the force of several cleavages among the Catalans and within the PCE more generally. There were cleavages between those who wanted greater autonomy (indeed, even independence) vis-à-vis Madrid and those who did not; those who wanted a return to a more closed, traditional party and those who did not; those whose "Eurocommunism" emphasized consensual policies and participation in parliament, and those who stressed mass mobilizations and a grass-roots experiment with democracy; and, finally, those who were willing to justify virtually any action taken by the Soviet Union, those who—while critical—nevertheless ultimately saw the PSUC and PCE on the side of the Socialist bloc, and a minority that insisted on a radical critique of the Soviet Union and Eastern Europe and a further distancing from the parties in power there.

I V

Events at the PSUC Congress underscored the severity of the Communist crisis, sharpening the tone of debate within the PCE. Carrillo now came under sharp attack. This occurred against a backdrop of continued Communist failure to catch up to the PSOE (the syndical elections in late 1980 confirmed a drop in support for *Comisiones* and a strengthening of the UGT)[34] and of a deepening political crisis in Spain. Military discontent and increasingly bitter wrangling within the UCD contributed first to Suárez's resignation as premier in January and then to an attempted coup a month later.

As the dominant figure in the party since the late 1950s and the architect of its policies, Carrillo was now blamed for failing to force through a *ruptura* with the institutions of the Francoist era, and for allowing both Suárez and the Socialists to outmaneuver the PCE. Prior to the Ninth Congress a number of dissidents had strongly criticized the draft versions of Theses 1, 3, 4, and 5 for hardly mentioning the differences between the party's predictions and the actual course of events after the death of Franco.[35] But Carrillo had managed to sidestep those criticisms in early 1978 because, despite the poor Communist showing in June 1977, most party members by and large believed that PCE fortunes would soon improve. Indeed, Carrillo played on those sentiments at the Madrid provincial conference in March 1978 by arguing that the transition from the Franco era was still under way and could lead to a "political revolution."[36] Subsequent events revealed just how large the gap was between wish and reality and prompted renewed criticism. By 1980, it was not only a few intellectuals who voiced their opposition to Carrillo. A number of disappointed labor activists now joined the chorus. They had agreed to abide by the wage guidelines issued in the *Pactos de la Moncloa*, because the Communist leadership confidently predicted that those agreements would be the first step toward the "government of national concentration." Events did not follow suit. By late 1978, it was evident that the government had outmaneuvered the PCE and the *Comisiones*, using them to hold down wages and making no major political concessions. Compounding this tactical failure was the growing economic crisis, which led to a further groundswell of discontent with the PCE's politics of consensus. Although as we have seen the national party tried to compensate by advocating a combination of consensus and mobilization politics, many Communists thought this smacked too much of the tactical sleight-of-hand for which Carrillo was so well known. Thus, labor leaders in Cataluña were less than enthusiastic and clearly uncomfortable in September 1978 when national *Comisiones* leaders urged the signing of new economic agreements. Labor activists in general were also much more vocal about what the Communists should demand in exchange, insisting that any agreement be signed for only a year (rather than for three, as proposed by the national PCE leadership), and rejecting the argument advanced by PCE leaders that an "exceptional" political situation required a toning down of confrontation.

The alliance policies Carrillo had pursued since 1977 were another target of criticism within the PCE. After June 1977, Carrillo had tried to use an emerging relationship between the Communists and the UCD to force the Socialists to agree to a "government of national concentration." Accordingly, the Communists pursued moderate policies, with the PCE playing a major role in fashioning the consensus that made possible the new Constitution. The PCE obviously hoped to use its moderation to gain access into the government, and to this it was the Socialists, not the UCD and Suárez, who were the principal obstacle. Thus the PSOE became the favorite target of the Communists, whose aggressive tactics became especially pronounced during the 1979 parliamentary elections. The strategy followed a certain logic and, furthermore, struck a responsive chord within the party, especially among more hard-line and traditional sectors. But an overtly anti-Socialist strategy could prosper only so long as Communist militants believed it would bring favorable results. By late 1979, with the consolidation of the PSOE and the UGT on the one hand and the setbacks the Communists and *Comisiones* had suffered on the other, there was growing concern among Communists over the political isolation of their party. Carrillo had never been explicitly anti-Socialist, of course. His "Eurocommunist" strategy had been publicly premised on close ties with the PSOE, and by a broader alliance with so-called "progressive" sectors, including the UCD. But he had tried too hard to be all things to all men on this question, criticizing the reformism of the PSOE yet calling it a necessary ally, then choosing to deal with Suárez and the UCD.

By 1980, these policies were under attack from distinct but often complementary directions. One group, hard-liners often associated with the labor wing of the PCE, objected to the "government of national concentration" strategy because it implied a more or less stable agreement with a conservative party, the UCD. Often bitter critics of Socialist "reformism" (it was to them that Carrillo had played during the 1979 campaign), these hard-liners did not particularly care for or trust the PSOE but talked of closer Communist-Socialist collaboration because they preferred traditional Left-Right dichotomies and formulations. A second group—whose most visible exponents were Executive Committee members Pilar Brabo and Carlos Alonso Zaldívar—also opposed too permanent an understanding with the UCD, but wanted the PCE to moderate its hostility toward the Socialists. Taking their cue from Carrillo's repeated insistence that Eurocommunism aimed to overcome the schism between Socialists and Communists that had developed after the October 1917 revolution, they sought to forge links with the PSOE. Although rejecting the idea of a Popular Front, Brabo, for example, insisted that "without advancing toward the unity of the Left it (was) not possible to advance toward [other] broader understandings."[37] This left-wing interpretation of the "historical compromise" strategy found favor in several Spanish regions. In Cataluña, for example, where the electoral and ideological distance separating Socialists and Communists was less pronounced than at the national level, and where a leftist regional government which included the Catalan centrist group *Convergencia* seemed more likely, the Socialists were perceived by many Communists as viable partners. As PSUC Secretary General Antonio Gutiérrez Díaz said: "The struggle in Cataluña is not directed against the Socialists." Or: "Our policy of concentration cannot be implemented *against* the PSOE."[38] As we have seen, similar attitudes existed in the Basque country, where Roberto Lertxundi pressed for eventual fusion with left-wing nationalist groups like *Euzkadiko Ezkerra*.

Alongside criticisms directed at Carrillo for his alliance choices,

there were questions raised regarding the foreign-policy orientation of the PCE. As we have seen, by the late 1970s Carrillo had
become one of the most forthright supporters of "Eurocommunism"; his book *"Eurocommunismo" y Estado* laid the foundations for a systematic challenge to Soviet domestic and international policies. No break in relations occurred, however. Unable to
squeeze much more advantage from his anti-Soviet international
policies and from initiatives like dropping Leninism from the PCE
program, Carrillo adopted after 1978 a lower profile vis-à-vis the
Soviet Union. On the one hand, he and Azcárate continued to defend their commitment to Eurocommunism: the PCE condemned
the trials of dissidents in Czechoslovakia, refused to attend the
Paris "peace" conference sponsored by the French and Polish
Communists, applauded the Mitterrand victory in France, rees-
tablished relations with the Chinese Communists, and called for
greater contacts with European Social Democratic and Socialist
parties.

But, if these were examples of the party's "official" posture,
there was also internal dissent. Earlier in this chapter, we quoted
a prominent Catalan Communist's perspective on international
questions. Numerous *agrupaciones* in Madrid, Asturias, and
Cataluña also approved resolutions supporting the Soviet intervention in Afghanistan, even as the PCE Executive Committee
condemned the action. It became fashionable again to laud the
Soviet Union and its accomplishments as well as to speak openly
of the pro-Soviet orientation of Executive Committee members
such as Armando López Salinas, Antonio Palomares, and Francisco Romero Marín. The Soviets, whose strategy vis-à-vis the
Spanish Communists was to attack Carrillo while continuing to
subsidize the Spanish party (in the form of commissions passed on
from mixed enterprises like Sovhispan, Prodag and CIEX, or of
equipment like the modern printing press given to the *Comisiones*
by the German Democratic Republic), were the beneficiaries,
though not the cause, of these developments. Obviously, some
members of the PCE were pro-Soviet, but, despite suggestions of
ample Soviet financial support, they were a distinct minority.
More numerous were the so-called Leninists, whose pressure led
the PCE leadership to sharpen its criticism of the United States and
of the possibility of Spanish entry into NATO as well as to support
more actively Third World revolutionary movements led by Cuba,
Vietnam, and Angola.

Carrillo's handling of internal party affairs and the question of what organizational principles should govern the party also provoked controversy within the PCE. During the 1960s and 1970s, Communist leaders had promised to transform the organization of the Communist party by modifying the much-vaunted principle of democratic centralism to permit greater internal discussion. Charges that old methods still held sway were voiced after the Central Committee decided to drop the party's traditional support for the Republic and its flag. The shift from sectoral to territorial *agrupaciones* also sparked debate, with professionals and intellectuals seeing the move as an effort to eliminate whatever power base they might have had within the PCE. Demands for greater internal democracy increased after the Ninth Congress. Many people who were active in labor affairs or in regional Communist organizations criticized Carrillo's highhandedness and the sclerotic control the Madrid-based apparatus exerted over the party. Many of the hard-line labor activists and the emerging pro-Soviet minority joined more "liberal" elements in pressing for revisions of party statutes so as to permit organized "currents of opinion" and assure them access to official PCE publications.[39] Distinct from these demands, but drawing support from some of the same individuals or groups, were Aragonese, Basque, and Catalan proposals for the party's "federalization." Because Carrillo opposed these proposals and because he personified the control the central apparatus was perceived to have over the party, he became a target in late 1980, and a number of younger cadres began publicly to call for his ouster.

The magnitude of the internal problems Carrillo faced became apparent at a Central Committee meeting in November 1981. The purpose of the meeting was to organize the Tenth PCE Congress for the following summer—a simple enough task. But a battle quickly broke out over a report Carrillo presented to the Central Committee.[40] Carrillo saw the document as a guideline for the pre-Congress discussion of the soon-to-be-elaborated Theses. In the document, he defended PCE policies since the legalization of the party and proposed several organizational amendments, among them the creation of the post of vice-secretary general. Reacting to mounting problems with the PSUC, he insisted that the PCE "remain a party and [not] become a federation of parties." The first notion alarmed those who thought Carrillo was trying to anoint a successor; the second worried those (like the Catalans and the

Basques) who wanted greater autonomy from the central party organization. More generally, Carrillo's analysis irritated those party leaders who, from the perspectives we have discussed, blamed Carrillo for the failures of the recent past. The debate over those issues became so heated in the Executive Committee that, of the thirty-four members, six abstained and three voted against using Carrillo's report as the basis for the pre-Congress debates. These nine then expressed their views to the full Central Committee. As the texts of the speeches indicate, there were few holds barred during the session.

An activist by temperament, and by no means ready to give up his position at the forthcoming PCE Congress, Carrillo used the ammunition provided by the Fifth PSUC Congress to counterattack. He prompted an Executive Committee resolution calling for an extraordinary Congress there, and joined Sánchez Montero in accusing the Soviets of meddling in PCE affairs. The choice, he said, was between the "Eurocommunists" and those who wanted to return to the Stalinist era. Although the situation was not quite so simple, reducing the problem to those terms was obviously advantageous to Carrillo. Moreover, the attempted military coup in February 1981 and the widespread fear that the King would be unable to stop the next one strengthened Carrillo's hand. Tamames and Pilar Brabo, members of the Executive Committee who, by arguing for more collective leadership, were most direct in their attacks on Carrillo, found themselves increasingly isolated. Others like Gutiérrez and Basque leaders who called for the "federalization" of the PCE also found their arguments weakened in a situation where the military looked with ill-disguised contempt at most demands for greater regional autonomy. Although Carrillo at times appeared conciliatory, he also cracked down organizationally, expelling Francisco García Salve from the Central Committee for criticizing party policies in public fora and warning the Catalans that, if t'.ey did not reaffirm their support for "Eurocommunism," he would sponsor another Communist party in Cataluña. The strategy worked. The Catalan Communists backed down from their overt challenge to the PCE. In May 1981, the PSUC Central Committee approved a statement reincorporating "Eurocommunism" into the party program, and a regional Conference in July 1981 confirmed that decision. At a July Congress in Valencia, anti-Carrillo leaders like Pilar Brabo, Emerit Bono, and Ernest García were kept out of the newly elected regional Central Committee; in Andalucía, Carrillo threw his support behind Felipe Al-caraz who was chosen the new Secretary General; and in Madrid, after a tumultuous provincial conference at which Carrillo lashed out at "renovators who charged he was abandoning his earlier commitment to 'Eurocommunism' in the face of internal pressures," Carrillo loyalist Adolfo Piñedo became provincial party head. Only in the Basque country, in Aragón, and in several other smaller regions did an anti-Carrillo majority emerge, but they did not have the votes to prevent Carrillo's eventual reelection or jeopardize his control over the Congress.

The PCE leadership meanwhile moved to reassert its control over party activists in the *Comisiones Obreras*. Dissident Central Committee members Fidel Alonso and Francisco García Salve were excluded from a May 1981 cadres' meeting called to determine the positions the Communists should adopt a few weeks later at the *Comisiones* Congress.[41] There, an alternate list headed by hard-liner Alfred Clemente won a surprising 25 percent of the delegates' votes, but the "official" list nevertheless won handily, presaging a less turbulent PCE Congress than many observers had anticipated earlier in the year and indicating the bulk of Communist labor activists still supported Carrillo and his policies.[42] Parallel to these efforts, PCE leaders also worked to convince party cadres in the *Comisiones* to rally behind the *Acuerdo Nacional sobre el Empleo* (National Accord on Employment—ANE) signed in June by the government, representatives of the UGT and CC.OO., as well as the principal employers' association. Although the ANE limited salary increases to between 9 and 11 percent, in exchange the unions received a government commitment to create an additional 350,000 jobs through public funds and to compensate the UGT and *Comisiones* with 2.5 billion *pesetas* for the *patrimonio sindical* taken over by the Franco regime.[43] This was a rather good deal, Communist leaders believed, given the political climate in Spain after the February 1981 coup attempt and the stagnating economy.

The Tenth PCE Congress met in late July 1981. Despite the unrest at regional and provincial party meetings, Carrillo was in command by the opening session. The four-hour report he presented in the name of the Central Committee was a strong defense of party policies since 1978.[44] The attempted military coup in February 1981, he argued, "had proven the Communists right" in their insistence on a "government of national concentration" and broad consensus policies. Painting a bleak scenario for Spain under a military dictatorship, he called on Communists and other parties to rally around the constitutional order. Carrillo spent most of his time discussing the internal PCE situation, however. He warned party members against engaging in a "nihilist confrontation" through which the Communists would "destroy their political patrimony." He came out strongly against permitting organized currents within the PCE, claiming the party suffered less from excessive centralization than from a weak apparatus and strong centrifugal tendencies. According to Carrillo, the party had committed two major organizational errors in the preceding four years. One was to weaken the *agrupaciones* by eliminating sectoral organizations for professionals and then allowing cadres to focus their activity "at the top and toward the top" rather than toward the base of the party. The other was for the leadership to believe that the "number and quality of Communist cadres" in the labor movement made it "unnecessary to have a permanent organ [in the leadership] . . . which would have responsibility for Communist syndical policy."

Although mildly self-critical, the report did not assuage Carrillo's more strident critics. These included a small but vocal pro-Soviet group most of whom were from Cataluña (they cast the sixty-four votes against his report) and a larger contingent of "Eurocommunist renovators" led by Pilar Brabo, Manuel Azcárate, and Carlos Alonso Zaldívar. The latter represented the most "liberal" wing within the PCE; their demands included greater democratization and decentralization within the party as well as a reaffirmation and deepening of the "Eurocommunist" identity of the PCE.[45] They were, however, in a minority at the Congress. The bulk of the delegates—689 of them, representing 70 percent of the total, approved his report—supported Carrillo. They represented loyalists from the labor movement and the apparatus. With Carrillo and his supporters in control,[46] the Theses presented by the outgoing Central Committee were approved with virtually no changes. The most divisive moments occurred during the debates preceding the vote on Thesis 7 (regarding internal party organization), when Executive Committee member Vicente Cazcarra, to the approval of most delegates, bitterly criticized the organizational proposals presented by the "renovators," who wanted to allow organized currents of opinion within the party and to "federalize" and "rejuvenate" it, as leading to the transformation of the Communist party into "a Social-Democratic party belonging to the Second International."

With the delegates rubberstamping the proposals made by the leadership, the debates over the party program and statutes were almost perfunctory. Much more interesting was the maneuvering over the choices for the new Central Committee. There, the "candidacy commission"—its five members included Nicolás Sartorius and Julián Ariza of the *Comisiones Obreras* as well as Jaime Ballesteros and Francisco Romero Marín representing the party apparatus—played a major role, excluding all but 14 "renovators" from the official list of 104 prospective Central Committee members it presented to the delegates. Of Carrillo's strongest critics in the Executive Committee—Pilar Brabo, Carlos Alonso Zaldívar, Manuel Azcárate, and Roberto Lertxundi—only the latter two were reelected to that body, Azcárate because to do otherwise would be interpreted as too great a concession to the Soviet Union, and Lertxundi because, as Secretary General of the Basque Communist party, he had an automatic spot on the Executive. The new Central Committee had a solid pro-Carrillo majority. Indirectly, however, the delegates to the Tenth Congress expressed a preference on his successor, with Nicolás Sartorius easily outpacing Jaime Ballesteros, the organizational secretary, in the votes he received for the Central Committee.[47]

V

The Tenth Congress signaled the passing of the era associated with the heroic period of clandestinity and the beginning of another marked by retrenchment, introspection, and uncertainty. Although Carrillo emerged from the Congress comfortably reelected as Secretary General, the Congress did not resolve the manifold crises affecting Spanish Communism. Indeed, tensions within the Catalan, Basque, and Madrid party organizations only increased, spilling over into the central apparatus as well.

The situation in Cataluña reflected the conflicts left unresolved since the Fifth PSUC Congress in early 1981. At that time, the delegates had dropped the phrase "Eurocommunism" from the party program, electing the "Leninist" Francisco Frutos as Secretary General, and a Central Committee about evenly divided between representatives of the *banderas blancas* and those with "Leninist" and hard-line (or pro-Soviet) tendencies.[48] This equilibrium paralyzed the Catalan party and led to bitter infighting throughout the party as well as in the Catalan *Comisiones Obreras* (CONC). Under pressure from Carrillo and the PCE, a working majority between the *banderas blancas* and the "Leninists" slowly developed in the Central Committee. Together, they sponsored a Central Committee resolution in May supporting the reintroduction of "Eurocommunism" into the PSUC program,[49] then voted at a special conference in July to readopt the term. Rather than calming the situation, the move only brought increased tension within the party, with the pro-Soviets and hard-liners working to sabotage the leadership. The open insubordination of Père Ardiaca (who, despite being PSUC President, led his *agrupación* in Lérida in voting against the May Central Committee resolution) led to his ouster in July.[50] Reports of physical and verbal violence directed against the *banderas blancas* at party meetings now became commonplace; local organizations in the Baix Llobregat and the Vallès Occidental, flagrantly violating the rules of democratic centralism, openly refused to accept the decisions taken by the Executive Committee.[51]

With the disintegration of the party every day more apparent, a faction of the "Leninists" (identified with Andreu Claret Serra, the editor of *Treball*) abandoned its efforts to mediate, urging instead a tightening of party discipline and the convocation of a new Congress, which Frutos announced in November would be held the following year. With that decision, the factional struggle shifted into high gear. The hard-liners, increasingly displaced within the Central Committee, hoped to gain a decisive victory at the Congress, and created a coordinating committee to direct the battle in the local *agrupaciones*.[52] The discovery of this parallel group, its existence again in further violation of democratic centralism, brought a sharp response from the PSUC Executive (firmly supported by Carrillo and the PCE). Ardiaca, former Organizational Secretaries Josep Serradell and Francesc Trives, Financial Secretary Fèlix Farré, and eight members of the PSUC Central Committee were summarily expelled; another fourteen members were separated from the party for a year; and, three more were suspended for three months.[53] Out with them went between forty and fifty (out of an estimated five hundred) Communist councilmen and mayors in Cataluña, who in March 1982 formed the core of a rival party, the *Partit dels Comunistes de Catalunya* (PCC).

With the hard-liners excluded and the year-end renewal of party membership cards an effective way of weeding out dissidents, a "sanitized" PSUC finally held its Congress in March 1982.[54] Its results—the election of Antonio Gutiérrez Díaz and Gregorio López Raimundo as Secretary General and President respectively, and the decision formally to recommit the PSUC to "Eurocommunism"—represented a major victory for Carrillo and opened the way for the renovation of the PSUC's tarnished public image. Whether the party would retain its electoral audience was not entirely clear, however. The events of the previous year had damaged the party, and the expulsion of the hard-line faction had seriously weakened the PSUC's presence among industrial workers.[55]

In the wake of the Tenth Congress, tension also escalated in the Basque Communist party. Earlier we noted how at the Congress, the proposals by PCE-EPK Secretary General Lertxundi for greater autonomy to regional party branches had been decisively defeated; and, instead, Lertxundi's principal rival and close Carrillo ally, Ignacio Latierro, had been appointed to the PCE Central Committee Secretariat. Perhaps provoked by this, and in any case more and more committed to developing closer links with *Euzkadiko Ezkerra*, Lertxundi now pressed ahead with plans for a merger with EE. Opponents of this initiative, (among them PCE-EPK President Ormazábal and many *Comisiones Obreras* leaders in the region) convinced party leaders in Madrid that Lertxundi's proposal would lead to the emasculation of the party in the Basque country.[56] Leaders of the PCE were not in principle opposed to fusion with other leftist organizations—the PSUC had been the product of such a merger in 1936—but feared EE would emerge the dominant partner (in the February 1980 regional elections EE received 9.6 percent of the vote while the PCE-EPK tallied only 3.9 percent), and the resulting organization would have little or no organic link with the PCE. Matters came to head in September and October when Lertxundi ignored warnings from the PCE Secretariat; it then dissolved the EPK Central Committee. Shortly thereafter, Lertxundi and several others were expelled from the national Central Committee.[57]

Meanwhile, the tension between Carrillo and the "renovators" only increased. The latter had been defeated at the Tenth Congress and their representatives removed from the Executive Committee. Only Azcárate remained (in charge of PCE international affairs), but he lost his editorship of the theoretical journal

Nuestra Bandera; other prominent "renovators" like Carlos Alonso Zaldívar and Pilar Brabo were dropped from their Secretariat positions. This only heightened their availability to the press and their willingness to make public statements. In response, Carrillo warned in September 1981: "And if someone wants to argue again, let him wait until the Eleventh Congress and there we can argue; but now is a time to work, and to work with discipline in order to implement the policies approved at the Tenth Congress."[58]

Conflict between the Carrillo leadership group and the "renovators" finally exploded over disagreement about the stance to be taken toward events in the Basque party organization. The "renovators" were openly supportive of Lértxundi, and, after his expulsion from the Central Committee, Azcárate, Brabo, and Alonso Zaldívar signed on as sponsors of a public meeting in Madrid at which Lertxundi and his EE counterpart, Mario Onaindía, explained why they wanted to merge their two organizations. Carrillo's response was swift: he demanded the "renovators" be expelled from the Central Committee, threatening to resign if his proposal were not accepted. In such a polarized atmosphere, various compromise efforts (most notably by Sartorius and Camacho, the latter noting "how easy it is to be 'Eurocommunist' to the outside while one does the opposite inside") failed, and the Central Committee approved their expulsions in November by a margin of sixty seven votes in favor to twenty four against and eight abstentions.[59] The expulsions had important repercussions throughout the country, but especially in the capital, where numerous "renovators" rallied around those expelled. For example, five of the nine councilmen elected on the Communist ticket in April 1979 had also sponsored the Lertxundi-Onaindía talk, and, when they refused to resign their posts, the PCE provincial committee expelled them from the party.[60] In solidarity with them, forty-one of the sixty Communists working in municipal governments throughout Madrid province resigned as well. Prominent hard-line *Comisiones* activists from Madrid, like Fidel Alonso, also publicly supported the "renovators," drafting a letter signed by three hundred Communist labor cadres. It decried "the climate of Stalinist purge" and "the scandalous situation" which "threatened to dilapidate the political capital obtained with so much sacrifice during the struggle against the [Franco] dictatorship."[61]

But, the *alliance contre nature* between "renovators" and hard-line activists was not the only, or even the most important, characteristic of the period immediately following the Tenth Congress. More significant was the spread of the cancer of dissent to the party apparatus itself. Azcárate, Brabo, and Alonso Zaldivar could hardly be described as intellectuals or "professionals"— they were key members of the apparatus who, especially the latter two, had been promoted into important positions within the PCE in the early 1970s by Carrillo himself.[62] That they now moved openly into the opposition suggested the depth of the crisis the PCE faced, a crisis that had extended to the prospective leaders of tomorrow.

The December 1981 military coup in Poland occurred against this backdrop. Official Spanish Communist reaction to it had been swift: the PCE Secretariat issued a statement describing the Jaruzelski coup as "an act in open contradiction to the essentials of socialism, Marxism and Leninism," and a unanimous Central Committee then insisted that "the failure of the Polish Unified Workers' Party [could] only be explained as the failure of the Soviet Union in exporting its political and economic models to other countries, and [as] the failure of the attempt to maintain those models against wind and tide."[63] Subsequently, Carrillo flew to Yugoslavia and Italy, and *Mundo Obrero* approvingly published a PCI declaration that was itself to become the object of vituperative attacks by *Pravda* and *Kommunist*. All in all, the PCE's rhetoric was vintage "Eurocommunist," but behind the facade of Central Committee unanimity lay profound differences of opinion over the Communists' international relationships and identity. Carrillo and the Central Committee majority had been unwilling to accept the Italian Communist judgment that the October 1917 revolution had lost is "propelling force," but they nevertheless saw in the events in Poland the failure of a "bureaucratized State" imposed by the Soviet Union. To the "renovators," however, this formulation was timid; it failed to account for the real sources and the nature of the Soviet dictatorship.[64] For their part, hardliners were mollified neither by the ritual references to Lenin nor by the charges that "imperialism" and "social-democratic sectors" had joined in "anti-Communist manipulation" of the Polish crisis. While Carrillo walked this tightrope, the Soviet Union increased its attacks on him. Contacts with PCE dissidents increased, and representatives of several Communist parties closely aligned with Moscow (among them the Czechs and the Portuguese) attended the constituent congress of the *Partit dels Communistes de Catalunya*.

The decline of the Communists and their internal squabbling

contrasted with the PSOE's growing self-confidence. As the UCD disintegrated (by midsummer over forty deputies, including Suárez, abandoned its ranks), the prospects for a Socialist victory in the upcoming elections increased. The hallmark of Socialist strategy was to downplay the calls for profound structural reforms. As a complement to this moderation, the PSOE flatly stated its refusal to form a government with the PCE after the next parliamentary elections. To this formal veto, the Communists responded by trying to compel the PSOE to accept them as partners in several regional governments. The PCE was successful in Asturias where, in April 1982, the Socialists granted the PCE one ministerial portfolio in exchange for Communist support of the PSOE candidate for the presidency of the regional *Junta*. Buoyed by this success, the Communists turned their attention to Andalucía, where regional elections were scheduled for May 1982. There, the Communists hoped to do well enough to compel the PSOE to rely on their support in the Andalucian parliament. The results shattered those illusions. Not only did the Socialists receive an astonishing 52.1 percent of the votes cast, but the PCE total shrank from 13.5 to 8.4 percent, as 150,000 of its 1979 voters either abstained or moved to the Socialist standard.[65] Because this pattern was likely to be repeated elsewhere, the Communists now had reason to fear that they might not even reach their 1977 totals in the next parliamentary elections.

The Andalucian election results provoked a major confrontation in the Spanish Communist leadership.[66] Vice-Secretary General Sartorius and Executive Committee member Marcelino Camacho openly blamed Carrillo for the debacle and demanded that negotiations begin immediately to secure the return of those expelled from the party or its leading organs in the previous two years. Camacho had been unhappy with the direction of PCE policies for some time; he especially feared the impact confrontations within the party were having on the *Comisiones Obreras*. Regarded as a political lightweight (and with his call for trade-union independence eliciting little support in the PCE), Camacho posed only a minor threat to Carrillo. Not so Sartorius. He was widely regarded as the *dauphin*, especially by the "renovators" who saw him as their last great hope. Hamlet-like,[67] Sartorius had been curiously ambivalent since being anointed Vice Secretary in September 1981, torn between support for the overall direction of Carrillo's policies and challenging his leadership. He calculated that the moment had finally come after the Andalucian elections, but in so doing misjudged. Many "renovators" (Alonso Zaldívar, Azcárate, Brabo, and Lertxundi) who might have supported him had been dropped from the Central Committee six months earlier, and those who remained were a small minority. The Catalans had had their disagreements with Carrillo, but they certainly did not want to negotiate with the expelled pro-Soviets. Younger party leaders from Asturias, Madrid, and Valencia, as well as Julián Ariza, more and more the strong man of the *Comisiones Obreras*, strongly supported Carrillo. After a marathon Central Committee meeting lasting nearly forty hours, Carrillo withdrew the resignation he had offered earlier, thus sidestepping for a time a bruising battle for the succession.

The October 1982 parliamentary elections proved a disaster for the Communist party. The PSOE won a most convincing victory, capturing 9.8 million votes (46 percent of the tally) and 201 of 350 seats in the Chamber of Deputies. Only Fraga Iribarne's Popular Alliance survived the Socialist tide, but its 106 seats and 25 percent of the vote placed it a distant second. The Socialist absolute majority and the UCD's debacle (it went from 168 seats in March 1979 to 13 in this election) shattered what hopes the Communists may have had of playing the PSOE and the Center off against each other. The dimensions of the Socialist victory—it made unnecessary any parliamentary agreement with the PCE—magnified the Communist defeat. The final count gave the PCE 824,000 votes (a mere 3.8 percent of the total) and 5 seats in the Chamber. Only Carrillo won a seat in Madrid province; the Communists elected one deputy (instead of 8 as in March 1979) from Barcelona; and, the PCE lost 1.1 million votes relative to the preceding elections.

The stunning electoral defeat sharpened tensions within the PCE and prompted Carrillo's resignation a week after the elections. With him passed an era, but the conflicts formed during the preceding four years remained. His nomination of Asturias Regional Secretary Gerardo Iglesias to succeed him won only 64 out of 85 Central Committee votes. With this undercurrent of opposition and a new congress expected, Iglesias will not have an easy time consolidating his position. Whether he is the person to lead the PCE as it battles to escape political oblivion remains to be seen.

Conclusion

SPANISH COMMUNISM enters the 1980s in crisis, having lost most of the political capital it accumulated while leading the opposition to Franco. Once aspiring to play a role comparable to that of the PCI in Italy and to emerge as the dominant force on the Left, the Communists have now become a marginal force in Spanish politics. Outstripped electorally by the Socialists by almost a twelve-to-one margin, divided internally along social, regional, and ideological lines, and having lost much of its "successor" generation, the PCE is searching for a role and an identity in Spain as well as in the international arena.

The Communists had adjusted to clandestine conditions better than other groups on the Left, gleaning a peculiar advantage because of the Franco regime's insistence that any manifestation of discontent or dissent was Communist-inspired or -controlled. To many Spaniards, the Spanish Communist party was a juggernaut capable of superhuman political and organizational feats, the only real opposition to Franco. To quote a prominent Spaniard, Pablo Picasso, on why he joined the PCE in the 1940s: "I am against Franco. The only way to show it was to join the [party]; that way I demonstrated that I belonged to the other side."[1] The PCE became a reference point for the increasingly politicized, post-Civil War generations of intellectuals, students, and labor elites that adopted antiregime positions. This status gave the party a psychological impetus which, along with the innovations its leaders—specifically Carrillo—made in the ideological and organizational spheres, and in its attitude toward the Church and the labor movement, suggested a significant role for the Communists in a democratic Spain.

But the Communist drive for national legitimacy and electoral success in post-Franco Spain fell short. One reason for its failure was the Civil War and its legacy. To the Communists, the war had been a heroic experience which, even though it ended in defeat, confirmed them as a major force in Spanish politics. The Communists also viewed the regime born out of that conflict as illegitimate, and saw its radical transformation as a necessity. That the party never abandoned these notions worked to its disadvantage among a population born largely after 1936, to whom the Civil War and the conflicts it had engendered were to be avoided at all costs. The PCE, in short, resuscitated too many unwelcome memories.

The ambiguities and contradictions in the Spanish Communist evolution over the previous twenty-five years weighed on the PCE. There is no doubt that the party, prodded by Carrillo, changed its policies in important ways during that period. But it is equally evident that the rituals, the language, the style, and the symbols the party clung to remained the same, confirming the Leibnizian dictum: *natura non saltit.*

The Communists were also unable to counter the effect that Admiral Luis Carrero Blanco's assassination in December 1973 and the Portuguese revolution in April 1974 had on the Spanish political elite. Both events strengthened the hands of reformers within and outside the regime. King Juan Carlos and Premier Adolfo Suárez, who could not be implicated in the worst excesses of the past, presented themselves as the natural choices for retaining the economic and material accomplishments of the Franco era while leading a peaceful and deliberate transition toward democracy. Their success in that venture allowed the PSOE not only to reactivate the historical memory Spaniards had of the party, but to develop an organization and a presence among broad sectors of the population. By 1977, the PSOE had assumed the role the PCE had coveted for itself: the party of democratic reform and orderly change. Whereas the PCI could bask in the memory of its role in the Resistance and claim a place as an architect of postwar Italian democracy, the PCE came out of clandestinity without a decisive victory over the Franco regime, without the boost provided to the PCI by the defeat of Fascism in Italy in 1945.

A major factor in the crisis Spanish Communism faces today has been the party's inability to establish a broad electoral base and carve a major role for itself in politics. The Communists are also having difficulty defining the nature of their relationship to the Soviet Union and to the international Communist movement. Much of the discussion has turned around the policy initiatives impelled by Carrillo during the 1970s. His pointed criticisms of Soviet foreign and domestic policies were accepted within the PCE largely because they promised to bring the Communists an electoral payoff. Unease among party members and cadres on this score was overcome by the strong sense of discipline then existing within the party. International detente discouraged polarization on the domestic scene and, thereby, helped Carrillo as well. But when the PCE registered no important gains electorally in 1977 and 1979, not only did the voices critical of Carrillo's "anti-Sovietism" assume a new prominence, but, in the process, discipline and party unity shattered. The worsening economic situation and the climate of confrontation between the United States and the Soviet Union made it easy for the traditional Communist language and reflexes in international politics to reemerge.

Redefining the Spanish Communist relationship to the Soviet Union inevitably involved the question of organizational and political identity, of what it meant to be a Communist—in Spain and elsewhere in Western Europe—in the last two decades of the twentieth century. During the 1970s Carrillo and other party leaders insisted that they had developed a new and profoundly different answer to that question. At the Tenth PCE Congress, however, the clock had been turned back: Carrillo insisted that a Communist should reject social democracy, unconditionally defend the October 1917 Russian Revolution, support national liberation movements in their struggle against imperialism, preserve democratic centralism as the cornerstone of the party, and manifest a will to transform society—even as he "became more democratic, as he [considered] democracy as something fundamental." But his vision is in many respects little more than a "revised standard version" of the traditional Communist model. As such it serves well during a time of retrenchment, rallying support from a Communist audience that, surveys show, perceives itself to be more radical than its leaders. Such a model limits the appeal of the party, however, and renders it more susceptible to an extreme leftist subculture whose votes, although small in absolute terms (1.5 percent of the total in 1977, 3.0 percent in 1979), are hardly dwarfed by the Communist total. Moreover, the inflection toward renewed sectarianism comes at a critical juncture, when patterns of electoral alignment that may hold for a generation are being formed and when the Socialists have convincingly established themselves as the premier party in Spain. Today, the PCE fails to excite the imagination or to present a program attractive to those sectors where the Communists traditionally have been strong, much less where they have always been weak.

Admittedly there will be room in Spain for a party that appeals to the dispossessed, the poor, those who are thoroughly alienated by industrialization and by the capitalist order. But this audience, the audience of a radical opposition party, makes up only a small portion of the Spanish population. Spain is an increasingly consumerized and Europeanized country, with a large middle-class and service sector, with a proletariat whose subcultural identity is declining, and with left-wing intellectuals who are no longer inspired by the Soviet example. For the PCE to have a chance to become a truly national party, then, it must transform itself further. It must drop its adherence to an internally autocratic model and break its political and psychological links with the Soviet Union. Otherwise, the many and varied Communist claims that they are committed to the democratic process remain empty professions. To the degree that the PCE has not yet renounced the ambition of fighting for and occupying the political and social space of democratic socialism—which is what "Eurocommunism" is all about—it must resolve these ambiguities or accept a role distinctly secondary to the Socialists. The membership hemorrhage the PCE has suffered, the decision to rely on working-class cadres as the cornerstone of party organization, and the bitter internecine struggles which have depleted the energies of the party suggest that the present Communist leadership, beginning with Carrillo and extending to his successor, Gerardo Iglesias, has lost the capacity and will to lead a further transformation and renewal of the PCE.

Further initiatives in that direction are made more difficult because the PCE is still involved in strengthening its structures at the regional, provincial, and local levels. The PCE must overcome numerous obstacles to its consolidation as a party. The shift of power from the legislative to executive branches, the growing complexity of the state and the expansion in the influence of the bureaucracy and of specialized interest groups, the growth of a professional salaried class for whom the socialization and recruitment functions of political parties are less relevant, the importance of the media rather than party organizations in reaching the electorate, and the personalization of political campaigns—none of these trends favors traditional party structures.

More specifically Spanish obstacles are the Francoist legacies of depoliticization and apathy, which have reinforced disdain for political parties and politicians and have reduced interest in civic affairs. Spanish parties (the PCE included) are having to create party structures, consolidate and expand partisan loyalties in a society that dispensed with them for forty years, even as the edifice of a corporatist, modern welfare-state was erected. Complicating the situation for the Communists had been their failure to adapt their policies and structures to regional demands. This a serious handicap in a country where the center-periphery cleavage remains important and has great disruptive potential.

The PCE's electoral failures, its difficulties in creating and consolidating party structures, its identity crisis, and the exhaustion of the myth of the October 1917 Bolshevik revolution have weakened the Communists to the point that many wonder whether the PCE will survive as a viable force in Spanish politics. And yet, while the obstacles the party faces are by no means easy to overcome, it would be unwise to conclude that the PCE cannot aspire to a larger share of the electorate.

I have emphasized the difficulties facing the Spanish Communist party in the 1980s, but some of the problems facing the PCE (especially those related to leadership change and succession) are not so different from those Socialists faced and successfully overcame ten years ago. Moreover, the Communists still have an important social presence in the labor movement. The advantage the *Comisiones* held over the UGT has been reduced significantly in the last five years, but it is unlikely that the Socialists will be able to become preponderant or eliminate Communist influence among workers altogether. Indeed, if the economic situation worsens in the next few years, and if the current "defensive" phase in Spanish trade unionism gives way to more aggressive tactics, a militant Communist posture could bring dividends in the labor arena. Unemployment currently stands at nearly 15 percent, and there are no prospects for quick improvement in the economy. Spanish entry into the European Economic Community is no longer a guarantee of rapid growth and will affect several regions and industrial sectors adversely in the years to come, increasing unemployment and pushing wages higher as integration proceeds. This situation could work to the disadvantage of the UGT, especially with the PSOE in government and committed to an austerity program.

Nevertheless, the current Communist electoral disadvantage vis-à-vis the PSOE is unlikely to diminish soon. Not only are the Socialists united (their leaders' lack of enthusiasm for unity of action with the Communists contrasting markedly with the attitude Pietro Nenni and other Italian Socialists had in the late 1940s), but the PCE is much weaker than the PCI was at the end of World War II. The Socialist alliance-strategy has been to maintain the municipal pact with the Communists while avoiding further entangling alliances at the national level. The strategy has worked so far, allowing the PSOE to consolidate a moderate image and to become the largest vote-getter in Spain. The prospects for closer Communist-Socialist collaboration during the 1980s depend on the PSOE's continued success in competing with the Center and Center-Right and in fending off the challenge posed by moderate and leftist regional parties in the Basque country and Cataluña.

The October 1982 parliamentary elections and the Socialists' overwhelming victory in them have transformed the Spanish political map. With the party system now essentially bipolar (between them the PSOE and AP hold 306 out of 350 seats in the Chamber of Deputies) and the future of a Centrist party uncertain, the Communists have been dealt a devastating blow. Not only have PCE electoral fortunes come to depend more than ever on mistakes the PSOE commits, but the Communists are now competing with a Socialist party that, having proven itself capable of winning an absolute majority in the *Cortes,* can rightfully claim to be the best and, given the allergy many Spaniards feel toward a Popular Front, perhaps the only chance the Left has for exercising power. The Communist dilemma is that they can only gain at the expense of the Socialists. Yet by weakening the PSOE, the PCE would undermine the prospects for the Left. Under present circumstances, and in the absence of a viable Centrist party, those who voted Socialist in 1982 can hardly be expected to shift to the Communist standard. The Communists therefore face an uphill struggle in their quest for a more important position on the Left and in Spanish politics. That they will work toward that end, that their efforts will enliven the politics of the Left over the next decade, is a virtual certainty. Success in the venture is problematic, however, and as the PCE and its leaders ponder their future, they must do so, as Antonio Gamsci once said, with the optimism of the will and the pessimism of the intellect.

Notes

Introduction

1. Santiago Carillo, *"Eurocomunismo" y Estado* (Barcelona: Editorial Grijalbo, 1977, p. 212.
2. Juan Linz, "Opposition in and under an Authoritarian Regime: The Case of Spain" in Robert A. Dahl (ed.), *Regimes and Oppositions* (New Haven: Yale University Press, 1973), pp. 188 ff.

1. The Past as Prelude

1. The reader interested in a fuller historical discussion may find the following books useful. Víctor Alba, *El Partido Comunista en España* (Barcelona: Editorial Planeta, 1979); José Bullejos, *La Comintern en España* (Mexico: Impresiones Modernas, 1972); David T. Cattell, *Communism and the Spanish Civil War* (Berkeley and Los Angeles: University of California Press, 1957); Fernando Claudín, *La Crisis del Movimiento Comunista* (Paris: Ediciones Ruedo Ibérico, 1970), particularly the section on Spain entitled "The Untimely Revolution," pp. 168–96; Eduardo Comín Colomer, *Historia del Partido Comunista de España* (Madrid: Editora Nacional, 1967); Dolores Ibárruri et al., *Historia del Partido Comunista de España* (Warsaw: Ediciones "Polonia," 1960); Joan Estruch, *Historia del PCE (1920–1939)* (Barcelona: Iniciativa Editoriales, 1978); Gerald Meaker, *The Revolutionary Left in Spain, 1914–1923* (Stanford: Stanford University Press, 1974); Pelai Pagès, *Historia del Partido Comunista de España* (Barcelona: Ediciones Ricou, 1978); and Angel Ruíz Ayúcar, *El Partido Comunista. 37 Años de Clandestinidad* (Madrid: Editorial San Martín, 1976).
2. Branko Lazitch, *Les Partis Communistes d'Europe* (Paris: Les Iles d'Or, 1956), p. 183.
3. For an analysis of Anarchism and its relation to others on the Left during this crucial decade, see Meaker and César M. Lorenzo, *Les Anar-*

chistes Espagnols et le Pouvoir, 1868–1969 (Paris: Editions du Seuil, 1969) and Gerald Brenan, *The Spanish Labyrinth* (London: Cambridge University Press, 1943), particularly pp. 131–202.

4. Luis Gómez Llorente's *Aproximación a la Historia del Socialismo Español (Hasta 1921)* (Madrid: Editorial Cuadernos para el Diálogo, 1972) provides a useful overview.

5. Ibid., p. 549.

6. Claudín, p. 603.

7. Ibid., p. 604.

8. The driving force behind the change appears to have been the German-Polish Non-Aggression Pact of January 1934. Stalin now began to understand the threat Hitler and Nazi Germany posed to Soviet security, and this realization led to a Russian rapprochement with the French government and then to the proposal (first voiced publicly in May 1934 by *Pravda* and republished shortly thereafter in *l'Humanité*) for anti-Fascist unity among the forces of the Left. See Claudín, pp. 134–44.

9. There are competing interpretations as to when the Spanish Communists shifted to Popular Front tactics. Dolores Ibárruri has claimed, for example, that despite "severe criticism" from the Comintern, the PCE began to pursue a policy of fostering closer ties with the Socialists a year before Stalin sanctioned such an initiative. Dolores Ibárruri, "The Seventh Congress of the Comintern and the Spanish Experience," *World Marxist Review* 8 (12) (December 1965):43–47. Most historiography on the Popular Front period rejects this argument however, with Victor Alba, for one, stressing that the Communists responded during 1933 and early 1934 to all Socialist suggestions for unity of action in the *Alianza Obrera* with vituperative scorn. Alba, p. 140.

10. For an analysis of this process, see Andrés de Blas Guerrero, *El Socialismo Radical en la Segunda República* (Madrid: Tucar Ediciones, 1978).

11. Claudín argues, however, that the Communist claim of 20,000 members in early 1936 had been exaggerated perhaps by as much as sevenfold.

12. George Orwell, *Homage to Catalonia* (New York: Harcourt, Brace & World, 1952), p. 67, makes the statement. For a useful compilation of Communist documents sketching out the PCE's position see José Díaz, *Tres Años de Lucha* (Paris: Colección Ebro, 1970).

13. Jackson, *The Spanish Republic and the Spanish Civil War, 1931–1939* (Princeton: Princeton University Press, 1965), pp. 403–04.

14. Carrillo claims in *"Eurocomunismo" y Estado* (Barcelona: Editorial Grijalbo, 1977), pp. 147–52, that party leaders did not know about what was going on.

15. Orwell, pp. 53–54 and Cattell, pp. 69–83.

16. Indeed, during his stay at the Aragon front where Anarchist militias were holding an important position against insurgent Nationalists, George Orwell noted only one Soviet-made piece in the Anarchist arsenal, a submachine gun. Orwell, p. 34. Also Franz Borkenau, *The Spanish Cockpit* (Ann Arbor: University of Michigan Press, 1963), pp. 179–80.

17. Claudín, p. 186.

18. Cattell, p. 184.

19. Claudín, pp. 195–97; Payne, p. 311; Cattell, p. 32.

20. Ignacio Fernández de Castro, *De las Cortes de Cádiz al Plan de Desarrollo* (Paris: Ediciones Ruedo Ibérico, 1968), p. 286.

21. See the evidence as sketched in Guy Hermet, *Los Comunistas en España* (Paris: Ediciones Ruedo Ibérico, 1972), p. 37–39.

22. See Dolores Ibárruri et al., pp. 211–47, for the official view of those years. For a contrast, see Ruíz Ayúcar, pp. 49–226.

23. A detailed account of the struggles among the exiled Popular Front parties may be found in José Borrás, *Políticas de los Exiliados Españoles, 1944–1958* (Paris: Ediciones Ruedo Ibérico, 1976).

24. Santiago Carrillo, "Somos el Partido de la Destrucción del franquismo y también el Partido de la Reconstrucción de una España grande y democrática," *Nuestra Bandera* (January–February 1946): 60. The party also came up with the proposal that a *gobierno de concentración nacional* should follow Franco, a notion later resurrected in the post-Franco era.

25. Santiago Carrillo, "La Situación de España y Nuestras Tareas después de la Victoria de las Naciones Unidas," *Nuestra Bandera* (June 1945): 18–19.

26. Líster, pp. 259–64.

27. Jesús Hernández, *La Grande Trahison* (Paris: Editions Flasquelle, 1953).

28. See the text in Enrique Líster, *Basta!* (Madrid: G. del Toro Editor, 1978), pp. 266–68.

29. Jorge Semprún, *Autobiografía de Federico Sánchez* (Barcelona: Editorial Planeta, 1977), pp. 38–39.

30. Líster, pp. 211–64.

31. The figure may be found in Gabriel Jackson, *The Spanish Republic and the Civil War, 1931–1939* (Princeton: Princeton University Press, 1965), p. 200.

32. Paul Preston, "The Anti-Franco Opposition: The Long March to Unity," in the book he edited, *Spain in Crisis* (London: Harvester Press, 1976), p. 135.

33. See the estimates for guerrilla actions and casualties in F. Aguado Sánchez, *El Maquís en España* (Madrid: Editorial San Martín, 1975), pp. 243–54.

34. On the October 1948 meeting with Stalin, see Andrés Sorel, *Guerrilla Española del Siglo XX* (Paris: Colección Ebro, 1970), pp. 69–70. Colección Ebro was the PCE publishing house in Paris on the rue de Belleyme. Another similar account may be found in Santiago Carrillo, *Demain l'Espagne* (Paris: Editions du Seuil, 1974), pp. 99–100.

35. For an interesting view on events of that time, see the book by José Gros, *Relatos de un Guerrillero Español* (Madrid: Editorial A.T.E., 1977), especially pp. 178–267. Gros has been a member of the PCE Central Committee and was a liaison between PCE headquarters in France and guerrillas operating in Spain.

36. Alba, pp. 259–61 for the text.

37. Líster, pp. 182–83.

38. Santiago Carrillo, *Demain l'Espagne*, p. 44. Also Alba, p. 70.

39. Alba, p. 140.

40. Líster, pp. 218–19.

41. Semprún, pp. 217–18.

42. *Mundo Obrero* (Paris), January 1956.

43. Semprún, pp. 219–23.

44. Carrillo apparently believes his opponents of the time saw Claudín as *recuperable* since he, unlike Carrillo, came from the Communist Youth. María Eugenia Yagüe, *Santiago Carrillo: Una Biografía Política* (Madrid: Editorial Cambio16, 1977), pp. 52–53.

45. The pamphlet of that title has no date or place of publication. For the reference to Uribe, see p. 26.

46. See Fernando Claudín, *Documentos de una Divergencia Comunista* (Barcelona: Iniciativas Editoriales, 1978), p. iii. As late as 1964, Carrillo still opposed the effort, urged by Claudín and Semprún, to analyze the Stalinist era more critically. In April of that year, he admitted "there had been political police, concentration camps, etc." in the Soviet Union, but insisted those institutions "were necessary and I am not sure they might not be in other socialist revolutions, even though these be realized under more favorable circumstances." From a speech in the Political Bureau, cited in Semprún, p. 280. See also pp. 277–79 for the negative reaction to a Semprún article in *Realidad* which insisted on the need to "liquidate the institutional [Stalinist] system."

47. Claudín, *Documentos*, pp. iv–v.

48. See the text of the speech delivered by Carrillo in April 1974 as translated in *Joint Publications Research Service* (Washington, D.C.), no. 26413, September 16, 1964, p. 22. Semprún, pp. 212–15, quotes from the original speech and contrasts that version with the one later published by the PCE.

2. The PCE and Spanish Catholicism

1. Gerald Brenan, *The Spanish Labyrinth* (New York and London: Cambridge University Press, 1943), pp. 37–56 presents a brilliant analysis of the place the Church occupied in Spanish society.

2. In part, this relative moderation on the Catholic question had its roots in the view that too militant an atheism, one which led to terrorism for example, was undesirable insofar as it would detract from other more important political tasks. Moreover, the Popular Front strategy followed by the PCE and other Latin European parties during the 1930s, at the instigation of Moscow, caused those parties to adopt a much less radical posture on any number of issues than that which party members or leaders, if given free rein, would have chosen. This was true on the Catholic question as on other issues, and for the most part the Spanish Communists followed here the policy of *main tendue* articulated by the French Communist leader Maurice Thorez.

3. See, for example, José Díaz, *Tres Años de Lucha* (Paris: Colección Ebro, 1970), p. 313; on the question of expropriation, pp. 163–64.

4. The text, entitled "Episcopado Español a los Obispos de todo el Mundo: Sobre la Guerra de España," may be found in Jesús Iribarren (ed.), *Documentos Colectivos del Episcopado Español, 1870–1974* (Madrid: Editorial Católica, 1974), pp. 220–42.

5. Construction of the National Catholic edifice began prior to the end of the Civil War with the abrogation of civil matrimonial statutes and the readmission of the Jesuit order to Spain. Subsequent decree laws abolished civil divorce and established once again a state subsidy to the clergy. In June 1941, Spain and the Vatican signed an agreement granting the government a role in the designation of bishops. For some time, however, the Vatican did not entirely reciprocate the interest Franco had in fusing Church and State in Spain, preferring to wait for clarification of the domestic and international situation. In the end, after the failure of a guerrilla struggle led by Loyalist forces in the country and the development of Soviet-American rivalry into Cold War, the Vatican acquiesced to

what Franco sought and in August 1953 signed the Concordat. José Chao, *Después de Franco, España* (Madrid: Ediciones Fellmar, 1976), pp. 69–72, makes an an exhaustive list of its provisions. Popularization of the term "National Catholic" is attributed to José María González Ruiz by Fernando Urbina in "Formas de Vida de la Iglesia en España: 1939–1975." His is the first chapter in Rafael Belda et al., *Iglesia y Sociedad en España, 1939–1975* (Madrid: Editorial Popular, 1977). See p. 85. Use of the term goes back to the 1940s, but without the later connotations.

6. See chapters 5 ("La Iglesia en el Sindicalismo Vertical") and 7 ("El Concordato de 1953: Expresión Jurídica de las Relaciones entre la Iglesia y el Nuevo Estado") in Belda et al., ibid., pp. 207–39 and 283–312.

7. Ramón Chao, *La Iglesia en el Franquismo* (Madrid: Ediciones Fellmar, 1976), p. 83.

8. Particularly those of 1951 (on the economic crisis and the general scarcity), of 1956 (on a more equitable distribution of income) and of 1960 (on the Stabilization Plan). Casimiro Martí, "La Iglesia en la Vida Política," in Belda et al., *Iglesia y Sociedad en España, 1939–1975*, pp. 155–56.

9. The exchange led to a public confrontation between Solís and Pla y Deniel with the latter expressing his support of the HOAC and the charges leveled against it.

10. Symptomatically, the first national meeting of the *Comisiones Obreras* organization took place at a religious house in June 1967, and when, five years later, police arrested the principal leaders of the CC.OO., they did so at a retreat house located in Pozuelo de Alarcón on the outskirts of Madrid.

11. Citizens of Euzkadi, as the Basque country is otherwise known, and Cataluña had been among the most staunch supporters of the Republican side during the Civil War, and in its aftermath those regions had been treated virtually as occupied territories by the victors. Striving to emasculate (this word is strong but accurate) Basque and Catalan culture, the regime forbade public use of its indigenous languages. In these efforts, Franco and his backers received the support of the national Catholic Church hierarchy through its presence in the field of education; the Church actively furthered the "hispanification" of Euzkadi and Cataluña in the years after 1939.

12. Raymond Carr and Juan Pablo Fusi, *España, de la dictadura a la democracia* (Barcelona: Editorial Planeta, 1979), p. 201.

13. Indeed the *Assemblea de Catalunya*, a regional coalition of twenty political and cultural organizations, held its constituent meeting with three hundred people in attendance in the middle of Barcelona city in November 1971. Catalan Catholic opposition to the regime had its symbolic focal point in the Benedictine abbey of Montserrat located high in the mountains outside the capital of the region. There, first under the direction of Dom Aureli Escarré and later under his various successors, the flame of Catalan culture was kept alive. Escarré gave an interview to *Le Monde* (November 14, 1963) in which, among other things, he declared "We have not had twenty-five years of peace, just of victory." For this, the government exiled him and he returned only shortly before his death in 1968. The magazine published at Montserrat, *Serra d'Or,* had an influence which extended much beyond a limited circulation—it played an important role in legitimizing *catalanismo* as a political phenomenon in opposition to the Franco regime.

14. Guy Hermet, "Les fonctions politiques des organisations ré-

ligieuses dans les régimes à pluralisme limité," *Revue Française de Science Politique* 23 (June 1973):439–73.

15. This was the case not only in France and Portugal but even more so in Italy where Catholic participation with Communists and Socialists in the Resistance after the signing of the September 1943 Armistice was an important political event. There, something called the *Movimento dei Cattolici Comunisti* emerged, and one of its guiding lights, Franco Rodano, subsequently played a role of some importance in the development of Italian Communist strategy toward the Christian Democratic party and in the formulation of the *compromesso storico*. Although at this time and for some years to come, the Spanish Communists looked more to their French counterparts for political guidance, they nevertheless saw in the Italian experience what might happen in their own country. See Carlo Felice Casula, *Cattolici-Comunisti e sinistra cristiana, 1938–45* (Bologna: Il Mulino, 1976).

16. This was the title of an article in *Nuestra Bandera*, no. 15 (February 1947):127–38.

17. *Programa del Partido Comunista de España (V Congreso)* (n.p., n.d.), p. 13.

18. Dolores Ibárruri, *Informe del CC al Quinto Congreso del PCE* (1954), pp. 98, 152.

19. M. Oriol, "Ignacio Fernández de Castro y la Tercera Revolución," *Nuestras Ideas*, no. 10 (January 1961): 82–95, at 84.

20. Already in 1956, Dolores Ibárruri had spoken favorably of the trends at work in the Catholic Action movement (Guy Hermet, *Los Comunistas en España* [Paris: Ediciones Ruedo Ibérico, 1972], p. 59), and in subsequent years the PCE had instructed its militants in the labor movement not to neglect any opportunity for developing contacts and unity of action with the Catholic activists.

21. He used the phrase in the book/interview *Demain l'Espagne* (Paris: Editions du Seuil, 1974), p. 166.

22. John XXIII, *Pacem in Terris* (New York: Paulist Press, 1963), paragraphs 159–60 (edited by William J. Gibbons, S.J.).

23. José Guerra Campos, "Precisiones sobre el ateísmo marxista," *Realidad*, no. 5 (May 1965):3–8. The reply by Azcárate is in the same issue:9–34.

24. One by José María González Ruíz argued for a convergence between Marxists and socialists. José María González Ruíz, "El humanismo atéo y el Díos bíblico," *Realidad*, no. 5 (November 1965):33–42. Spokesmen for the PCE regularly appeared in the pages of the Prague-based *World Marxist Review* to talk about the importance of dialogue and collaboration with Catholics as well. For example, Santiago Alvarez, "Towards an Alliance of Communists and Catholics," *World Marxist Review* 8 (June 1965):40–47 and also his "Once More on the Catholic-Communist Alliance," *World Marxist Review* 11 (September 1968):70–78.

25. Santiago Carrillo, *Después de Franco, Qué?* (Paris: Editions Sociales, 1965), pp. 75–83.

26. Santiago Carrillo, *Nuevos Enfoques a Problemas de Hoy* (Paris: Editions Sociales, 1967), pp. 116–39.

27. In his discussion of church-state relations, Carrillo defended and praised the actions taken by governments in Poland and Hungary against the Catholic Church and other religions. Ibid., pp. 121–22.

28. *Le Monde*, November 4, 1970. Carrillo had made a similar formula-

tion in late 1963, at a PCF Central Committee plenum. See *Los Marxistas Españoles y la Religión* (Madrid: Editorial Cuadernos para el Diálogo, 1977), p. 84.

29. For a brief sketch of CpS, see the articles by Enrique Miret Magadalena in *Triunfo* (Madrid), April 2, 1977.

30. The text of the so-called Avila document may be found in Alfredo. Fierro Bardaji and Reyes Mate Rupérez (eds.), *Cristianos por el Socialismo: Documentación* (Pamplona: Editorial Verbo Divino, 1977), pp. 151–56. As one internationally renowned CpS activist, the Italian priest Giulio Girardi, put it: "Love does not exclude the class struggle but rather demands it. We cannot love the poor without joining their battle for liberation." Cited in Alfonso C. Comín, *Fe en la Tierra* (Bilbao: Editorial Desclée de Brouwer, 1975), p. 219.

31. See, for example, Reyes Mate, *El Desafío Socialista* (Salamanca: Ediciones Sígueme, 1975), pp. 39 and 48–77.

32. Nicholas Lobkowicz (ed.), *Marx and the Western World* (Notre Dame, Ind.: University of Notre Dame Press, 1967), p. 307. The comment is made by the editor in his chapter "Marx's Attitude Toward Religion."

33. Mate, *El Desafío Socialista*, p. 148.

34. Fierro and Mate, p. 156.

35. Some of its most prominent members like Reyes Mate, who wrote several books on the subjects discussed here, were independents. On the other hand, Juan N. García Nieto, a Jesuit priest who taught at ESADE in Barcelona, and participated actively in the *Comisiones Obreras*, had always been close to the Catalan Communist party. Another prominent member, Mariano Gamo, a priest in one of the satellite working-class cities which sprang up around Madrid during the period of intense economic development in the 1960s, would eventually run for Parliament on the ticket of the Maoist *Organización Revolucionaria de Trabajadores* in June 1977. And Alfonso Carlos Comín, the author of such books as *Per Una Estrategia Sindical* and *Fe en la Tierra,* was a member of the Catalan extreme Left group *Bandera Roja* before joining the PSUC in 1974. Other individuals like the ex-Jesuit theologian José María Díez Alegría and José María González Ruíz—might not have been formal members, but they were close to CpS and participated actively in its meetings and debates.

36. Alfonso C. Comín, *Fe en la Tierra,* p. 189.

37. Ibid., pp. 251–54.

38. Cited in Alfonso C. Comín, *Cristianos en el Partido, Comunistas en la Iglesia* (Barcelona: Editorial Laia, 1977), p. 74.

39. *Mundo Obrero,* March 19, 1975.

40. Federico Melchor, "Pero Pueden los Cristianos ser Comunistas?," *Nuestra Bandera,* nos. 79–80 (March–June 1975):22–29.

41. Ignacio Gallego, *Desarrollo del Partido Comunista* (Paris: Colección Ebro, 1976), pp. 177–90.

42. A variation on this theme was the statement made at the Madrid party school in October 1976 by fellow Executive Committee member José Sandoval, the man responsible for cultural and ideological affairs in the party, to the effect that religion would inevitably disappear once the social conditions justifying it had been eliminated. Alfonso C. Comín, *Cristianos en el Partido, Comunistas en la Iglesia* (Barcelona: Editorial Laia, 1977), p. 68.

43. "Declaración del Comité Central del Partit Socialista Unificat de Catalunya," dated September 1976. Also to be found in the Appendix, pp. 201–11 of Comín, *Cristianos*.

44. Manuel Sacristán, "La Militancia de cristianos en el P.C.," *Materiales*, no. 1 (January–February 1977):101–12.

45. The phrase is used by Juan José Ruíz Rico in his *El Papel Politico de la Iglesia Católica en la Espaã de Franco* (Madrid: Editorial Technos, 1977), p. 189.

46. These ranged from the pro-regime *Unión Democrática Española* headed by former Minister of Education Federico Silva Muñoz to José María Gil Robles' *Federación Popular Democrática*, right-of-Center but in the moderate opposition, and extended on the Left to Ruíz Giménez and his *Izquierda Democrática*. For brief but useful histories and analyses of the programs of FPD, ID, and UDE, see *Ya* (Madrid), August 12, 14 and 15, 1976. Also José Chao, *Después de Franco, España* (Madrid: Ediciones Fellmar, 1976), pp. 137–68.

3. The PCE and Labor

1. Ignacio Fernández de Castro and Antonio Goytre, *Clases Sociales en España en el Umbral de los Años '70* (Madrid: Siglo XXI, 1974), p. 281.

2. Ramón Bulnes, "Del Sindicalismo de Represión al Sindicalismo de Integración," *Horizonte Español 1966*, Vol. II, pp. 285–91. Also Eduardo Martín and Jesús Salvador, *Los Enlaces Sindicales* (Barcelona: Editorial Laia, 1976), p. 184.

3. The first started with a general strike in the Basque country and spread to other parts of the country, paralyzing some thirty thousand textile workers in Cataluña; the second began as a boycott of public transportation in Barcelona, spreading in subsequent weeks to the Basque country, and even to Madrid.

4. José María Maravall, *Dictatorship and Political Dissent: Workers and Students in Franco Spain* (London: Tavistock Publications, 1978), p. 69. In that last year, security forces also captured the Secretary General of the UGT in Spain, Tomás Centeno Sierra. He died under mysterious circumstances in the Madrid headquarters of the *Dirección Nacional de Seguridad*.

5. José Borrás, *Políticas de los Exiliados Españoles 1944–1958* (Paris: Ediciones Ruedo Ibérico, 1976), pp. 252–53.

6. Lluis Fina, "Político salarial i lluita de classes sota el franquisme," *Materiales* (Barcelona), no. 7 (January–February 1978):107.

7. For a detailed discussion of the process, see Joan Clavera et al., *Capitalismo Español: de la Autarquía a la Estabilización, 1939–1959* (Madrid: Editorial Cuadernos para el Diálogo, 1978). The industrial workers numbered approximately 2.5 million in 1940 and grew to nearly 5 million by 1964. Those placed under the category of *asalariados agrícolas*, on the other hand, dropped by five hundred thousand in the same period. See, José Félix Tezanos, *Estructura de Clases en la España Actual* (Madrid: Ediciones Cuadernos para el Diálogo, 1975), p. 47. For a general discussion of Spanish social structure, see Ignacio Fernández de Castro and Antonio Goytre, *Clases Sociales en España*.

8. Luis C. Nuñez, *Clases Sociales en Euzkadi* (San Sebastián: Editorial Txertoa, 1977), p. 163.

9. Clavera et al., *Capitalismo Espanol*, p. 248.

10. Jon Amsden, *Collective Bargaining and Class Conflict in Spain* (London: Weidenfeld and Nicholson, 1972).

11. These posts had been open to plant-level election since 1944 and 1953 respectively, but, insofar as *enlaces* and *jurados* had scant opportunity to function as representatives of their fellow workers, they had been of little importance.

12. Fernández de Castro, *Clases Sociales en España*, pp. 125–55.

13. Amsden, p. 62. Whereas in 1958 the new system affected fewer than twenty thousand workers, by 1962 that number had risen to 2 million.

14. Ibid., p. 92. For a statement by the ASO, see *Alianza Sindical Obrera: Nuestras Raíces, Nuestro Presente, Nuestro Futuro* (Ediciones Iberia, n.d.)

15. José Castaño Colomer, *La JOC en España* (1946–1970) (Salamanca: Ediciones Sígueme, 1978), pp. 90–92.

16. José María Maravall, *Dictatorship and Political Dissent*, p. 81. Lenin had suggested such a course in many of his writings and particularly in *"Left-Wing" Communism, An Infantile Disorder*. Georgi Dimitrov had emphasized the importance of such tactical flexibility in his principal speech to the Seventh Comintern Congress in 1935, and the Italian Communists had followed a similar policy during the Popular Front phase.

17. See, for example, the article which appeared in *Mundo Obrero*, October 15, 1957.

18. Amsden, pp. 94–95 and 99–100.

19. Fernando Claudín indicates the phrase *comisión obrera* first appeared in a PCE document in 1955, at which time the party urged these be made permanent. Lucio Magri et al., *Movimiento Obrero y Acción Política* (Mexico: Ediciones Era, 1975), p. 91. The PCE continued to talk of the *comisiones de obreros* as a base for the OSO until 1962. See *Nuestra Bandera*, no. 35 (IV Trimester, 1962):12–13.

20. Amsden, p. 96.

21. They were ready, PCE Secretary General Santiago Carrillo insisted, "to extend themselves even further and embrace in a shorter or longer space of time all of the working class." *Después de Franco, Qué?* (Paris: Editions Sociales, 1965), p. 34.

22. Useful selections of *Comisiones Obreras* documents may be found in *CC.OO. en sus Documentos (1958–1976)* (Madrid: Ediciones HOAC, 1977); Marco Calamai, *Storia del Movimento Operaio Spagnol dal 1960 al 1975* (Bari: DeDonato Editore, 1975); and, Vicente Romano, *Spain: The Workers' Commissions, Basic Documents 1966–1971* (Canadian Committee for a Democratic Spain, 1973).

23. For example, the modification of Article 222 of the Penal Code distinguished between political and economic ones and did not equate the latter with military sedition. They had also been particularly buoyed by the widely publicized remarks some young industrialists made to the effect that the present syndical structures were anachronistic and acted as a brake on economic development. See "Una Nueva Mentalidad? Jóvenes Patronos Españoles," *CRI*, no. 3 (October–November 1965):105.

24. Jesús Sanz Oller, *Entre el Fraude y la Esperanza, Las Comisiones Obreras de Barcelona* (Paris: Ediciones Ruedo Ibérico, 1972), p. 80.

25. *Le Monde* (Paris), March 16, 1967.

26. For a penetrating analysis upon which I draw heavily for my conclusions, see José María Maravall, *El Desarrollo Económico y la Clase Obrera* (Barcelona: Ediciones Ariel, 1970), pp. 109–68.

27. A leading PCE activist, Central Committee member, and former political commissar during the Civil War, Carlos Elvira González ran the offices of the *Delegación Exterior de Comisiones Obreras* in Paris and served as a major conduit for such funds. Another member of the PCE, Serafín Aliaga Lledo, a former Anarchosyndicalist, lived in Prague and as the International Secretary of the CC.OO. was the point man for contacts with the Czech-based WFTU.

28. *USO en sus Documentos, 1960–1975* (Madrid: Ediciones HOAC, 1976), p. 49 quoting from *Por un Sindicalismo de Clase. Qué es la USO?* (May 1975), pp. 21–22.

29. Characteristically, a splinter group like the *Partido Comunista (internacional)*, after splitting from the PCE/PSUC in April 1967, left the *Comisiones Obreras* as too "reformist" in May 1968 to set up something called the *Comisiones Obreras Revolucionarias*. Another group called *Bandera Roja* and active in Cataluña set up a rival *Coordinadoras de Sectores*. Even the AST, which unlike many other extreme Left groups entered rather than left *Comisiones* during this period, would also eventually part company with the PCE and boycott the meetings of the *Coordinadora General*.

30. Text in Calamai, *Storia del Movimento Operaio*, pp. 240–44.

31. See, for example, Santiago Carrillo, *Nuevos Enfoques a Problemas de Hoy* (Paris: Editions Sociales, 1967), pp. 41–50.

32. See the Executive Committee statement in *Mundo Obrero*, June 15–30, 1968. Also Santiago Alvarez, "The New Working Class Movement in Spain," *World Marxist Review*, 9 (December 1966):52.

33. José Antonio Díaz, *Luchas Internas en Comisiones Obreras, Barcelona 1964–1970* (Barcelona: Editorial Bruguera, 1977), pp. 25–34 and 44–48.

34. Most of those groups sought to overcome their organizational weakness vis-à-vis the PCE. A similar judgment would have to be made about their calls for *asambleismo* and their arguments that *Comisiones* leaders should serve only so long as they were not in jail and retained the confidence of their fellow workers. The anti-PCE thrust of insisting on the permanent revocability of leaders is evident, even if it drew on a justified disenchantment with the bureaucratization of what was once a spontaneous and independent working-class movement.

35. *CRI*, nos. 39–40, p. 60. Also Manuel Ludevid, *El Movimiento Obrero en Cataluña bajo el Franquismo* (Barcelona: Editorial Avance, 1977), p. 29.

36. The struggle between the two organizations did not involve broad masses of people. Indeed in 1968, at a time when both the CONC and COLB were locked in battle and called for a general strike against the regime, the latter had no more than three dozen militants actively involved in the labor movement in Barcelona. José Antonio Díaz, *Luchas Internas en CC.OO.*, pp. 38–39.

37. José María Maravall, *El Desarrollo*, pp. 169–229.

38. That year, it was the Metro in Madrid and construction in Seville and Granada; 1971, Harry Walker and SEAT in Barcelona and construction in Madrid; 1972, Bazán and Citröen-Hispana in El Ferrol and Vigo respectively; 1973, construction in Madrid and HUNOSA in Asturias; and 1974, in the Baix Llobregat and Standard in Madrid.

39. Some reports place the number of *enlaces sindicales* who lost their jobs for one reason or another in the period 1966 to 1975 at between thirty and fifty thousand. The lower figure is in Josep Picó, *El Moviment Obrer al Pais Valencia sota el Franquisme* (Valencia: Editorial Eliseu Climent, 1977), p. 26. The higher one is cited in *Boletín de la UGT,* no. 362 (September 1975) and in *El Correo Catalán* (Barcelona), June 17, 1975. On two occasions, the government arrested high-ranking leaders of the organization: Marcelino Camacho, Nicolás Sartorius, and Francisco García Salve and seven others fell into the hands of police while at a clandestine meeting of the *Coordinadora General* in June 1972 (this became the now-famous Proceso 1001 which attracted international attention and notoriety); a year later, police detained Rafael Pillado, Amor Deus, and twenty-one other Galician activists in El Ferrol.

40. Alfredo Tejero, "Auge y Crisis de Comisiones Obreras," *Materiales,* no. 3 (May–June 1977):45. For a flavor of the PCE documents on this matter, see the Central Committee statement and the Carrillo article "Salir a la Superficie" in *Nuestra Bandera,* no. 65 (III Trimester 1970):3–10 and 11–17 respectively.

41. Ernest Martí (Joaquim Sempere), in "Primeras Reflexiones en torno a las Elecciones Sindicales," *Nuestra Bandera,* no. 67 (II Trimester 1971):18, described such calls as *liquidacionismo con ropaje revolucionario.*

42. *Cambio16* (Madrid), July 7, 1965 for a discussion of the problems with the statistics. Also, ibid., October 27, 1975.

43. *Comisiones* won approximately 40 percent of the total number of *enlace* posts and and UGT 25 to 30 percent in 1978.

44. This was particularly the case in the metallurgical sector in Barcelona, Seville, Madrid (in the latter province, during the strikes of late 1975 and early 1976, the provincial *Unión de Trabajadores y Técnicos* paid the fines for those arrested for illegal labor activities and, at the height of the movement, the strike leaders grouped in the *Asamblea Provincial del UTT Metal* met openly in the offices of the national metallurgical union in downtown Madrid) and in the Baix Llobregat, where *Comisiones* activists captured important posts in the *comarcal* and *rama* levels of the *sindicato vertical.*

45. For example, at the top of a pyramidal structure based on 1,300,000 metallurgical workers, stood a president of the *Sindicato del Metal.* Thirty-nine people elected him.

46. See the thrust of remarks in Isidor Boix and Manuel Pujadas, *Conversaciones Sindicales con Dirigentes Obreros* (Barcelona: Editorial Avance, 1975).

47. Such as the one in June 1966 which declared the CC.OO. "are not today, and do not pretend to become tomorrow, a trade union." *Documentos Básicos de Comisiones Obreras* (DECO, n.d.), p. 1.

48. Thus, a bitter article in the PSUC weekly *Treball*—for the Boix views found their strongest support in Cataluña and to a lesser extent in the Basque country—decried the *concepción liquidacionista* and the *orientación legalista* which supposedly animated his arguments, January 5, 1976.

49. See the texts and speeches in "Segunda Conferencia del PCE," *Nuestra Bandera,* no. 81 (October 1975). Also important because it was a speech to party labor activists is Santiago Carrillo, "Las Tareas del Movimiento Obrero para que el Franquismo Desaparezca También," *Nuestra Bandera,* no. 82 (November 1975). It was a special issue with

only his speech in it. See also the report to the Third PSUC Central Committee plenum in October 1975 by Gregorio López Raimundo. Its title, "La Huelga General y el Papel Dirigente de la Clase Obrera" (n.p., n.d.).

50. *Nuestra Bandera*, no. 83 (January–February 1976):43–57.

51. See, for example, the *Documento de los 101* and the *Manifiesto de la Unidad Sindical* (both from January 1976) in *CC.OO. en sus Documentos 1958–1976* (Madrid: Ediciones HOAC, 1977), pp. 1–4 and 5–30.

52. The recent Portuguese experience—the Communist-controlled front called *Intersindical* had parlayed with the help of allies in the radical military their penetration of the vertical syndicates into control of the labor movement—weighed heavily on their minds. The Spanish Communists, of course, had criticized the PCP for its excessively aggressive behavior during the most turbulent months of the Portuguese revolution, but non-Communist trade union leaders did not forget that prior to this PCE leaders had praised the strategy and tactics the PCP followed in the labor movement. See the article by Gregorio López Raimundo, "La Experiencia del Bajo Llobregat," *Nuestra Bandera*, no. 76 (September–October 1974):40.

53. Jesús Prieto provides a good overview of the whole affair in *Cuadernos para el Diálogo*, June 19, 1976.

54. For the most important texts approved there, the reader should consult *Asamblea General de CC.OO.* (Barcelona: Editorial Laia, 1976).

55. For a discussion of the *unitarios*, see Fernando Almendrós Morcillo et al., *El Sindicalismo de Clase en España (1939–1977)* (Barcelona: Edicions 62, 1978), pp. 191–208. The PTE is the *Portido del Trabajo de España*.

56. Symptomatic of this complex was the statement Julián Ariza made during a speech to the *Asamblea General* where he declared that *Comisiones* "was not interested in having the workers see [it] as just one more trade union." See his speech entitled "Sobre la Alternativa y la Unidad Sindical" in *Asamblea General de CC.O.*, p. 61.

57. Francisco Frutos, "El nuevo movimiento obrero, Apuntes para un debate," *Materiales*, no. 7 (January–February 1978):73–84. There was a certain irony in having José María Rodríguez Rovira insist in the *Gaceta de Derecho Social*, no. 75 (July 1977), that it "would be an error . . . to view the Councils as something above the Trade Unions." Cited in Angel Fernández Lupión, "Algunas Notas sobre el futuro sindical en nuestro país," *Argumentos*, no. 4 (September 1977):16.

4. Ideology and Organization in the PCE

1. Santiago Carrillo, *"Eurocomunismo" y Estado* (Barcelona: Editorial Grijalbo, 1977), p. 23.

2. Membership figures available for 1937 indicate that the PCE had become an overwhelmingly middle-class organization: of the 300,000 members of the party claimed that year only 35 percent came from the industrial working class, and even that figure inflated the number of people of working class origin since it included an unspecified number of artisans and small shopkeepers. See the discussion in Guy Hermet, *Los Comunistas en España* (Paris: Ediciones Ruedo Ibérico, 1972), pp. 36–39.

3. In 1960, the PCE described the overthrow as coming after a series of well-coordinated strikes—*huelga general política* leading to the *huelga*

nacional—which would paralyze the country, but by mid-1976 even this mildly revolutionary approach had been cast aside, and the term *ruptura pactada* had entered the Spanish Communist lexicon: a formal agreement between the opposition and reformers within the regime to change the form and substance of government. The PCE did not look to the armed forces to play and active role in this enterprise. The thrust of its efforts aimed to insure military neutrality or, what was the same thing, its disengagement from the regime during the crisis. For example, Fabio Espinosa, "El Ejército en el Momento Político Actual," in *VIII Congreso* (Bucharest, 1972), pp. 233–49. This policy assumed another dimension after the Portuguese revolution in 1974–75 and the radicalization of the *Movimento das Forças Armadas*, namely, preventing a rightist reaction within the Spanish military.

4. Santiago Carrillo, *Después de Franco, Qué?* (Paris: Editions Sociales, 1965), pp. 15–99.

5. The PCE further argued that failure to destroy the economic power of the monopolies or to begin the construction of the *democracia política y social* immediately upon the overthrow of Franco would result in the installation of a new dictatorship in the country. This formulation was very similar to that of the Portuguese Communists. In their case, this assessment led ultimately in 1975 to the argument that the alternatives facing the country were either fascism or revolution. The Spanish were more careful. The *democracia política y social* would be a lengthy transitional stage, lasting for several decades during which time there would be a plurality of parties and broad freedom of expression, criticism and assembly. *VIII Congreso*, pp. 338–39.

6. *Programa Manifiesto del PCE* (n.p., n.d.) approved at the Second National Conference in September 1975. For a more general statement of the economic policies to be followed during the *democracia política y social*, see *Un Futuro para España: La Democracia Económica y Política* (Paris: Colección Ebro, 1967), particularly pp. 119–201.

7. Their owners would be paid compensation. The PCE Program Manifesto, although silent on the critically important question of what specific formula would be used in determining their remuneration, justified such a payment on the grounds that "the working class finds it cheaper, when possible, to pay a compensation, however unjust it may be from the point of view of equality, to a group of property owners who would otherwise be difficult to replace." *Programa Manifiesto*, p. 40.

8. See Santiago Carrillo, "La Lucha por el Socialismo Hoy," in *Problemas del Socialismo* (Paris: Colección Ebro, 1969), pp. 20–31.

9. The latter had made science the "central productive force" in the world and would bring about the eventual elimination of any distinction between intellectual and physical labor. Manuel Azcárate, "Algunas Consecuencias del Nuevo Papel de la Ciencia," *Realidad*, no. 23 (June 1972):3. Azcárate, of course, was not the first to advance this notion. Soviet theorists from Lenin on, including Khrushchev in the 1961 CPSU statutes, proposed the elimination of all distinctions between physical and mental work and the establishment of an "all-peoples' state." The USSR was declared to be such a state in the early 1960s.

10. Santiago Carrillo, *Demain l'Espagne* (Paris: Editions du Seuil, 1974), p. 180.

11. See the pamphlet "Algunos Aspectos de la Alianza de las Fuerzas del Trabajo y de la Cultura" of the PSUC Barcelona Committee, February 1973.

12. Emilio Quirós (Jaime Ballesteros), "Nuevas Características y Tareas del Frente Teórico y Cultural," in *VIII Congreso*, p. 223.

13. *Programa Manifiesto*, p. 31. Also Santiago Carrillo, *Demain l'Espagne*, pp. 186 and 189, as well as *Después de Franco, Qué?*, p. 91.

14. *Demain l'Espagne*, p. 190.

15. Individuals like Rudolf Hilferding of the Austro-Marxist school had already begun to describe and analyze this evolution in the second decade of this century.

16. Carrillo, *"Eurocomunismo,"* pp. 59–62.

17. Azcárate, p. 17. Santiago Carrillo's *"Eurocomunismo" y Estado*, published in early 1977 prior to the legalization of the party, contains the most explicit and complete statement the Spanish Communists have yet made on their strategy with respect to the state and bourgeois society. There, Carrillo urged the PCE and other forces on the Left to concentrate their efforts on undermining those ideological and coercive apparatuses (the former include the Church, the educational system, the judiciary and mass media; the latter, the armed forces and other organs of "direct" repression) which have traditionally functioned as sustaining elements of the existing order. Those apparatuses can, in his words, be "transformed and used, if not totally, then in part against the power of the state monopoly capitalist system" (p. 141).

18. Carrillo, *"Eurocomunismo,"* p. 103.

19. Such a view, it should be stressed, became official PCE doctrine only in the mid-1970s. At the Eighth PCE Congress in April 1972, party leaders held to the idea that a dictatorship of the proletariat had not become anachronistic, even while insisting that it was the "broadest and most complete democracy." See the report Carrillo presented to the Eighth PCE Congress, "Hacia la Libertad," in *VIII Congreso*, p. 81. Despite ambiguities which we shall take up shortly, the substance of the Spanish Communist evolution on this score went beyond that of the French and Portuguese parties which also dropped the phrase.

20. For an exposition of this thesis, Nicolás Sartorius, *El Resurgir del Movimiento Obrero* (Barcelona: Editorial Laia, 1975), pp. 52–87 and 99–113.

21. As might be expected, the programmatic redefinitions supported by Carrillo and others in the PCE leadership were sharply criticized both within and outside the party. Some of these harbored either pro-Soviet or pro-Chinese sympathies and railed against the abandonment of pristine Leninist principles. Enrique Líster, for example, accused of Carrillo of being nothing more than a *euro-oportunista*. Other, more significant criticisms came from the group coalescing around Manuel Sacristán and the journal *Materiales* and former PCE Executive Committee member Fernando Claudín.

See the articles "A Propósito del libro de Santiago Carrillo, 'Eurocomunismo' y Estado," *Materiales*, no. 4 (July–August 1977):5–18; Antoni Domenèch, "Crisis del capitalismo, 'eurocomunismo,' perspective revolucionaria," no. 5 (September–October 1977):43–58; and Manuel Sacristán, "A Propósito del 'eurocomunismo,'" no. 16 (November–December 1977):5–14; Julio Rodríguez Aramberri, "La Contradicción del estado burgués," no. 7 (January–February 1978):7–30. Also in the latter issue, the articles "Sobre Algunos Aspectos del Proyecto de Programa del PSUC" by Francisco Fernández Buey (31–46) and "Nota sobre la 'alianza de las fuerzas del trabajo y de la cultura'" by Jácobo Muñoz (47–51).

Although by no means in total agreement with each other, Claudín and Sacristán criticized what they saw as the theoretical eclecticism and vacuousness into which the PCE was falling and the pollyannaish view of the state propounded by the Communist leaders. Sacristán and his supporters decried the notion that the socialization of the *aparato del estado* would be effected by the entry of people from lower classes into the state. This, they claimed, overestimated the probable success of efforts to penetrate the state apparatus: not only had most parts of the state been impregnated by a profit-making logic, making them unusable for socialist purposes, but most of the critical decision-making centers had been shifted from domestic to multinational points. Muñoz, "Nota sobre la 'alianza de las fuerzas del trabajo y de la cultura,'" p. 50.

PCE advocacy of a relatively long transition period characterized by relative social peace (the *democracia política y social*) also came under fire as unrealistic. As shrewd a politician as Carrillo could not believe in this scenario and held to it only for propagandistic reasons, Claudín insisted; with its strong anticapitalist thrust the *democracia* could not be held for long at the merely antimonopolist level. Fernando Claudín, *Eurocomunismo y Socialismo* (Madrid: Siglo 21, 1977), pp. 119–32.

Also attacked was the supposed "proletarization" of the *fuerzas de la cultura*, a concept upon which so many of the positions adopted by the PCE hinged. This was, in the view of the critics, at best a *tendential* process, and qualitative modifications were necessary in technology, science, and the organization of the work-place before these could serve the socialist society. Muñoz, "Nota sobre 'la alianza,'" p. 50.

22. Freedom of assembly, he declared to the first Comintern Congress in 1919, was "an empty phrase in the most democratic of bourgeois republics." Cited in Claudín, *Eurocomunismo y Socialismo* (Madrid: Siglo XXI, 1977), p. 92. The quote is from V.I. Lenin, *Collected Works* (Sp. ed.), Vol. 28, p. 462.

23. *VIII Congreso*, pp. 338–39. More recently, Santiago Carrillo called on the Communists to have "a more fundamental appreciation of democracy," and Manuel Azcárate, in a remarkable essay in the journal *Argumentos* declared that "liberty was a *metapolitical* necessity of social progress." (Emphasis mine) The references are to "Eurocomunismo," p. 110, and "El Tema de las Libertades Hoy" in *Argumentos*, no. 1 (May 1977):14, respectively.

24. See *Le Monde*, July 14–15, 1977 for the text of the one with the PCI and *Mundo Obrero;* March 10, 1977, for the one from the tripartite summit in Madrid. The Communist draft constitution is in *Nuestra Bandera*, no. 86 (March–April 1977):57–59.

25. See, for example, the interview Carrillo gave to *La Stampa* (Turin), December 14, 1974. The PCE's ideas on this score draw heavily but nevertheless diverge, as do those of the PCI, from the original Gramscian concept of hegemony as equivalent to the dictatorship of the proletariat.

26. Santiago Carrillo, "Eurocomunismo," pp. 129–31. See also his *Escritos sobre Eurocomunismo* (Madrid: Forma Ediciones, 1977), Vol. I pp. 84–86.

27. Indeed, they were less than reassuring about their hegemonic intentions (or lack thereof) when they cited the Popular Front as the prototype of the "new political formation" and, more startlingly, as a situation where there was "a permanent and free contrast of opinions." See the introduction Carrillo wrote for José Díaz, *Tres Años de Lucha* (Paris: Colección Ebro, 1970), p. ix.

28. See Ignacio Gallego, *El Desarrollo del Partido Comunista* (Paris: Colección Ebro, 1976), Sartorius has claimed the PCE has (see *El Sindicalismo de Nuevo Tipo* [Barcelona: Editorial Laia, 1977], p. 45) "the most perfected, scientific, and refined instrument for analysis" in Marxism-Leninism. The last phrase in the sentence is from Jaime Ballesteros, "El Partido Comunista en los Umbrales de la Democracia," *Nuestra Bandera*, no. 85 (n.d.):15.

29. For example, Nicolás Sartorius bluntly stated that "the autonomy of the labor movement is only real if there exist worker parties and these fulfill their leading role." *El Resurgir del Movimiento Obrero* (Barcelona: Editorial Laia, 1975), p. 76. Also Marcelino Camacho, *Charlas en la Prisión* (Barcelona: Editorial Laia, 1976), p. 16, and Sartorius, "Movimiento y Organización," *Nuestra Bandera*, no. 83 (January–February 1976):56.

Certainly, the PCE has not been as forthrightly disdainful of mass movements as Lenin in *What is to be Done?*, but the theoretical prism through which it viewed labor still held as a fundamental premise the condescending notion that such movements (and, more generally, the working class) were objects into which consciousness had to be instilled. Sartorius, to take the most prominent labor ideologue of the party, could thus write about the "eminently dialectical" relation which needed to be established between party and trade union (Nicolás Sartorius, *El Sindicalismo de Nuevo Tipo*, pp. 155–56). As Carrillo noted, when push comes to shove, Communists active in *Comisiones*, whether at the base or in leading bodies, "owed themselves to the party." There may be some controversy over whether my quote of the Carrillo phrase is taken out of context. I do not think so. Here is the paragraph in question:

> The militants of the Party who act in *Comisiones Obreras*, although they have a latitude while acting in these and trying to achieve a unitary synthesis which in each moment responds to the collective interests of the workers, are not, personally independent of the Party; they cannot pay homage to simple, elementary spontenaiety, [thus] lowering the role of revolutionary conscience. They respond for their work to the *Comisiones Obreras;* but as Communists they respond as well to the Party and owe themselves to it. So long as the Party does not infringe on its own principles, its own line, with mistaken decisions, there is no danger that any conflict emerge between those double responsibilities. If some [conflict] does emerge it is because something has failed in the labor *partidaria* which has to be checked.

This is from Santiago Carrillo, *Hacia el Post-Franquismo* (Paris: Colección Ebro, 1974), p. 76. All that is known about PCE and *Comisiones* relations during the Franco era suggests a very close relationship of mutual support between the two. Even so, the Communist labor leader Marcelino Camacho dared to insist that "never in any Central Committee of the party are the tactics, program or anything of the *Comisiones Obreras* discussed." *Cambio16*, November 6, 1977, p. 46.

30. Ignacio Gallego, *El Partido de Masas* (Madrid: Editorial Cénit, 1977), pp. 17–23.

31. Santiago Carrillo, *"Eurocomunismo,"* p. 208.

32. Ibid., p. 212.

33. Ibid., pp. 105 and 208.

34. Manuel Azcárate, "El Movimiento Revolucionario Internacional," p. 70 in Tomás García and Manuel Azcárate, *Temas de Política y Sociedad: Cuestiones Internacionales* (Madrid: Editorial Cénit, 1977).

See also Azcárate, "Problemes i Perspectives d l'eurocomunisme," *Taula de Cunvi* (Barcelona), Extra no. 1 (June 1978):24–33.

35. Santiago Carrillo, *Escritos sobre Eurocomunismo*, vol. 1, p. 39. This is taken from a September 1973 Central Committee report.

36. *Mundo Obrero*, October 22, 1969. Cited in Hermet, *Los Comunistas en España*, p. 155. See also Carrillo in *Nuevos Enfoques a Problemas de Hoy* (Paris: Ediciones Sociales, 1967), p. 182, when he warned that a socialist government would move forcefully against "any actions which tend to subvert the new social order."

37. Fernando Claudín, "The Split in the Spanish Communist Party," *New Left Review* (London), no. 71 (November–December 1971):76.

38. *Mundo Obrero*, February 27, 1974 and January 19, 1977. The foreign policy bulletin of the PCE, *Información Internacional*, no. 6 (February 1977):10–12 carried the text of the Charter 1977 document.

39. Santiago Carrillo, *Demain l'Espagne* (Paris: Editions du Seuil, 1974), p. 146.

40. See his "Libertades Políticas y Socialismo" in *Alkarrilketa 2*, no. 2 (1970):13–15. Azcárate, it should be said in the interest of fairness, has told the author he no longer holds to that opinion.

41. See the discussion in Franco Ferrarotti, "The Italian Communist Party and Eurocommunism," in Morton A. Kaplan, ed., *The Many Faces of Communism* (New York: The Free Press, 1978), pp. 43–47. Also Donald L.M. Blackmer, "Continuity and Change in Italian Communism," in Donald L.M. Blackmer and Sidney Tarrow, eds., *Communism in Italy and France* (Princeton: Princeton University Press, 1975), pp. 34–40.

42. See Santiago Carrillo in his *Informe del Comité Central* (Sixth PCE Congress, December 1955), p. 99.

43. A close reading of the Spanish and Communist press in recent years as well as conversations with PCE members leads me to the conclusion that in early 1977 the Communists were lucky if they had 35,000 members. The emigré Communist organization had approximately 7,000 of these. Other important PCE centers were in Madrid (7,000), Barcelona (5,000), and Asturias (3,000). In Cataluña, the PSUC had fewer that 5,000 members in February 1977, according to an official document of the Barcelona provincial organization. Apparently, in Madrid, 80 percent of PCE members entered after April 1977. *Diario16*, March 17, 1978.

44. Another important step in this respect came on the crucial issue of defining the rights and obligations of party membership. Thus, Santiago Carrillo in his report to the Central Committee talked about the necessity of accepting varying degrees of involvement in party life and of a party composed of *adherentes, militantes*, and *cuadros*. See the report Carrillo delivered to the PCE Central Committee meeting in Rome in July 1976 entitled *De la Clandestinidad a la Legalidad* (n.p., n.d.), pp. 61–64.

45. Thus, in Madrid, the provincial leadership associated with Executive Committee member Víctor Díaz Cardiel dissolved the highly politicized and critical lawyers' *agrupación*, blasting the undue influence professionals and intellectuals had in the *dirección política* of the party and warning of the risks this entailed for the "de-naturalization" of the PCE. The phrase is taken from the opening speech he gave in March 1978 at the Madrid provincial conference at which the author was present. See also the *Informe sobre la Política Organizativa* (n.p., n.d) presented at the conference, pp. 7–8.

46. One of the few exceptions—aside from Carrillo and his book/interview *Demain l'Espagne*—is Manuel Azcárate in the interview he

gave to *El País Semanal* (Madrid), April 2, 1978, pp. 10–13. One reason he consented to questions on this period was in part to rebut the charges leveled at him and others in the Spanish Communist leadership by Jorge Semprún in the *Autobiografía de Federico Sánchez* (1977). Speculation on events during this time is only fueled by Spanish Communist unwillingness to address questions on this score forthrightly.

47. Enrique Líster, *Basta!* (Madrid: G. del Toro Editor, 1978), pp. 245–49. Líster has become a passionate opponent of Carrillo, so we have to take his accounts with a grain of salt. Nevertheless, the charges ring true, given the general paranoia in the Soviet Union in the late 1940s and early 1950s.

48. The phrase is cited in José Borrás, *Políticas de los Exiliados Españoles: 1944–1958* (Paris: Ediciones Ruedo Ibérico, 1956), p. 50. See also the editorial written by Santiago Carrillo in *Nuestra Bandera*, no. 4 (1950) and quoted in Líster, *Basta!*, pp. 233–37.

His was certainly not an isolated case. Spanish Communist guerrillas, acting under instruction from the leadership, executed a dissident Communist leader, León Trilla, in 1945. Hermet, *Los Comunistas en España*, p. 50. He notes that the PCE claims Trilla was a criminal acting under the cover of the guerrilla struggle against Franco. Trilla had been a deputy to Heriberto Quiñones in the early 1940s and there may have been a settling of accounts. See Líster, *Basta!*, pp. 238–39.

Joan Comorera, the first Secretary General of the PSUC, and some Basque Communists tried to break the control exercised over their respective regional parties by the parent PCE organization, For their trouble they were expelled in 1948 and accused of being Titoists. At the height of the campaign against Comorera, the clandestine Communist transmitter *Radio España Independiente*, in what was tantamount to a death sentence for anyone living in Spain, accused him of "being openly at the service of the Francoist police and serving in the repugnant role of informant." The text of the broadcast by *Radio España Independiente* and other information may be found in Líster, *Basta!*, pp. 228–33.

49. Santiago Carrillo, *La Situación en la Dirección General del Partido y los Problemas del Reforzamiento del Mismo* (n.p., August, 1956).

50. For documents relating to this split, see Fernando Claudín, *Documentos de una Divergencia Comunista* (Barcelona: Iniciativas Editoriales, 1978). A more personal and passionate account may be found in Jorge Semprún, *Autobiografía de Federico Sánchez* (Barcelona: Editorial Planeta, 1977). Sánchez was Semprún's *nom de guerre*. The analysis contained in this paragraph relies primarily on these books.

51. In any case and whatever his reasons, Carrillo forced the suspension of Claudín and Semprún from their posts in the Executive Committee and then opted at an April 1964 meeting of cadres in the Parisian suburb of Stains to violate a tacit agreement not to discuss the issues in public until the Central Committee had had a chance to ratify that suspension by openly attacking the two men. He rejected their demands for a general discussion and the distribution of the rival platforms. In early 1965, coinciding with the announcement of their expulsion, a Claudín text was published in the theoretical journal *Nuestra Bandera*: it was in small print with an official rebuttal in much larger letters interspersed throughout the pages.

52. Immediately after learning that Warsaw Pact forces had entered Prague, Marcelino Camacho, who was in jail at the time, convened the

group composed of Communist party members and sympathizers and explained why the intervention had been necessary; shortly thereafter, he learned of the decision taken by the Executive Committee and rectified the mistake. Francisco Garcia Salve, *Por qué somos comunistas* (Madrid: Penthalon Ediciones, 1982), p. 76.

53. *Estatutos del Partido Comunista de España—Aprobados en su VIII Congreso*, 1972 (n.p., n.d.).

54. See, for example, *Mundo Obrero*, April 11, 1973. There it is said that "fractions lead to nothing but self-elimination in politics." Also Ignacio Gallego, "El Centralismo Democrático en el Partido," *Nuestra Bandera*, no. 65 (III Trimester 1970):18–24, and Jaime Ballesteros, "El Partido Comunista en los umbrales de la democracia," *Nuestra Bandera*, no. 85 (n.d.):13–18.

55. Santiago Carrillo, *Demain l'Espagne* (Paris: Editions du Seuil, 1974), p. 121.

56. The best articles to appear on the PSUC in the Spanish press in 1977 were those by Alfons Quintà in *El País* (Madrid) and Enrique Sopena in *Informaciones* (Madrid). I rely here on the typology developed by Quintà.

57. "Socialistes i Comunistes Davant la Democracia," *Taula de Canvi*, no. 2 (November–December 1976):51.

5. The Foreign Policy of the PCE

1. Ignacio Gallego, "La Lucha contra el Titoismo es un Deber Revolucionario de los Comunistas," *Nuestra Bandera*, no. 4 (February–March 1950):169–91.

2. *Mundo Obrero*, November–December 1956.

3. See the article by Juan Diz (Manuel Azcárate) entitled "Sobre las Posiciones Revisionistas de la Liga de los Comunistas de Yugoeslavia" in *Nuestra Bandera*, no. 21 (July 1958):53–74.

4. *Scinteia* (Bucharest), April 15, 1966. Also, in *Nuestra Bandera*, nos. 49–50 (May–June 1966):87–88.

5. *Pravda* (Moscow), September 16, 1963.

6. See the text in *Nuestra Bandera*, no. 37 (III/IV Trimester 1963):45.

7. Santiago Carrillo, *Nuevos Enfoques a Problemas de Hoy* (Paris: Editions Sociales, 1967), p. 140.

8. *Izvestia* (Moscow), December 12, 1967.

9. Santiago Carrillo, "La Lucha por el Socialismo Hoy," *Nuestra Bandera*, no. 58 (June 1968):41. The call for a new offensive thrust in all aspects of a Communist party's work was evident in many of Carrillo's writings, and he obviously considered it necessary not only for the PCE but other parties as well.

10. *Mundo Obrero*, May 1, 1968.

11. See the document issued on the Bratislava conference in *Nuestra Bandera*, no. 53 (III Trimester 1968):105–16.

12. *Le Monde*, October 23, 1970. This incident is recounted in a lengthy article by K. S. Karol.

13. *FBIS* (Western Europe), January 3, 1969, p. X2.

14. Ibid., July 3, 1969, p. X1, and *Mundo Obrero*, October 7, 1969. The inordinate length of time it took the party to convey the news formally to its organizations suggests that behind-the-scenes maneuvering was taking place. It is, for example, known that at the June 1969 Moscow Confer-

ence, representatives of the CPSU (including at least Boris Ponomarev) met with the heads of the Spanish delegation, Santiago Carrillo and Dolores Ibárruri, in an effort to convince them to modify PCE criticism of Soviet actions. Líster, *Basta!*, p. 70 and 99–100. María Eugenia Yagüe, *Santiago Carrillo* (Madrid: Editorial Cambio16, 1977), pp. 128–29. Interestingly, the speech delivered by Carrillo at the conference was much milder than one might have expected and, unlike the Communist parties of Australia, Italy, San Marino, and Reunion, the PCE approved the Basic Document issued at the conclusion of the meeting. Similarly, Enrique Líster has revealed that in the wake of his expulsion from the Spanish party delegations from the Central Committee met with Eduardo García several times between April and October, the last time just as the issue of *Mundo Obrero* announcing his resignation was being distributed. Líster, *Basta!*, p. 90.

15. Líster, ibid., pp. 56–57.

16. The phrase is from a letter sent by the Executive Committee to Líster which the latter quotes in *Basta!*, p. 137.

17. "Le Ultime Vicende del PC Spagnolo," *Rinascita* 27 (February 6, 1970):10–11.

18. *Rinascita* 27 (October 23, 1970):23–24.

19. *Scinteia*, June 15, 1969 and December 8, 1970.

20. *L'Humanité* (Paris), November 4, 1970.

21. *Nuestra Bandera*, no. 60 (December 1968–January 1969):55–62.

22. *Mundo Obrero* (dissident), June 1–15 1971. Perhaps the most significant aspect of the meeting was that the French delegation headed by Raymond Guyot, a member of the PCF's Politburo, sided with the forces arrayed in opposition to the dissidents. That even the French Communists, the most conservative of the major nonruling Communist parties, were actively moving to defend Carrillo and Ibárruri indicated that the dissidents had a difficult, if not impossible, road ahead.

23. Ibid., October 1–15, 1972.

24. Ibid., June 5, 1971.

25. For the contents of the article, see *FBIS* (Western Europe), May 28, 1971, pp. X1–2; June 4, 1971, pp. X1–2; and June 14, 1971, pp. X1–2.

26. The previous summer, a five-man Central Committee delegation had returned from Moscow, having secured mention in a communiqué that the "PCE was at present the principal force—not the only one, but the principal one—of the Spanish revolutionary present and of its democratic and socialist future." *Mundo Obrero*, September 7, 1972.

These concessions so exacerbated differences within the dissident group that its ranks split in late 1972. The group's Central Committee met in January 1973 and voted to dismiss Eduardo García, Agustín Gómez, and Alvaro Galiana (the "three G's" in the Spanish lexicon of the time) from their posts on the Executive Committee. The Líster faction, victors in the internal dogfight, criticized García and his followers for setting a "dogmatic-sectarian" policy whose objective, they claimed, was to turn the dissidents into a pressure group for the USSR. See Líster's speech to the newly named *Partido Comunista Obrero Español* in *Nuestra Bandera* (dissident-Líster), April 1974, pp. 3–35.

García, who continued to publish his own version of the party newspaper *Mundo Obrero* and organized subsequently a group called *PCE-VIII y IX Congreso*, in turn charged Líster with anti-Sovietism. Both accusations were by and large absurd, but they nevertheless reflected the different notions each leader had of the role dissidents should play. García conceived of that role as a catalyst to activate a broader movement within the party to correct the deviations made by Carrillo and his obdurate supporters, while Líster (and the documents his group published after the split confirm this) was against such a passive role and thought that, even if the Soviets did not understand the importance of quickly dealing with Carrillo and the other "revisionists," he would at least fashion his own revolutionary, orthodox party in much the same way that pro-Soviet Communists had "bolshevized" the old-time Socialist parties in the early 1920s.

27. "Más Problemas Actuales del Socialismo," *Nuestra Bandera*, no. 59 (II Trimester 1970):41–53.

28. See the text of his speech in *Conferencia Internacional de los Partidos Comunistas y Obreros* (Prague: Editorial Paz y Socialismo, 1969), pp. 381–94.

29. See Ernest Martí, "Problemas Ideológicos y el Frente Cultural," *Nuestra Bandera*, no. 64 (II Trimester 1970) as translated in *FBIS* (Western Europe), August 27, 1970, pp. X1–4 and September 3, 1970, pp. X1–4. And Juan Diz, "La Lucha Antidogmática," *Nuestra Bandera* no. 65 (III Trimester, 1970):73–81.

30. Santiago Carrillo, in fact, declared that the socialist countries had become the "rear guard" of the international working class movement in the contemporary era. *Demain l'Espagne* (Paris: Editions du Seuil, 1974), p. 149.

31. *Mundo Obrero*, December 10, 1979.

32. The articulation of this strategy and model has been given the appellation of Eurocommunism by the Yugoslav expatriate Frane Barbieri, who apparently coined the term in June 1975 when he described in the Milan newspaper *Il Giornale* the positions adopted by the PCI and PCE at Livorno.

33. For example, Juan Gómez, "Algunas Verdades Elementales Sobre la Integración," *Nuestra Bandera*, no. 31 (July–August 1961):37–52. Contrast his "Sobre el Mercado Común Europeo," *VIII Congreso del PCE* (Bucharest, 1972):207–16.

34. Manuel Azcárate, "Sobre Algunos Problemas de la Política Internacional del Partido," in ibid., pp. 183–206.

35. For the version broadcast by Radio Moscow, see *FBIS* (Soviet Union), February 16, 1974, pp. A1–10. Azcárate's report may be found in *Nuestra Bandera*, no. 72 (1973):15–30.

36. *Pravda*, October 16, 1974.

37. *Triunfo* (Madrid), July 3, 1976.

38. Gregorio López Raimundo, "Reflexiones Sobre la Revolucion Portuguesa," *Treball* (Barcelona), May 21, 1974.

39. *Mundo Obrero*, May 8, 1974.

40. Ibid., June 4, 1974.

41. Eusebio Mujal-León, "The PCP and the Portuguese Revolution," *Problems of Communism* 26 (January-February 1977):21–41.

42. *Il Manifesto* (Rome), November 1, 1975.

43. See, for example, the article entitled, "Una Necesidad Nacional: Que Desaparezcan las Bases Yanquis en España" by Enrique Líster (at the time in charge of international affairs for the PCE) in *Mundo Obrero*, October 1, 1960, and "Por la Cancelación de los Acuerdos Militares con los EE. UU.," a statement of the Central Committee in *Nuestra Bandera*, nos. 56–57 (III–IV 1967–1968):154–56.

44. *Mundo Obrero*, July 31, 1974.

45. See, for example, a Carrillo interview in the *New York Times*, August 7, 1976 and also in *Cuadernos para el Diálogo*, July 17, 1976.
46. *L'Humanité*, February 9, 1974. For extracts of the Carrillo speech, see *Dossier API* (Barcelona), no. 9, March 1974, pp. 13–14.
47. Press conference mimeograph, March 3, 1977 (n.p., n.d.), p. 4.
48. See, in particular, chapter 6, "Sobre la Dictadura del Proletario" in *"Eurocomunismo" y Estado* (Barcelona: Editorial Grijalbo, 1977).
49. "Contrary to the Interests of Peace and Socialism in Europe, Concerning the book *"Eurocommunism" and the State* by Santiago Carrillo, General Secretary of the Communist Party of Spain," *New Times* (Moscow), no. 26 (June 1977):9–13.
50. Fernando Claudín, "Eurocommunisme: L'Aggression Sovietique," *Politique Hebdo* (Paris), July 4–10, 1977, p. 6.
51. Gian Carlo Pajetta, head of the delegation and someone who had never developed good relations with either Carrillo or Azcárate, remarked upon his return from Moscow that the Italian party was "against sacred texts and . . . did not like the idea of Carrillo becoming at one stroke the prophet of Eurocommunism simply because he wrote a book." *Cuadernos para el Diálogo*, July 16, 1977.
52. *L'Humanité*, July 7, 1977.

6. The PCE and the Politics of Transition

1. For a useful overview of these groups, see Xavier Raufer's article in *Est et Ouest* (Paris), March 16–31, 1976, pp. 12–20.
2. With respect to the PSOE, I have relied on selected issues of *El Socialista* published biweekly in Brussels and Toulouse and various books. Among them, Felipe González and Antonio Guerra, *Socialismo es Libertad y Notas para una Biografía* (Barcelona: Ediciones Galbá, 1978); José Manuel Arija, *Nicolás Redondo* (Madrid: Editorial Cambio 16, 1977); Ramón Chao, *Después de Franco, España* (Madrid: Ediciones Fellmar, 1976), pp. 211–32; and, Sergio Vilar, *La Oposición a la Dictadura* (Barcelona: Editorial Aymá, 1976), pp. 165–81.
3. The effort was widely publicized in early 1978 as a result of reporting done on the polemics caused by publication of Jorge Semprún's *Autobiografía de Federico Sánchez* (Barcelona: Editorial Planeta, 1977). See *Cambio16*, January 22, 1978.
4. Thus, at one point Santiago Carrillo compared the Spanish Communist position in late 1971 to that of the PSOE in 1930. Santiago Carrillo, in an interview with *La Nouvelle Critique* (Paris), October–November 1977, p. 24. The thrust of his message was clear to those who knew something about Spanish history: 1930 was the year before the instauration of the Second Spanish Republic, and, in the June 1931 Constituent Assembly elections, the PSOE had emerged as the dominant party on the Left, capturing 105 out of 470 seats.
5. *International Herald Tribune* (Paris), September 27, 1974.
6. Santiago Carrillo, *Nuevos Enfoques a Problemas de Hoy* (Paris: Editions Sociales, 1967), pp. 25–32, 95–101, and 111–16.
7. See the report Carrillo presented in the name of the Central Committee in *VIII Congreso del PCE* (Bucharest, 1972), pp. 21–31.
8. *Mundo Obrero*, September 5, 1973.
9. Ibid., May 8, 1974.
10. The PSOE leadership had some difficulty enforcing the decision to

abstain once this *Junta Democrática* took shape. In places like the Canary Islands, the party federation initially joined the *Junta* and left only after intense pressure from the national organization.

11. See the text of the declaration in *Mundo Obrero*, July 29, 1974.

12. *Mundo Obrero*, September 18, 1974, carried a commentary on a Reuters news dispatch to this effect.

13. The British Communist newspaper, *Morning Star* (London), March 24, 1976 cited unofficial sources to the effect that the UMD had a membership which included 461 captains, 11 majors, 54 lieutenant colonels, 21 colonels, and 5 general officers.

14. The Communists recognized this difference in the Portuguese and Spanish situations early on, and they wanted the armed forces in Spain to remain neutral and not become actively involved in politics. See the statement by Executive Committee member Santiago Alvarez in *Nuestra Bandera*, no. 75 (May–June 1974):33.

15. The text of their manifesto can be found in the *Mundo Obrero* (June 15–30, 1973 issue) put out by the pro-Soviet faction then challenging Carrillo.

16. The *Junta*, spurred on by the PCE, demanded the self-exile of the newly crowned King Juan Carlos while a referendum was organized to decide the fate of the monarchy and the immediate constitution of a provisional government with the participation of all the opposition.

17. Carrillo first used the expression in his report to the Eighth PCE Congress in August 1972. See *VIII Congreso del PCE* (Bucharest, 1972), p. 7. However, Luis Ramírez may have come up with the expression initially. See *Horizonte Español 1972* (Paris: Ediciones Ruedo Ibérico, n.d.), vol.1, p. 1.

18. Interview with Carrillo in *l'Humanité* (Paris), October 25, 1976.

19. *Mundo Obrero*, 3d week of April, 1975.

20. See Victor Díaz Cardiel et al., *Madrid en Huelga, Enero 1976* (Madrid: Editorial Ayuso, 1976).

21. *Mundo Obrero*, April 9, 1976.

22. *El Europeo* (Madrid), June 19, 1976.

23. José María Gil Robles, "Esquema de un Camino Hacia la Democracia" (Madrid), May 1976.

24. *Newsweek*, April 26, 1976.

25. The first reference is to remarks in *Cuadernos para el Diálogo* (Madrid), July 10, 1976; the second, to *Mundo Obrero*, July 14, 1976.

26. The point is made in Eugenio Nasarre's "Ponencia sobre Estrategia Política," mimeograph, October 12, 1976 delivered at a meeting of the Christian Democratic leadership at Miraflores.

27. Santiago Carrillo, "De la Clandestinidad a la Legalidad," July 1976, pp. 9–11.

28. *Mundo Obrero*, September 15, 1976.

29. Ibid., October 27, 1976.

30. General statements of the Communist position in this regard may be found in Dolores Ibárruri, *España, Estado Multinacional* (Paris: Editions Sociales, 1971) and in Santiago Alvarez, "Notas sobre el Problema Nacional en España," *Nuestra Bandera*, no. 84 (March–April 1976):13–25.

31. *Mundo Obrero*, July 7, 1976 carried an article by Ernest Martí (Joaquim Sempere of the PSUC Executive Committee) making this point.

32. Ibid, June 11, and July 26, 1976.

33. Manuel Azcárate, *"Nuestra Bandera,* Hoy," *Nuestra Bandera,* no. 85 (n.d.):3.

34. *Cuadernos para el Diálogo,* June 19, 1976. The *Manifiesto de la Unidad Sindical* issued in January 1976 may be found in *CC. OO. en sus Documentos, 1958–1976* (Madrid: Ediciones HOAC, 1977), Appendix, pp. 5–30.

35. Carlos Elvira, "De la Ruptura Democrática al Sindicalismo Unitario," *Nuestra Bandera,* no. 83 (January–February 1976):26–30.

36. *Mundo Obrero,* October 6, 1977.

37. *Informaciones,* January 27, 1977.

38. *Cambio16,* May 1, 1977 and *El País,* May 24, 1977.

39. Santiago Carrillo, "Informe Presentado al CC," mimeograph, April 1977.

40. *Informaciones,* March 14, 1977.

41. *Mundo Obrero,* April 16, 1976. The move, in any case, was not without its historical ironies. In December 1967, in one of the first public signs of disagreement with the Soviet Union, Carrillo had taken the Soviets to task for publishing an article in *Izvestia* suggesting that a monarchy-led transition might be a viable path to the post-Franco era. The PCE, then at the height of its insistence that the opposition could bring the regime down by means of a *huelga general,* vehemently rejected a stance reality would force it to accept ten years later.

42. *Cuadernos para el Diálogo,* May 28, 1977.

7. The Search for Political Space

1. *Cuadernos para el Diálogo,* May 28, 1977.

2. See, for example, Santiago Carrillo's report to the PCE Central Committee in July 1976 entitled *De la Clandestinidad a la Legalidad* (n.p., n.d.), pp. 9–11.

3. The "Proyecto de Acuerdo Constitucional del PCE" *Nuestra Bandera,* no. 86 (March–April 1977):57–59.

4. *Mundo Obrero,* April 20, 1977.

5. *Diario16,* April 30, 1977.

6. For a consideration of the PSOE's resurgence, see my chapter entitled "The Spanish Left: Present Realities and Future Prospects" in William E. Griffith (ed.), *The Western European Left* (Lexington: D.C. Heath Books, 1979).

7. The phrase appeared in the principal report approved at the Third Conference of the Madrid provincial organization in April 1976 (mimeograph, p. 18). There is some question whether Communist leaders really believed what they were saying after a certain point, but they continued to make such statements.

8. See the article by Angel Mullor, the PCE Central Committee press secretary, in *El País,* June 11, 1977.

9. *Mundo Obrero,* June 16, 1977.

10. Ibid., June 22, 1977.

11. A complete version of his report to the Central Committee session in late June may be found in *Mundo Obrero,* June 29, 1977.

12. These are from the results of a survey by Data, S.A. cited by Juan Linz in his chapter entitled "A Sociological Look at Spanish Communism" in George Schwab (ed.), *Eurocommunism: The Ideological and*

Political-Theoretical Foundations (Westport, Ct.: Greenwood Press, 1980), p. 250.

13. Santiago Carrillo, *"Eurocomunismo" y Estado,* p. 212.

14. For example, *El País,* May 31, 1977, and *Mundo Obrero,* May 25, 1977.

15. Jaime Ballesteros, "El Partido Comunista en los umbrales de la democracia" in *Nuestra Bandera,* no. 85 (n.d.)13–18.

16. *El País,* May 11, 1977.

17. The figures have been published in Victor Pérez Díaz, *Clase Obrera, Partidos y Sindicatos* (Madrid: Fundación del Instituto Nacional de Industria, 1980), p. 109. There are other estimates. José María Maravall, "Political Cleavages in Spain and the 1979 General Election," *Government and Opposition* 14, no. 3 (Autumn 1979):305, suggests approximately 60 percent of the *Comisiones'* voters in 1978 voted PSOE in 1977. Samuel Barnes, Antonio López Pina, and Peter McDonough, "The Spanish Public in Political Transition," *British Journal of Political Science* 11, no. 1 (January 1981):76, indicates the PCE received 3 percent of the 1978 UGT vote and 46 percent of that from *Comisiones* voters. The PSOE, they estimate, captured 75 percent of the UGT and 24 percent of the CC.OO. 1978 vote.

18. Marcelino Camacho cautioned about the possible rise of a Pinochet in Chile, and Carrillo railed against those "who do not see what is right in front of their noses." *Diario16* (Madrid), September 1, 1977, and *Mundo Obrero,* August 16, 1977, for the statements by Camacho and *Mundo Obrero,* Sept. 8–14, 1977 for that of Carrillo.

19. A detailed discussion of Communist initiatives may be found in my "The PCE in Spanish Politics," *Problems of Communism* 27 (July–August 1978):15–37.

20. Carrillo at one point remarked that González and the PSOE were behaving like amateurs in politics. González answered back in an interview with *Le Monde,* October 16, 1977, that he wondered how Carrillo could emit such a judgment given his track record: "When I am his age, have his experience, and his degree of professionalism, I would not want to be at the head of a party which collected 9 percent of the vote."

21. See the Santiago Carrillo speech at the Festival of the PCE, as reported in *Mundo Obrero* in its October 20–26, 1977 issue.

22. At the outset, the Communists were full of bravado. "The party will control the fulfillment of the accords," declared *Mundo Obrero* in its October 20–26 issue.

23. In midsummer 1976 it had come out that 21 out of 27 people on the CC.OO. National Secretariat were members of the PCE and, later that summer during a visit to the USSR, Marcelino Camacho put his foot in his mouth by giving an interview to *TASS* in which he extolled life in that country. *Cambio16,* September 6, 1976.

24. Estimated variously at between 6.2 and 8 billion pesetas, the *patrimonio sindical* became particularly important in light of the heavy borrowing the UGT had engaged in from West German and Spanish banks, using it as collateral. The UGT claims this amount. See *Boletín de la UGT,* 1st week March 1978. The government used a much lower 1.5 billion peseta figure. *Cambio16,* February 12, 1978.

25. For the text of the electoral norms, see *Mundo Obrero,* December 29, 1977–January 4, 1978.

26. The statistics used in preparing this analysis are drawn from Victor

Pérez Díaz, *Clase Obrera, Partidos y Sindicatos* (Madrid: Fundación del Instituto Nacional de Industria, 1979), pp. 76, 78, and 85. *El País,* March 28, 1978, reported the percentages as CC.OO. 38 and UGT 31. Julián Ariza of the *Comisiones'* National Secretariat, writing in *Nuestra Bandera,* no. 94, p. 47, claimed 44–46 percent for the CC.OO. and 27–28 percent for the UGT. Several weeks later, an article in *Mundo Obrero* (August 10–16, 1978) indicated that out of 178, 540 delegates chosen and verified up to that point, 36.9 percent had no affiliation, and 13.4 percent were classifiable as independents.

27. *Mundo Obrero,* November 10–16, 1977. The PCE has been very unclear what Carrillo was to have said. In remarks reported by *Corriere della Sera,* the Secretary-General of the PCE was quoted as saying that his speech contained "more or less the same ideas as Berlinguer's." *Corriere della Sera* (Milan), November 4, 1977. Some people in the Italian party were critical of what they perceived as Carrillo's tendency to grandstand. Gian Carlo Pajetta, for example, made some disparaging remarks about Carrillo's having an "Iberian temperament" (*El País,* November 4, 1977); and in an interview a few days later after the uproar in Moscow (*Corriere della Sera,* November 8, 1977), Pajetta, wanting to distinguish between PCE and PCI attitudes, remarked that "[the Italian Communist] verdict, even when it is critical, and . . . our stances, even when they are different, are never connected to propagandistic motives or concessions to this or that adversary." During his trip to the United States, Carrillo, when asked about possible differences with the PCI, was cautious. Talking about differences of style between himself and PCI leaders, he often speculated on the impact operating next to the Vatican has had on Italian political parties.

28. *La Stampa* (Turin), February 26, 1978.

29. *Diario16,* March 27, 1978, and *El País,* March 28, 1978.

30. *Diario16,* March 17, 1978. See also the article by Fernando López Agudín in *Triunfo* (Madrid), March 18, 1978.

31. The closest vote came on a motion to postpone the decision on Thesis 15 until an extraordinary congress had been convened to debate the issue. This motion failed only after Simón Sanchéz Montero of the National Executive Committee made a forceful speech against the proposal.

32. *IV Congreso del Partit Socialista Unificat de Catalunya (Recull de Materials i d'Intervencions)* (Barcelona: Editorial Laia, 1978), p. 51. This was done before Carrillo announced that the PCE would probably drop Leninism, and the failure to coordinate matters on this score had serious consequences.

33. See the excellent article by Enrique Sopena, *Informaciones* (Madrid), April 6, 1978.

34. The text is carried in *Mundo Obrero,* April 20, 1978.

35. Eurocommunistologists might argue about the underlying significance of the ordering of the words "Marxism," "revolution," and "democracy" in the final version. The original proposal was for the program to say that the PCE is a "Marxist, democratic, and revolutionary party." The final version, after lengthy debates in the commission, read slightly differently: "The PCE is a Marxist, revolutionary, and democratic party."

36. *La Calle* (Madrid), April 17–23, 1979.

37. *Cambio16,* February 18, 1979.

38. See José Félix Tezános, "Analisis sociopolítico del voto socialista en las elecciones de 1979," *Sistema*, no. 31, July 1979:111.
39. This was Fernando Claudín in *El País*, March 15, 1979.
40. *Mundo Obrero*, February 27, 1979.
41. Ibid., March 2, 1979.
42. For a more detailed analysis of the Communist showing in the principal regions and areas of Spain, see my "The Electoral Space of Spanish Communism" in Howard R. Penniman (ed.), *Spain at the Polls* (Washington, D.C.: American Enterprise Institute, forthcoming).
43. José Félix Tezanos, "El Espacio político y sociológico del socialismo," *Sistema*, no. 32, September 1979: 54. The PCE had improved on its 1977 performance in this regard. Then, it had received 75 percent of its vote from men and only 25 percent from women. See Monica Threlfall, "Socialismo y electorado femenino," ibid., p. 23.
44. Ibid., p. 54.
45. Ibid., p. 56.
46. Ibid., p. 56. The breakdown was 24.6 percent skilled and 6.8 unskilled. For the PSOE, it was 18.3 and 6.0 percent respectively.
47. Victor Pérez Díaz, *Clase Obrera*, p. 162.
48. José María Maravall, "Political Cleavages," p. 24.

8. Crisis and Retrenchment

1. See the González interview in *Zona Abierta* (Madrid), September 1979, p. 12.
2. See, for example, the reports in *El País*, October 28 and November 16, 1978, as well as in *La Vanguardia*, March 30, 1979.
3. *El País*, September 18, 1979.
4. A discussion of the agreement's principal points may be found in *Cambio16*, July 22, 1979.
5. *Mundo Obrero*, December 11–13, 1979 carried a lengthy critique of the Statute. For other comments, *Cambio16*, December 9, 1979, and January 6, 1980.
6. For the Communist reaction, see *Mundo Obrero*, January 6, 1980. The text may be found in *El País*, January 6, 1980.
7. *El País*, June 29, 1979. For a disclaimer by Sartorius, see *Mundo Obrero*, June 30, 1979. Reaction to his statement was sufficiently unfavorable (with Redondo harshly criticizing its "lightness and immaturity") that Sartorius backed down a few days later. Seeking to reemphasize its moderation, *Comisiones* then initiated talks with the third largest union in the country, the *Unión Sindical Obrera*, and with representatives of small- and medium-sized enterprises that stood outside the CEOE.
8. *El País*, December 21, 1979.
9. *El País*, November 11, 1979, reported that some labor cadres in the Central Committee had unsuccessfully urged the PCE to boycott the debates surrounding the Workers' Statute.
10. Julián Ariza used the phrase in *Mundo Obrero Semanal*, September 20–26, 1979.
11. For a discussion of the strike and its aftermath, see the articles in *Mundo Obrero*, May 8, 9, and 18, 1980; in *Mundo Obrero Semanal*, May 15–21, 1980; in the PSUC weekly, *Treball*, April 24, May 8, 15, and 22, 1980; and in *La Calle*, May 6–12, 1980.

12. *La Calle*, May 20–26, 1980.

13. *Mundo Obrero*, June 18, 1980.

14. For an interesting discussion, see the various collaborative projects involving Samuel H. Barnes, Peter McDonough, and Antonio López Pina. Especially, "The Spanish Public and the Transition to Democracy," *British Journal of Political Science* 11, no. 1 (January 1981) and "Democracy and Disenchantment" by McDonough and López Pina in Paul Allen et al., (eds.), *Mass Politics in Industrial Societies* (Princeton: Princeton University Press, 1982).

15. See the Carrillo speech to the Central Committee meeting in Córdoba in May 1978 (n.p., n.d.). Also, Carlos Rodríguez, "Lo específico del eurocomunismo en España" in *Argumentos*, September 1979, pp. 9–12; and articles in *Mundo Obrero*.

16. *Mundo Obrero*, July 27, 1977.

17. See the Santiago Carrillo report to the PCE Central Committee in April 1974 as reprinted in *Escritos sobre el Eurocomunismo* (I) (Madrid: FORMA Ediciones, 1977), p. 74.

18. *Cambio16*, February 12, 1978.

19. *Mundo Obrero Semanal*, January 30–February 5, 1981 carried Carrillo's speech to the meeting and his defense of party policies. For the Assembly's Resolutions, ibid., February 13–19, 1981.

20. In sum, as Carrillo finally admitted in mid-1980, the Communists had lost "the nearly messianic certainty (they had had) in other times as to the victory of [their] cause." *Mundo Obrero Semanal*, August 8–14, 1980. For an excellent journalistic account of the PCE crisis through late 1982, see Pedro Vega and Peru Erroteta, *Los herejes del PCE* (Barcelona: Editorial Planeta, 1982).

21. An interesting discussion of the situation in the Basque Party may be found in *La Calle*, October 28–November 3, 1980.

22. See the exchange between Soto and Romero in *Mundo Obrero*, June 27 and 28, 1980.

23. The figures are from the analysis of the Communist voter and his attitudes prepared by Juan Linz entitled "A Sociological Look at Spanish Communism," manuscript, 1979. An abbreviated version may be found in George Schwab (ed.), *Eurocommunism: The Ideological and Political-Theoretical Foundations*, pp. 217–68.

24. *Mundo Obrero*, December 19–25, 1980.

25. For a more thorough analysis, see my *"Catalanismo*, the Left and the Consolidation of Centrism in Spain," *World Affairs* 143 (Winter 1980–81):298–317.

26. The analysis in the preceding paragraph draws heavily from reporting in *Treball*. See especially its June 26, 1980 issue and the articles by Txiki Laorden and Manuel Ludevid.

27. See the speeches by López Raimundo and Gutierrez Díaz in *Reunión del Comité Central*, April 26–27, 1980, and their replies to questions and criticisms.

28. Ibid., pp. 35–37.

29. See the partial transcript in *Mundo Obrero*, June 3, 1980.

30. *El País*, October 30 and November 7, 1980. Also *Mundo Obrero Semanal*, December 5–11, 1980, for the official PSUC statement on this issue.

31. After the Catalan Congress, a former editor of *Treball*, Ignasi Riera, charged that "in the 'pro-Sovietization' of the PSUC it was possible to see very direct and [why not?] financed influences." Simón Sánchez Montero

of the PCE Executive Committee echoed these charges, as did Carrillo when he accused the Soviets of engaging in "political terrorism." *Cambio16*, April 6, 1981.

32. *Hoja del Lunes* (Barcelona), December 29, 1980.

33. For information on the Congress, see *Treball*, December 24, 1980–January 9, 1981; *La Calle*, January 13–19, 1981; *Mundo Obrero Semanal*, January 9–15, 1981; and *El País*, January 6, 1981.

34. Syndical elections had been celebrated from mid-March to December 31, 1980 with the participation totalling 3.4 million workers (approximately 54 percent of those eligible). According to the Ministry of Labor, the national results showed the *Comisiones* in first place with 30.8 of the delegates elected, but the margin separating the CC.OO. from the UGT (29.3) shrank to less than 2 percent. As one headline put it, "CC.OO. came in first, but the UGT won." (*Cambio16*, January 19, 1981). Compared to 1978, *Comisiones* lost 3.6 percent of its delegates and in 12 of 16 provinces, while the UGT increased its delegate share by 7.4 percent and lost ground only in the Basque country. As in 1978, these figures were disputed by the Communists. But even in the totals they cited showed *Comisiones* electing significantly fewer delegates than before. In factories with fewer than 250 employees, in fact, the CC.OO. dropped from 43 to 35 percent of the delegates elected, and the UGT increased its share from 27 to 30 percent. See *Mundo Obrero Semanal*, December 19–25, 1980. Only in Cataluña did the *Comisiones* hold its ground. *Comunicación* (Barcelona), December 20, 1980.

35. For example, the speech José María Mohedano made in March 1978 preceding the Madrid provincial conference (n.p., n.d.).

36. Ricardo Lovelace quoting Carrillo in *La Calle*, January 27–February 2, 1981

37. See *Nuestra Bandera*, no. 101 (1979): 29.

38. For the first quote, see his report to the Central Committee, *Informe del Secretario General*, October 7–8, 1978, p. 35; for the second, an interview in *Mundo Obrero Semanal*, March 15–21, 1979.

39. See the articles in *Mundo Obrero Semanal* by Ernest García and Antonio Elzora, in June 5–11 and June 12–18, 1980, respectively.

40. The text of the Carrillo report is in *Mundo Obrero Semanal*, November 4–13, 1980. Partial but substantial texts of speeches by the Executive and Central Committee members are in ibid., November 14–20 and 21–27, 1980. For further reporting, see *El País*, November 5, 1980.

41. *El País*, May 17, 1981. García Salve, who would eventually try to organize a rival Communist party, described the meeting as "a scheme put together by cronies who want to manipulate the Communist party."

42. A useful discussion of the *Comisiones* Congress may be found in *La Calle*, June 23–29, 1981, and *Cambio16*, June 29, 1981.

43. *Mundo Obrero Semanal*, May 29–June 4, 1981, remarked that the *Comisiones* "were firmly decided this time around not to be kept out of the final agreements." Coverage of the ANE provisions was ample in the Spanish press; a summary is in *Cambio16*, June 15, 1981.

44. *Mundo Obrero*, July 28, 1981, carried the full text.

45. The name caught on after 250 critics published a document in *El País* (June 3, 1981) entitled "Eurocomunismo y renovación."

46. *El País*, July 29 through August 4, 1981, carried detailed reports on the Congress. Also *Mundo Obrero Semanal*, August 7–13 and 14–20, 1981.

47. Sartorius received 838 out of 1,079 possible votes (giving him third

place behind Ibárruri and Camacho), while Ballesteros won 647 delegate votes, putting him in twenty-first place.

48. By early 1981, the distinction between "pro-Soviet" and "hard-line" factions had virtually disappeared, a consequence of the polarization taking place within the PSUC and, to a lesser extent, in the rest of the PCE.

49. For the text, see *Treball*, May 21–27, 1981.

50. Ardiaca argued that the Central Committee resolution was not binding because it went against the line approved at the Fifth PSUC Congress. He further identified himself with those who "did not want to abandon [their] Communist identity and [who] feel a sense of solidarity with all Communists in the world." *Treball*, July 9, 1981.

51. *Treball*, October 28–November 4, 1981, and *El País*, October 28, 1981. For a chronology of the crisis as it built up, consult *Treball*, March 18–24, 1982.

52. In early December 1981, Frutos distributed to the PSUC Central Committee copies of notes taken by one of the participants at the secret meeting. *Treball* (Supplement), December 11, 1981. Frutos was particularly wounded by what he felt was a betrayal on the part of the hardliners. Ibid., December 17–24, 1981.

53. *La Vanguardia*, December 6, 1981, discussed the positions those who were expelled had within the PSUC. On the councilmen, *Treball*, February 5–11, 1982.

54. On the Sixth Congress, *Treball*, March 25–31, 1982, and April 1–14, 1982, and the coverage in *El País* and *La Vanguardia*.

55. The decline in PSUC working class cadres is revealed in the diminished percentage of workers among the delegates selected for the Sixth Congress. Whereas at the Fourth Congress in November 1977 approximately 38 percent of the delegates had working class backgrounds, in April 1982 this percentage had dropped to 23 percent. *Treball*, April 15, 1982.

56. The letters and communiqués exchanged between the national party and its Basque branch may be found in *Mundo Obrero Semanal*, November 6–12, 1981. The Spanish Communist leadership had already shown who it supported by publishing an article by Ormazábal (in ibid., October 9–15, 1981) and refusing to do the same for Lertxundi. Labor cadres, especially those with immigrant backgrounds, resented Lertxundi's haste. One worker at the Babcock-Wilcox plant in Bilbao said: "We have not negotiated, we have renounced." *Cambio16*, November 9, 1981.

57. The formal fusion of the Lertxundi group with *Euskadiko Eskerra* took place in March 1982. See *El País*, March 21, 1982, and *Cambio16*, March 22, 1982.

58. The quote is from his speech at the annual PCE Festival in September. *Mundo Obrero Semanal*, October 2–8, 1981.

59. *La Calle*, November 1–10–16, 1981, carried an excellent discussion of the debates that took place in the PCE Central Committee. See also *El País*, especially November 25, 1981.

60. The Madrid provincial committee under the leadership of Adolfo Piñedo took an extremely harsh line on internal dissent. See his interview in *Mundo Obrero Semanal*, November 27–December 3, 1981. Carrillo openly supported him in this, insisting on the need for the PCE to control those it elected. Ibid., December 4–10, 1981. The resignations of those with municipal responsibilities came in January 18, 1982. *El País*, January 10, 1982. One consequence of the intraparty squabble was the further

weakening of the PSOE-PCE municipal entente in Madrid, with the Socialists using the resignation of councilmen to take the Urban Planning portfolio from the PCE.

61. *Mundo Obrero (Extraordinario para Madrid)*, November 1981, carried the text of the letter. Labor activists were reacting not only to the loss of Communist identity (*señas de identidad* in the PCE jargon) but to the poor economic situation. There was a high unemployment throughout Spain and virtually no growth in the Spanish economy in 1981. Official figures indicated approximately 2 million unemployed (about 14 percent of the active labor force).

62. Pilar Brabo was 38 years old; she had been a member of the PCE for 17 years and of the Executive Committee since 1970. At the time of the PCE's legalization in April 1977, she was the third or fourth-ranking figure in the party and had an extremely close relationship with Carrillo. She was the filter through which Secretariat decisions and party issues were brought to his attention. Carlos Alonso Zaldívar, 35 years old, had been in the PCE for fifteen years and had risen to a position of prominence as a protege of Brabo. He was one of the more open members of the leadership, having become a member of the Executive in 1976.

63. *Mundo Obrero Semanal*, December 18–24, 1982, and January 1–8, 1982.

64. For example, in the article by Pilar Brabo in *El País*, February 2, 1982 or in the piece by Antonio Elorza in *La Calle*, January 27–February 2, 1982. Significantly, the PCE Central Committee statement talked about "continuing the process opened by the October Revolution."

65. For the results of the Andalucian elections, see *El País*, May 25, 1982.

66. *Mundo Obrero Semanal*, June 18–24, 1982 carried some of the speeches made at the Central Committee meeting. Also the coverage in *El País*, June 11 through 14, 1982.

67. The characterization is made by Azcarate in a forthcoming book entitled *La Crisis del eurocomunismo* (Madrid: Editorial Argos Vergara.) An excerpt is in *El País*, June 13, 1982.

Conclusion

1. La Vanguardia, March 17, 1982.

Bibliography

Alba, Victor. *El Partido Comunista en España*. Barcelona: Editorial Planeta, 1970.

Alfaya, Javier. "Galicia: La Explicación no es Unicamente el Miedo." *Argumentos*, no. 3 (July 1977):26–29.

Aliaga, Serafín. "Los Dirigentes Anarquistas al Servicio de la Reacción Española y del Imperialismo Yanqui." *Nuestra Bandera*, no. 28 (June–July 1948):541–50.

Alianza Sindical Obrera. *Alianza Sindical Obrera: Nuestras Raíces, Nuestro Presente, Nuestro Futuro*. Ediciones Iberia, n.d.

Almendros Morcillo, Fernando, et al. *El Sindicalismo de Clase en España (1939–1977)*. Barcelona: Ediciones 62, 1978.

Almerich, Paulina, et al. *Cambio Social y Religión en España*. Barcelona: Editorial Fontanella, 1975.

Alvarez, Santiago. "Towards an Alliance of Communists and Catholics." *World Marxist Review* 8 (June 1965):40–47.

———. "The New Working Class Movement in Spain." *World Marxist Review* 9 (December 1966):49–53.

———. "Once More on the Catholic-Communist Alliance." *World Marxist Review* 11 (September 1968):70–78.

———. "Notas Sobre el Problema Nacional en España." *Nuestra Bandera*, no. 84 (March–April 1976):13–25.

Amsden, Jon. *Collective Bargaining and Class Conflict in Spain*. London: Weidenfeld and Nicholson, 1972.

Arija, José Manuel. *Nicolás Redondo*. Madrid: Editorial Cambio16, 1977.

Asamblea General de CC.OO. Barcelona: Editorial Laia, 1976.

Azcárate, Manuel. "Libertades Políticas y Socialismo." *Alkarrilketa* 2, no. 2 (1970):13–15.

———. "Sobre Algunos Problemas de la Política Internacional del Partido." *VIII Congreso*. Bucharest, 1972.

———. "Algunas Consecuencias del Nuevo Papel de la Ciencia." *Realidad*, no. 23 (June 1972):3–10.

————. "El Movimiento Revolucionario Internacional." In *Temas de Política y Sociedad: Cuestiones Internacionales.* Edited by Manuel Azcárate and Tomás García. Madrid: Editorial Cénit, 1977.

————. "El Tema de la Libertades Hoy." *Argumentos,* no. 1 (May 1977):12–17.

————. "Problemes i Perspectives de l'Eurocomunisme." *Taula de Canvi,* Extra no. 1 (June 1978):24–33.

Bailby, Edouard. *España Hacia la Democracia?* Barcelona: Editorial Argos, 1977.

Ballesteros, Jaime. "El Partido Comunista en los Umbrales de la Democracia." *Nuestra Bandera,* no. 85 (n.d.):13–18.

Bardaje Fierro, Alfredo and Mate Rupérez, Reyes, ed. *Cristianos por el Socialismo: Documentación.* Pamplona: Editorial Verbo Divino, 1977.

Barnes, Samuel H., et al. "The Spanish Public in Political Transition." *British Journal of Political Science* 11 (January 1981):49–80.

Belda, Rafael, et al. *Iglesia y Sociedad en España, 1939–1975.* Madrid: Editorial Tecnos, 1977.

Blackmer, Donald L. M. and Tarrow, Sidney, eds. *Communism in Italy and France.* Princeton: Princeton University Press, 1975.

de Blas Guerrero, Andrés. *El Socialismo Radical en la Segunda Republica.* Madrid: Tucar Ediciones, 1978.

Boix, Isidor and Pujadas, Manuel. *Conversaciones Sindicales con Dirigentes Obreros.* Barcelona: Editorial Avance, 1975.

Borja, Jordi. "Socialistes i Comunistes davant la Democracia." *Taula de Canvi,* no. 2 (November–December 1976):35–51.

Borkenau, Franz. *The Spanish Cockpit.* Ann Arbor: University of Michigan Press, 1963.

Borrás, José. *Políticas de los Exiliados Españoles, 1944–1958.* Paris: Ediciones Ruedo Ibérico, 1976.

Brenan, Gerald. *The Spanish Labyrinth.* London: Cambridge University Press, 1943.

Bullejos, José. *La Comintern en España.* Mexico: Impresiones Modernas, 1972.

Bulnes, Ramón. "Del Sindicalismo de Represión al Sindicalismo de Intergración." *Horizonte Español 1966, Volume II.*

Calamai, Marco. *Storia del Movimento Operaio dal 1960 al 1975.* Bari: De Donato Editore, 1975.

Camacho, Marcelino. *Charlas en la Prisión.* Barcelona: Editorial Laia, 1976.

Caro, Antonio; Cuesta, Juan; Díaz, María Dolores; et al. *Prueba de Fuerza entre el Reformismo y la Ruptura.* Madrid: Elías Querejeta Ediciones, 1976.

Carr, Raymond and Fusi, Juan Pablo. *España, de la Dictadura a la Democracia.* Barcelona: Editorial Planeta, 1979.

Carrillo, Santiago. "La Situación de España y Nuestras Tareas después de la Victoria de las Naciones Unidas." *Nuestra Bandera* (June 1945):18–19.

————. "Somos el Partido de la Destrucción del Franquismo y también el Partido de la Reconstrucción de una España Grande y Democrática." *Nuestra Bandera* (January–February 1946): 45–67.

————. *La Situación en la Dirección del Partido y los Problemas del Reforzamiento del Mismo.* (n.p.) August 1956.

————. "Informe del Comité Central." *Sexto Congresso del PCE.* December 1959.

———. *Después de Franco, Qué?* Paris: Editions Sociales, 1965.

———. *Nuevos Enfoques a Problemas de Hoy.* Paris: Editions Sociales, 1967.

———. "Mas Problemas Actuales del Socialismo." *Nuestra Bandera,* no. 59 (III Trimester 1968):41–53.

———. "La Lucha por el Socialismo Hoy." *Nuestra Bandera,* no. 58 (June 1968):11–15.

———. *Problemas del Socialismo.* Paris: Colección Ebro, 1969.

———. Report to the 8th PCE Congress. "Hacia la Libertad" in *VIII Congreso.* Bucharest, 1972.

———. *Hacia el Post-Franquismo.* Paris: Colección Ebro, 1974.

———. *Demain L'Espagne.* Paris: Editions du Seuil, 1974.

———. "Las Tareas del Movimiento Obrero para que el Franquismo Desaparezca También." *Nuestra Bandera,* no. 82 (November 1975):3–35.

———. *De la Clandestinidad a la Legalidad.* Speech delivered to the PCE Central Committee meeting. Rome, July 1976.

———. *Escritos sobre Eurocomunismo.* Madrid: Forma Ediciones, 1977.

———. *"Eurocomunismo" y Estado.* Barcelona: Editorial Grijalbo, 1977.

Castaño Colomer, José. *La JOC en España (1946–1970).* Salamanca: Ediciones Sígueme, 1978.

Casula, Felice. *Cattolici-Comunisti e Sinistra Cristiana, 1938–45.* Bologna: Il Mulino, 1976.

———. *Communism and the Spanish Civil War.* Berkeley and Los Angeles: University of California Press, 1955.

Cattell, David T. *Soviet Diplomacy and the Spanish Civil War.* Berkeley and Los Angeles: University of California Press, 1957.

CC.OO. en sus Documentos (1958–1976). Madrid: Ediciones HOAC, 1977.

Chao, José. *Después de Franco, España.* Madrid: Ediciones Fellmar, 1976.

Chao, Ramón. *La Iglesia en el Franquismo.* Madrid: Ediciones Fellmar, 1976.

Claudín, Fernando. "Dos Concepciones de la Via Española al Socialismo." In *Horizonte Español,* Vol. I, pp. 58–100. Paris: Ruedo Ibérico, 1966.

———. *La Crisis del Movimiento Comunista.* Paris: Ediciones Ruedo Ibérico, 1970.

———. "The Split in the Spanish Communist Party." *New Left Review,* no. 71 (London), November–December 1971: 75–99.

———. Magri, Lucio; Quijano, Aníbal; Rossanda, Rossana. *Movimiento Obrero y Acción Política.* Mexico: Ediciones Era, 1975.

———. *Eurocomunismo y Socialismo.* Madrid: Siglo XXI, 1977.

———. "Eurocommunisme: L'Aggression Sovietique." *Politique Hebdo* (July 4–10, 1977): 4–6.

———. *Documentos de una Divergencia Comunista.* Barcelona: Iniciativas Editoriales, 1978.

Clavera, Joan; Esteban, Joan M.; Monés, M. Antonio; Montserrat, Antoni; Hombravella, J. Ros. *Capitalismo Español: de la Autarquía a la Estabilización 1939–1959.* Madrid: Editorial Cuadernos para el Diálogo, 1978.

Comín, Alfonso C. *Cristianos el el Partido, Comunistas en el Iglesia.* Barcelona: Editorial Laia, 1977.

———. *Fe en la Tierra.* Bilbao: Editorial Desclée de Brouwer, 1975.

"Contrary to the Interests of Peace and Socialism in Europe. Concerning

the book 'Eurocommunism' and the State by Santiago Carrillo, General
    Secretary of the Communist Party of Spain." *New Times* (Moscow), no.
    26 (June 1977):9–13.
Comín Colomer, Eduardo. *Historia del Partido Comunista de España.*
    Madrid: Editora Nacional, 1967.
Los Cristianos y la Política. Madrid: Servicio Editorial del Arzobispado
    de Madrid-Alcalá, 1977.
Díaz, José. *Tres Años de Lucha.* Paris: Colección Ebro, 1970.
Díaz, José Antonio. *Luchas Internas en Comisiones Obreras, Barcelona
    1964–1970.* Barcelona: Editorial Bruguera, 1977.
Díaz Cardiel, Victor, et al. *Madrid en Huelga, Enero 1976.* Madrid: Edi-
    torial Ayuso, 1976.
Diz, Juan. [Manuel Azcárate] "Sobre las Posiciones Revisionistas de la
    Liga de los Comunistas de Yugoeslavia." *Nuestra Bandera*, no. 21 (July
    1958):53–74.
———. "La Lucha Antidogmática." *Nuestra Bandera*, no. 65 (III Trimes-
    ter, 1970):73–81.
Domenech, Antoni. "Crisis del Capitalismo, 'Eurocomunismo,' Perspec-
    tiva Revolucionaria." *Materiales*, no. 5 (September–October
    1977):43–58.
Elvira, Carlos. "De la Ruptura Democrática al Sindicalismo Unitario."
    Nuestra Bandera, no. 83 (January–February 1976):26–30.
Espinosa, Fabio. "El Ejercito en el Momento Político Actual." In *VIII
    Congreso*, Bucharest, 1972, pp. 233–49.
Estruch, Joan. *Historia del PCE (1920–1939).* Barcelona: Iniciativa Edi-
    toriales, 1978.
Fernández Buey, Francisco. "Sobre Algunos Aspectos del Proyecto de
    Programa del PSUC." *Materiales*, no. 7 (January–February 1978):31–
    46.
Fernández de Castro, Ignacio. *De las Cortes de Cádiz al Plan de Desar-
    rollo.* Paris: Ediciones Ruedo Ibérico, 1968.
———. "Tres Años Importantes: 1961–1962–1963." *Cuadernos de Ruedo
    Ibérico*, no. 16 (December–January, 1968):81.
——— and Goytre, Antonio. *Clases Sociales en España en el Umbral de
    los Años '70.* Madrid: Siglo XXI, 1974.
Fernández Lupión, Angel. "Algunas Notas Sobre el Futuro Sindical en
    Nuestro País." *Argumentos*, no. 4 (September 1977):14–17.
Ferrarotti, Franco. "The Italian Communist Party and Eurocommunism."
    In *The Many Faces of Communism.* Edited by Morton A. Kaplan. New
    York: The Free Press, 1978.
Fina, Lluis. "Politica Salarial i Lluita de Classes Sota el Franquisme."
    Materiales (January–February 1978):105–30.
Frutos, Francisco. "El Nuevo Movimiento Obrero. Apuntes para un De-
    bate." *Materiales*, no. 7 (January–February 1978):73–84.
Gallego, Ignacio. "La Lucha contra el Titismo es un Deber Rev-
    olucionario de los Comunistas." *Nuestra Bandera*, no. 4 (February–
    March 1950):169–91.
———. "El Centralismo Democrático en el Partido." *Nuestra Bandera*,
    no. 7 (January–February 1978):73–84.
———. *El Desarrollo del Partido Comunista.* Paris: Colección Ebro,
    1976.
———. *El Partido de Masas.* Madrid: Editorial Cenit, 1977.
Gallo, Max. *Historia de la España Franquista.* Paris: Ediciones Ruedo
    Ibérico, 1972.

García Salve, Francisco. *Por qué somos comunistas.* Madrid: Ediciones Penthalon, 1982.

Gil Robles, José María. "Esquema de un Camino Hacia la Democracia." Madrid: n.p., May 1976.

Gimbernat, José Antonio, and Rodríguez de Lecea, Teresa, ed. *Los Marxistas Españoles y la Religión.* Madrid: Editorial Cuadernos para el Diálogo, 1977.

Gómez, Juan. "Algunas Verdades Elementales Sobre la Integración." *Nuestra Bandera,* no. 31 (July–August 1961):37–52.

———. "Sobre el Mercado Común Europeo." *VIII Congreso del PCE.* Bucharest, 1972, p. 233–48.

Gómez Llorente, Luis. *Aproximación a la Historia del Socialismo Español (Hasta 1921).* Madrid: Editorial Cuadernos para el Dialogo, 1972.

González, Felipe and Guerra, Antonio. *Socialismo es Libertad y Notas para una Biografía.* Barcelona: Ediciones Galbá, 1978.

González Ruíz, José María. "El Humanismo Ateo y el Dios Bíblico." *Realidad,* no. 5 (November 1965):33–42.

Guerra Campos, José. "Precisiones sobre el ateísmo marxista." *Realidad,* no. 5 (May 1965):3–8.

Hacia el III Congreso del Partido Comunista de Euzkadi. (n.p., n.d.).

Hermet, Guy. *Los Comunistas en España.* Paris: Ediciones Ruedo Ibérico, 1972.

———. "Les fonctions politiques des organisations religieuses dans les regimes à pluralisme limité." *Revue Française de Science Politique* 23 (June 1973):439–73.

Hernández, Jesús. *La Grande Trahison.* Paris: Editions Flasquelle, 1953.

Horizonte Español 1972. Paris: Ediciones Ruedo Ibérico, Vol. 1. n.d.

Ibárruri, Dolores. *Informe del CC al Quinto Congreso del PCE.* 1954.

———. "The Seventh Congress of the Comintern and the Spanish Experience." *World Marxist Review* 8 (December 1965):43–47.

———. *España, Estado Multinacional.* Paris: Edicions Sociales, 1971.

———., et al. *Historia del Partido Comunista de España.* Warsaw: Ediciones 'Polonia,' 1960.

Iribarren, Jesús, ed. *Documentos Colectivos del Episcopado Español, 1870–1974.* Madrid: Editorial Católica, 1974.

Jackson, Gabriel. *The Spanish Republic and the Civil War, 1931–1939.* Princeton: Princeton University Press, 1965.

John XXIII. *Pacem in Terris.* New York: Paulist Press, 1963.

Lazitch, Branko. *Les Partis Communistes d'Europe.* Paris: Les Isles d'Or, 1956.

Linz, Juan. "An Authoritarian Regime: Spain." In *Cleavages, Ideologies and Party Systems.* Edited by Erik Allardt and Yrjo Littunen. Helsinki: The Academic Bookstore, 1964.

———. "The Party System of Spain: Past and Future." In *Party Systems and Voter Alignments: Cross-National Perspectives.* Edited by Seymour M. Lipset and Stein Rokkan. New York: Free Press, 1967.

———. "Opposition in and under an Authoritarian Regime: The case of Spain." In *Regimes and Oppositions.* Edited by Robert A. Dahl. New Haven, Conn. and London: Yale University Press, 1973.

———. "A Sociological Look at Spanish Communism." In *Eurocommunism: The Ideological and Political-Theoretical Foundations.* Edited by George Schwab. Westport: Greenwood Press, 1981.

Líster, Enrique. "Una Necesidad Nacional: Que Desaparezcan la Bases Yanquis en España." *Mundo Obrero,* October 1, 1960.

──────. *Basta!* Madrid: G. del Toro Editor, 1978.

Lobkowicz, Nicholas. "Marx's Attitude Toward Religion." In *Marx and the Western World.* Edited by Nicholas Lobkowicz. Notre Dame, Ind.: University of Notre Dame Press, 1967.

López, Emilio. *Nacionalismo Vasco y Clases Sociales.* San Sebastián: Editorial Txertoa, 1976.

López Raimundo, Gregorio. "La Experiencia del Bajo Llobregat." *Nuestra Bandera,* no. 76 (September–October 1974):35–40.

──────. *La Huelga General y el Papel Dirigente de la Clase Obrera.* Report to the 3rd PSUC Central Commitee plenum, October, 1975.

Lorenzo, Cesar M. *Les Anarchistes Espagnols et le Pouvoir, 1868–1969.* Paris: Editions du Seuil, 1969.

Ludevid, Manuel. *El Movimiento Obrero en Cataluña Bajo el Franquismo.* Barcelona: Editorial Avance, 1977.

McDonough, Peter and López Pina, Antonio. "Democracy and Disenchantment in Spanish Politics." In *Mass Politics in Industrial Societies.* Edited by Paul Allen Beck et al. Princeton: Princeton University Press, 1982.

Magri, Lucio, et al. *Movimiento Obrero y Acción Política.* Mexico: Ediciones Era, 1975.

"Manifiesto de la Unidad Sindical." *CC.OO. en sus Documentos 1958–1976.* Madrid: Ediciones HOAC, 1977, pp. 5–30.

Maravall, José María. *El Desarrollo Económico y la Clase Obrera.* Barcelona: Ediciones Ariel, 1970.

──────. *Dictatorship and Political Dissent: Workers and Students in Franco Spain.* London: Tavistock Publications, 1978.

──────. "Political Cleavages in Spain and the 1979 General Election." *Government and Opposition* 14, no. 3 (Autumn 1979):299–317.

Martí, Casimiro. "La Iglesia en la Vida Política." In *Iglesia y Sociedad en España, 1938–1975.* Edited by Rafael Belda, et al. Madrid: Editorial Popular, 1977.

Martí, Ernest. [Joaquim Sempere] "Problemas Ideológicos y el Frente Cultural." *Nuestra Bandera,* no. 64 (II Trimester 1970).

──────. "Primeras Reflexiones en torno a las Elecciones Sindicales." *Nuestra Bandera,* no. 67 (II Trimester 1977):14–22.

Martín, Eduardo and Salvador, Jesús. *Los Enlaces Sindicales.* Barcelona: Editorial Laia, 1976.

Mate Rupérez, Reyes. *El Desafío Socialista.* Salamanca: Ediciones Sígueme, 1975.

Meaker, Gerald. *The Revolutionary Left In Spain, 1914–1923.* Stanford: Stanford University Press, 1974.

Melchor, Federico. "Pero, Pueden los Cristianos ser Comunistas? *Nuestra Bandera,* nos. 79–80 (March–June 1975):22–29.

Montiel, Félix. "Con los Católicos que quieren liquidar el fascismo en España, podemos y debemos estar unidos." *Nuestra Bandera,* no. 15 (February 1974):127–38.

Mujal-León, Eusebio M. "The PCP and the Portuguese Revolution." *Problems of Communism* 26 (January–February 1977):21–41.

──────. "The PCE in Spanish Politics." *Problems of Communism* 27 (July–August 1978):15–37.

──────. "The Domestic and International Evolution of the Spanish Communist Party." In *Eurocommunism and Detente.* Edited by Rudolf L. Tökés. New York: New York University Press, 1978.

―――. "The Spanish Left: Present Realities and Future Prospects." In *The Western European Left*. Edited by William E. Griffith. Lexington: D.C. Heath Books, 1979.

―――. "*Catalanismo*, the Left and the Consolidation of Centrism of Spain." *World Affairs* 143 (Winter 1980/81):298–317.

―――. "The Search for Political Space." In *Spain at the Polls, 1977 and 1979*. Edited by Howard R. Penniman. Washington, D.C.: American Enterprise Institute, 1982.

Muñoz, Jacobo. "Nota Sobre la 'Alianza de la Fuerzas del Trabajo y de la Cultura.'" *Materiales*, no. 7 (January–February 1978):47–51.

Nuñez, Luis C. *Clases Sociales en Euzkadi*. San Sebastián: Editorial Txertoa, 1977.

Oriol, M. "Ignacio Fernández de Castro y la Tercera Revolución." *Nuestras Ideas*, no. 10 (January 1961):82–95.

Orwell, George. *Homage to Catalonia*. New York: Harcourt, Brace & World, Inc., 1952.

Pagès, Pelai. *Historia del Partido Comunista de España*. Barcelona: Ediciones Ricou, 1978.

Partido Comunista de España. *Un Futuro para España: La Democracia Económica y Política*. Paris: Colección Ebro, 1967.

―――. VIII Congreso. Bucharest, 1972.

―――. *Estatutos del Partido Comunista de España―Aprobados en su VIII Congreso*, 1972 (n.p., n.d.).

―――. "Segunda Conferencia del PCE." *Nuestra Bandera*, no. 81 (October 1975).

―――. "El Proyecto de Constitución." *Nuestra Bandera*, no. 86 (March–April 1977):57–59.

―――. *Informe Sobre Política Organizativa*. Presented at the Madrid Provincial Conference in March 1978.

―――. *Noveno Congreso del Partido Comunista de España, 19–23 Abril 1978*. Barcelona: Editorial Grijalbo, 1978.

Partit Socialista Unificat de Cataluna. "Algunos Aspectos de la Alianza de las Fuerzas del Trabajo y de la Cultura." Barcelona: PSUC Barcelona Committee, February 1973.

―――. *IV Congres del Partit Socialista Unificat de Catalunya (Recull de Materials i d'Intervencions)*. Barcelona: Editorial Laia, 1978.

Payne, Stanley G. *The Spanish Revolution*. New York: W. W. Norton & Co., 1970.

Pércz Díaz, Victor. *Clase Obrera, Partidos y Sindicatos*. Madrid: Fundación del Instituto Nacional de Industria, 1980.

Petschen, Santiago. *La Iglesia en la España de Franco*. Madrid: Ediciones Sedmay, 1977.

Picó, Josep. *El Moviment Obrer al Pais Valenciá sota el Franquisme*. Valencia: Editorial Eliseu Climent, 1977.

"El Proyecto de Constitución." *Nuestra Bandera*, no. 86 (March–April 1977):57–59.

Quirós, Emilio [Jaime Ballesteros]. "Nuevas Características y Tareas del Frente Teórico y Cultural." In *VIII Congreso*. Bucharest, 1972.

Rama, Carlos M. *La Crisis Española del Siglo XX*. Mexico: Fondo de Cultura Económica, 1960.

Relayo, Juan. "Una Nueva Mentalidad? Jovenes Patrónos Españoles." *Cuadernos de Ruedo Ibérico*, no. 3 (October–November 1965):103–6.

Rodríguez, Carlos. "Lo específico del eurocomunismo en España." *Argumentos*, no. 29 (September 1979):9–12.

Rodríguez Aramberri, Julio. "La Contradicción del Estado Burgués." *Materiales*, no. 7 (January–February 1978):7–30.

Romano, Vicente. *Spain: The Workers' Commissions, Basic Documents 1966–1971*. Toronto: Canadian Committee for a Democratic Spain, 1973.

Ruíz Ayúcar, Angel. *El Partido Comunista, 37 Años de Clandestinidad.* Madrid: Editorial San Martín, 1976.

Ruíz Rico, Juan José. *El Papel Político de la Iglesia Católica en la España de Franco.* Madrid: Editorial Tecnos, 1977.

Sacristán, Manuel. "La Militancia de Cristianos en el P.C." *Materiales*, no. 1 (January–February 1977):101–12.

————. "A Próposito del 'Eurocomunismo.'" *Materiales*, no. 16 (November–December 1977):5–14.

Sánchez Montero, Simón. *El Estado.* Madrid: Editorial Cénit, 1977.

Sandri, Renato. "Le Ultime Vicende del PC Spagnolo." *Rinascita* 27 (February 6, 1970): 10–11.

Sanz Oller, Jesús. *Entre el Fraude y la Esperanza, Las Comisiones Obreras de Barcelona.* Paris: Ediciones Ruedo Ibérico, 1972.

Sartorius, Nicolás. "Movimiento y Organización." *Nuestra Bandera,* no. 83 (January–February 1976):43–57.

————. *El Sindicalismo de Nuevo Tipo.* Barcelona: Editorial Laia, 1977.

————. *El Resurgir del Movimiento Obrero.* Barcelona: Editorial Laia, 1975.

Selznick, Philip. *The Organizational Weapon.* New York: McGraw-Hill, 1952.

Sempere, Joaquim. "Sobre la Tradició Comunista i la seva Vigencia." *Nous Horitzons,* no. 36 (October 1977):7–18.

Semprún, Jorge. *Autobiografía de Federico Sánchez.* Barcelona: Editorial Planeta, 1977.

Tarancón, Enrique. *Los Cristianos y la Política.* Madrid: Servicio Editorial del Arzobispado de Madrid-Alcalá, 1977.

Tejero, Alfredo. "Auge y Crisis de Comisiones Obreras." *Materiales* (May–June 1977):37–48.

Tezános, José Félix. *Estructura de Clases en la España Actual.* Madrid: Ediciones Cuadernos para el Diálogo, 1975.

————. "Analisis sociopolítico del voto socialista en las elecciones de 1979." *Sistema,* no. 31 (July 1979):105–22.

————. "El Espacio político y sociológico del socialismo." *Sistema,* no. 32 (September 1979):51–76.

Thomas, Hugh. *The Spanish Civil War.* New York: Harper & Row, 1961.

Threlfall, Monica. "Socialismo y electorado femenino." *Sistema,* no. 32 (September 1979):19–34.

Tucker, Robert C. *The Marxian Revolutionary Idea.* New York: W. W. Norton & Co., 1969.

Urbina, Fernando. "Formas de Vida de la Iglesia en España: 1939–1975." In *Ilgesia y Sociedad en España, 1939–1975.* Edited by Rafael Belda, et al. Madrid: Editorial Popular, 1977.

USO en sus Documentos, 1960–1975. Madrid: Ediciones HOAC, 1976.

Vega, Pedro and Erruteta, Peru. *Los herejes del PCE.* Madrid: Editorial Planeta, 1982.

Vilar, Sergio. *La Oposición a la Dictadura.* Barcelona: Editorial Ayma, 1976.

Yagüe, María Eugenia. *Santiago Carrillo: Una Biografía Politica.* Madrid: Editorial Cambio16, 1977.

Index

S
(
1